Global Surveillance and Policing

Global Surveillance and Policing
Borders, security, identity

edited by

Elia Zureik and Mark B. Salter

WILLAN
PUBLISHING

Published by

Willan Publishing
Culmcott House
Mill Street, Uffculme
Cullompton, Devon
EX15 3AT, UK
Tel: +44(0)1884 840337
Fax: +44(0)1884 840251
e-mail: info@willanpublishing.co.uk
website: www.willanpublishing.co.uk

Published simultaneously in the USA and Canada by

Willan Publishing
c/o ISBS, 920 NE 58th Ave, Suite 300,
Portland, Oregon 97213-3786, USA
Tel: +001(0)503 287 3093
Fax: +001(0)503 280 8832
e-mail: info@isbs.com
website: www.isbs.com

First published 2005

ISBN 1-84392-160-X paperback
ISBN 1-84392-161-8 hardback

British Library Cataloguing-in-Publication Data

A catalogue record for this book is available from the British Library

Project managed by Deer Park Productions, Tavistock, Devon
Typeset by GCS, Leighton Buzzard, Beds.
Printed and bound by T.J. International Ltd, Padstow, Cornwall

Contents

Acknowledgements

We would like to thank the Social Sciences and Humanities Research Council of Canada for making this collaboration possible, through the generous funding of the Globalization of Data Project, of which this is a part. In particular, we wish to thank David Lyon and Yolande Chan for their support of this project. We value their friendship, encouragement, and thoughtful input, as well as that of other colleagues and collaborators in the project. We would also like to thank Joan Sharpe, whose superlative logistical, organizational, and personal skills have been invaluable in organizing the workshop and in seeing to it that the manuscript for this book stayed on track. We also acknowledge with gratitude the organizational and intellectual input of graduate students throughout this project. We thank Anna Dekker for her skillful editing of the manuscript and her punctuality which made the task of working with her a joy.

Elia Zureik and Mark B. Salter
Kingston and Ottawa, Ontario

Notes on contributors

Katja Franko Aas is senior researcher at the Institute of Criminology and Sociology of Law, University of Oslo. She has written extensively on the use of information and communication technologies in contemporary penal systems, including *Sentencing in the Age of Information: from Faust to Macintosh* (Cavendish/Glasshouse Press 2005). She is currently completing a book for SAGE Publications entitled *Globalization and Crime*.

Colin J. Bennett received his Bachelor's and Master's degrees from the University of Wales, and his PhD from the University of Illinois at Urbana-Champaign. Since 1986 he has taught in the Department of Political Science at the University of Victoria (British Columbia, Canada), where he is now Professor. His research has focused on the comparative analysis of information privacy protection policies at the domestic and international levels, published in three books: *Regulating Privacy: Data Protection and Public Police in Europe and the United States* (Cornell University Press 1992); *Visions of Privacy: Policy Choices for the Digital Age* (University of Toronto Press 1999, with Rebecca Grant); and *The Governance of Privacy: Policy Instruments in the Digital Age* (Ashgate Press 2003, with Charles Raab).

John W. Donaldson is a research associate at the International Boundaries Research Unit (IBRU) in the Department of Geography at the University of Durham (United Kingdom). IBRU works to enhance the resources available for the peaceful resolution of problems associated with international boundaries on land and at sea, including their delimitation, demarcation and management. At IBRU Mr Donaldson has authored boundary reports for the US government's National Geospatial-Intelligence Agency (formerly NIMA) and has assisted in research for several current international boundary arbitrations. His articles have appeared in *Geopolitics* and *Jane's Intelligence Review,* and he has presented papers on a variety of boundary-related issues to several international conferences. Currently pursuing a PhD at the University of Durham, Mr Donaldson holds a BA degree from Southern Methodist University (USA) and a MA degree in International Boundaries from the University of Durham.

Jonathan Finn is Assistant Professor in the Department of Communication Studies at Wilfrid Laurier University. His research focuses on the intersections of visual and scientific practices with particular emphasis on the use of visual representation in forensic science and surveillance systems.

Don Flynn is the policy officer for the Joint Council for the Welfare of Immigrants, an independent UK immigration rights group. He has worked in the field of immigration law and policy for the past 25 years, covering developments in both the UK and the wider European Union. He has written extensively on New Labour's approach to immigration policy and is currently working on the situation of migrant workers in the UK and the European Union under 'managed migration' policies.

Nancy Lewis is an Assistant Professor of Sociology and Criminal Justice at State University of New York, at Potsdam. Her areas of interest include feminist criminology and women in policing. Her interest in police use of surveillance as social control is related to a seminar she leads for senior undergraduate students at Potsdam College. Her work has appeared in the journals *Women Studies Quarterly, Violence Against Women* and in an edited collection on policing in Canada by Dennis P. Forcese (ed.), *Police: Selected Issues in Canadian Law Enforcement.*

David Lyon is Director of the Surveillance Project and Professor of Sociology at Queen's University in Kingston, Ontario, Canada. He is the author of several books on surveillance, the most recent of which is *Surveillance after September 11* (Polity Press 2003).

Willem Maas has a PhD in Political Science from Yale University and is Assistant Professor of Politics and European Studies at New York University. In his research, Dr Maas focuses on citizenship, European integration, migration, sovereignty, federalism, and democratic theory and elections. At NYU, he teaches the graduate and undergraduate research seminars in European Studies and graduate courses on European citizenship, comparative European politics and the European Union.

Gary T. Marx is a lapsed sociologist, Professor Emeritus MIT, and an electronic (garymarx.net) – and occasionally itinerant – scholar. He is the author of *Protest and Prejudice and Undercover: Police Surveillance in America*, and of articles in all the usual, and some unusual, places. He is the founder of the Bainbridge Island and Scottsdale Bike and Kayak Club.

Benjamin J. Muller recently completed his PhD at Queen's University Belfast. His research focuses broadly on the post-9/11 securitization of citizenship and migration, homeland security strategies, biometric technologies, biopolitics and theories of international relations. He has published in various academic journals, and since September 2003 has taught International Security and European Studies in the Department of Political Science at the University of Victoria, Canada.

Hélène Pellerin is Associate Professor in the School of Political Studies, University of Ottawa. Her research interests involve the management of migration flows at regional and international levels and the current GATS negotiations around migration. She has published several articles on these issues. The most recent of these are 'Economic integration and security', *Choices*, 10(6), July 2004; and 'Borders and Migration controls in the European Union' in J. DeBardeleben (ed.), *Soft or Hard Borders? Managing the Divide in an Enlarged Europe* (Ashgate 2005).

Mark B. Salter teaches globalization, security and global mobility in the School of Politics at the University of Ottawa. He is author of *Barbarians and Civilizations in International Relations*, and *Rights of Passage: the passport in international relations*, and several articles and chapters on border security and identity documents.

John Torpey is Professor of Sociology at the City University of New York Graduate Center. He is the author of *The Invention of the Passport: Surveillance, Citizenship, and the State* (Cambridge University Press 2000; translated into Portuguese with a Japanese translation in process); and editor (with Jane Caplan) of *Documenting Individual Identity: The*

Development of State Practices in the Modern World (Princeton University Press 2001); of *Politics and the Past: On Repairing Historical Injustices* (Rowman & Littlefield 2003); and (with Daniel Levy and Max Pensky) of *Old Europe, New Europe, Core Europe: Transatlantic Relations after the Iraq War* (Verso 2005). His book *Making Whole What Has Been Smashed: On Reparations Politics* will be published by Harvard University Press in late 2005.

Elia Zureik is a Professor of Sociology at Queen's University in Kingston, Ontario, Canada. His published work focuses on privacy, surveillance in the workplace and biometrics. Recently he has been researching information technology and nation-building in Palestine.

Chapter 1

Global surveillance and policing: borders, security, identity – Introduction

Elia Zureik and Mark B. Salter

There is no doubt that the mobility of people, data and goods is emerging as a defining feature of life in late modernity. The talk about globalization and the disappearance of space notwithstanding, borders in their geo-graphical, spatial and virtual forms have become increasingly central for understanding the life chances of people. If for Marx the capitalist state exercised monopoly over the means of production, and for Weber the state exercised monopoly over the organized means of violence, for John Torpey (2000) the modern state exercises monopoly over the means of movement. If there was a move towards a borderless world, the terrorist attacks of 11 September 2001 have managed to dash any such hopes.

Since the 9/11 attacks in North America and the accession of the Schengen Accord in Europe, students, scholars, politicians and pundits have been increasingly concerned with the passages of people, goods and information across borders. In response, states have fundamentally changed the ways that they police and monitor this mobile population and personal data. In this highly topical anthology we assemble a number of prominent scholars from disciplines across the social sciences, all working on the common problem of policing and surveillance at physical and virtual borders. *Global Surveillance and Policing* combines theoretical discussions of how we think of policing and surveillance at borders with empirical case studies.

Gathering at a workshop held at Queen's University (Kingston, Ontario, Canada) under the aegis of the Globalization of Personal Data

Project funded by the Social Sciences and Humanities Research Council of Canada, scholars, researchers and activists discussed the ways in which the modern state attempts to control its mobile population and data flows. This collection offers both a theoretical frame and empirical cases for the study of borders and the flow of personal information which are accessible to students and scholars in sociology, political science, geography and public administration who are concerned with state power, bureaucracies, borders and border management, and homeland security in an age of terror. One of the great strengths of this collection is that there is no other anthology on this subject which examines the study of physical and virtual borders simultaneously. Furthermore, similar works on this topic do not address a post-9/11 world, which has fundamentally changed the global mobility regime and the way that states police their borders.

The themes of the papers in this volume capture various dimensions of borders, and indeed they highlight the relevance of Gary Marx's rephrasing in this volume of General Douglas MacArthur's often quoted words: 'old borders never die, they just get rearranged'. But in noting the flexibility of borders, one should also note that in the process people and their identities are deconstructed and rearranged as well.

Contributors to this volume come from a variety of disciplines and theoretical traditions. Our mutual concern with various forms, processes and institutions of surveillance provides the impetus for this collection. We might point to Foucault's writings on the topic of surveillance as a broad grounding for this analysis. Foucault examined the concomitant evolution of industrial and institutional techniques of modern governance through an investigation of how productive, healthy, moral bodies were constructed, schooled, policed and harnessed for labour and public order. His investigation of how the penal system in particular led to the evolution of a disciplinary society provides a model for this study in which we examine how mobile bodies are produced and policed (1977). Foucault was also instrumental in elaborating how a disciplinary society might evolve that used surveillance as a primary machine for the construction of docile citizens. While Lyon, among others, argues that the panopticon model is ambiguous and, on its own, inadequate as the basis of surveillance theory, he also acknowledges that it remains a powerful reminder that power is not solely repressive, but also constitutive. In examining the institutions of surveillance, Bigo has presented a modification of Foucault's panopticon as the 'banopticon' in which, rather than the criminal being encircled and institutionalized, modern societies encircle and institutionalize the 'normal' and exclude the 'abnormal' (Bigo 2002). Lyon puts forward the argument that the effect of a generalized surveillance is a 'social sorting' that has only intensified after the terror attacks of 9/11 (2001, 2002, 2003). In analysing how the state and private authorities monitor and police populations, several different avenues of research present themselves.

Haggerty and Ericson discuss how the governmental modality of surveillance has become oriented around the idea of 'risk' and 'risk management'. In particular, they argue that a new form of 'surveillant assemblage' functions to 'abstract […] human bodies from their territorial settings, and separate them into a series of discrete flows. These flows are then reassembled in different locations as discrete and virtual "data doubles"' (2000: 605). It is this prompting, among others, that has led us in this collection to examine the simultaneous flows of data and persons across borders to understand better the relationship between the mobile body and its data shadow. In addition to abstract data, we also examine the documents of identity which provide the grounding for surveillance. Torpey's work was seminal in his investigation of the history of the passport (2000), later supplemented by Salter's account of the evolution of international cooperation surrounding the global mobility regime of passports and visas (2003). This collection extends this research with chapters by Lyon, Muller, Torpey and Salter which push this agenda forward. In examining the object of surveillance, Zureik and others have explored the importance of biometrics – the conversion of the body into data (Zureik 2004). Muller situates biometric technology within a political framework in the current volume and in a forthcoming work. Muller highlights the role of the biometrics industry in framing the debate around security, identity and borders. Nancy Lewis argues in this volume that in responding to political and cultural pressures, the police have resorted to using the latest in surveillance technologies such as biometrics and DNA testing in a dragnet fashion, and in the process have expanded policing functions to include non-criminal activities at a cost to human rights.

The current collection brings together a number of these threads of investigation to weave a complex story about the current practices of surveillance and their implications for policy and policy study.

Our shared concern about surveillance has also led us to the border. Let us set out some commonly accepted precepts: Borders are important and understudied. While all borders are important, some borders are more important than others. Inter-state borders – of various significance – are central to the global mobility regime, the international system in both political and economic spheres, and to national identity. Inter-state frontiers always reflect the over-determination of economic, military and cultural boundaries. That said, the metaphor of the border is over-used

3

to the extent that our thinking about borders is often clouded – although Marx goes a long way to providing a typology of borders in the current volume. Marx reminds us that borders are the subject of a variety of disciplinary investigations, in addition to a few inter-disciplinary forays. Crossing the disciplines of anthropology, sociology, political science and human geography within this collection, the border itself is opened up as an extremely productive site of study.

The presumed isomorphism among sovereignty, nationality and territory has been undone by transportation, communications and population flows commonly called 'globalization'. Airports, for instance, deterritorialize the border, while immigration databases virtualize it. Nevertheless, the border of a state is central to its definition; as Anderson suggests, 'the frontier is the basic political institution' (1996: 1). To draw an analytical distinction between the policing of population and the policing of territory (although in practice the two functions are often carried out in concert and are certainly mutually reinforcing), we might separate the frontier and the boundary of a state. Thus we can understand the policing of human movement across borders as a boundary-maintenance procedure and the policing of territorial rights across borders as a frontier-maintenance procedure. One sees the difference clearly in the kinds of institutions which arise to structure each of these different governmental roles. This analytical division is especially salient now, when many POEs (Ports of Entry) and checkpoints or security nodes – border policing – occur outside the territory of the state – or inside the territory of the state (in addition to being at the frontier). Albert and Brock have described this as a 'debordering' process because border functions are increasingly distant from territorial frontiers (1996: 62–3). For the most part, this collection focuses on the border and the control and policing of population rather than territory, although Donaldson's work provides an interesting counterpoint by detailing both kinds of lines.

It is our contention that as the policing function of the border is undermined or interrupted, a more general policing of the population must take place, as Lyon and Salter have suggested. The image of a controlled border allows for the construction of the national space as smooth space, safe space and domestic space. In the macro-politics of the inside/outside dynamic, the anxiety of the internal other may be generalized into policing as the external other is contained by the army and the international border. As these two forces and threats intertwine, Bigo suggests, we see the forces of army and police coordinate to 'lower [...] the level of acceptability of the other' (2001: 111). To our mind, this is a reconfiguration of the national sense of 'safe' space – a vital part of national territoriality. Within a globalized, post-9/11 world, revolutions in transportation, technology, and policing make the border an essential site of study.

Our core argument in this volume is fourfold:

1) That the new dynamics of global policing and surveillance should be a central concern of modern policy makers and policy studies;

2) That this project to understand the processes, institutions and experiences of control – such as identity cards, censuses, passports, etc. – requires a multi-disciplinary effort;

3) That the border itself is an under-studied and under-theorized important site of politics; and

4) That we must examine the paths, processes and institutions of the movement of data and information just as much as we examine the paths, processes and institutions of the movement of persons.

In an age of globalization, how do world governments, and often private corporations, attempt to mitigate the inherent uncertainty of increasingly mobile populations? How might we account for the ease of some persons jetting around the world with little concern other than the choice of an aisle or window seat alongside the tyranny of the local in which the majority of the world's population is tied to the natal home? Similarly, how might we explain the movement of our personal data, often without our explicit knowledge? We would suggest that there are three dimensions which illustrate the dynamics of state policing, surveillance and the differential mobilities of data and persons. We might gauge the freedom of mobility (of data and persons) as being conditioned by state capacity for surveillance, state inclination demonstrated by policing environment, and the characteristics of the different mobile (bodily or informational) populations. This three-dimensional space allows us to conceptualize the varying degrees of control and constitution of states and individuals as they cross international borders.

State surveillance capacity is determined by the resources available, including not only the budgetary, material or geographic restraints, but also political will. Distinct from the ability of the state to control its border, we must also examine the degree to which the state polices its citizens and its borders. Finally, as Salter has argued elsewhere, the characteristics of the mobile subject are crucial in determining the permeability of an international border, determined by class, nationality and other social scripts (Salter 2003, 2004).

Thus, we can characterize the freedom of mobility of particular individuals or information packets across different jurisdictions – allowing

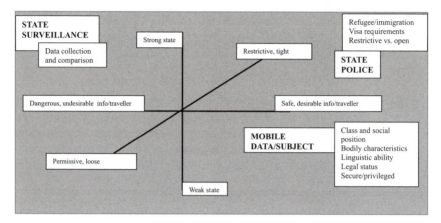

Figure 1.1   Dimensions of Control at the Border

for different permeabilities in different government jurisdictions. The various authors examine questions of technology, biometrics, identity, police cooperation, private surveillance, data and information sharing, airports and territorial borders.

Our collection is organized into four broad themes. Marx, Salter and Pellerin discuss typologies and theories of borders and border maintenance. Lyon, Muller and Lewis analyse the intersection of biometric and surveillance technologies through both empirical and theoretical lenses. Bennett, Finn and Torpey investigate the North American context – although Bennett examines private data tracks while Finn and Torpey trace governmental programs. Aas and Donaldson look at the persistence and even reprioritization of borders to states from a theoretical and empirical stance. Flynn and Maas investigate the European case through assessments of British and a potential European citizenship. From sociology, criminology, political science, communications, border studies and activist groups, these authors represent an important multi-disciplinary effort to parse the effects of state policing and surveillance at the border.

Marx offers a theoretical investigation into the 'operating principle' of a social barrier through exploring how risk, communications and surveillance technologies condition, alter and undermine different kinds of borders. By drawing upon the notion of systems in sociological theory, Marx points out that 'forms of surveillance can be usefully viewed as techniques of boundary maintenance'. Through his typology, we see that borders are manifest in spatial, institutional, temporal and bodily ways. Salter examines the over-determined politics of the state border through an examination of the various legal, economic, cultural and social functions it fulfils, in terms of the policing of a mobile population and the construction of a particular mobile citizen/subject. The airport is taken as an exemplar of the international border through the application of anthropological models of 'rites of passage'. Pellerin elaborates the political economy aspect of the international border in the context of state securitization, focusing on the way in which the regulation of border permeability is conditioned by labour markets, economic forces and continental integration. In adding economic information as data which travel, Pellerin productively expands the informational context in which states make decisions regarding freedom of movement. She argues that despite suggestions of trends towards deterritorialization as a result of economic globalization, we are in fact witnessing a reterritorialization of economic space.

The precise intersection of personal and data mobility is found in the national identity card, and the transmission of biometric information between governments and government agencies. Lyon's comparative approach to the national identity card issue illustrates the degree to which political will and political culture affect the adoption of wide-scale schemes. Taking into account the technological capacity of states, he suggests that with the increased ability to gather and use personal data, the border – both personal and virtual – is potentially everywhere. Muller also examines the technological capacity of states to 'know' their population, but uses the frame of security to ask, 'What is the political space of biometrics?' He argues that the construction of biometrics as an inevitable evolution of policing has displaced some crucial political debates about the value and possible abuses of such information. Bennett examines this dynamic of privacy/surveillance through a study of his own data trail generated from an airline ticket. This innovative project plots the trajectory of Bennett's data as he physically crosses the country, generating an empirically grounded view of the actual dangers of surveillance. Bennett concludes by cautioning against the use of 'totalizing metaphors' in discussing surveillance. Surveillance is a contingent thing. In his detailed description of what happens to the information collected about him as an air traveller coming to the workshop that generated the chapters of this volume, Bennett shows that it is not beyond reach to deconstruct one's digital persona as it is assembled at crossing points such as an airport. Lewis continues this empirical investigation in the realm of police cooperation, which she argues holds for information-sharing across borders among different agencies – a thesis supported also by the 9/11 Commission Report and the Auditor-General's report on Canadian anti-terror policies. For both Bennett and Lewis, the as-yet-untapped potential for data-sharing has not manifested itself or led to the kind of total surveillance warned by others.

Finn also evaluates the collection of data in the North American context through the new National Security Entry-Exit Registration System that has recently been upgraded through the US-VISIT program to require the fingerprinting and photographing of every foreign entrant to America (except Canadians). He argues that the selective application of these programs to some mobile bodies and not to others suggests the construction or description of benign or potentially criminal travellers, which has implications in terms of rights and freedoms as well as the creation of American and foreign identities. Torpey makes the point that European empires used the colonies to experiment with methods of social control before they imported these to the mother country, as Germany did in Southwest Africa and its subsequent extension of similar methods of population control in dealing with the Jewish population in Germany. A pertinent example is the point made by Timothy Mitchell (1988), who notes that Jeremy Bentham's visit to Egypt in the nineteenth century was prompted by his desire to assist the Turkish ruler of Egypt at the time to instill obedience and discipline in the Egyptian population through surveillance techniques. Thus, Bentham's 'panoptic principle was devised on Europe's colonial frontiers with the British empire, and examples of the panopticon were built for the most part not in Northern Europe, but in places like colonial India' (Zureik 2001: 211).

In contrast to European empires, though, the 'American hegemonic empire' practised extralegal methods of surveillance in the 'penal colonies' by engaging in both outlawed practices in the mother country and at the same time by exporting other illegal methods of social control which were introduced in US prisons, as occurred in the prisons of Guantanamo Bay and Abu Ghraib. From the point of view of the incarcerated, border and citizenship do not seem to matter whether the prisoner is inside the US or outside it. With an increase in the privatization of the military, Torpey asks if it is still the case that the modern state has a monopoly over the use of legitimate means of violence. The confluence of liberal democracy and penal colonies prompted Torpey to argue that a more apt description of the United States would be to call it an 'imperial republic'.

Several authors take the question of borders themselves seriously in examining the broader context of globalization. Donaldson provides some important and new empirical surveys of the territorial borders in such diverse cases as India/Pakistan, Israel/Palestine, Bangladesh/India, Botswana/Zimbabwe, Malaysia/Thailand and Saudi Arabia/Yemen. From a firm foundation he argues that border defence and security measures are not decreasing – especially in zones of conflict or dispute. Aas examines the changing notions of territoriality within the context of a potential 'space of flows' evidenced by globalization and the 'era of space' typified by the sovereign state. She avoids over-simplification and argues that conflicting political, economic and social trends reinforce the symbolic need for state borders. Aas points out that state borders can be elsewhere, beyond the state. She shows how Britain, for example, is stationing its police authority in continental European cities to forestall the entry of what it considers to be unwanted subjects, and how Norway, in the name of security, is adopting stringent measures to curtail the entry of asylum seekers. Flynn questions this symbolic dimension of borders and the national identities they secure through a study of British immigration policy, which regulates the permeability of the UK border to foreigners. In the uneven history of British citizenship, Flynn asserts a bureaucratic rationale behind a 'fuzzy' notion of citizenship which will challenge contemporary theories of citizenship as a legal status which fixes the uncertainty of populations in flux. Maas is more sanguine about the EU experiment, and analyses the move towards common citizenship in Europe and the removal of borders in the context of various tensions among the EU states. While Europe may not be a 'fortress' for Europeans, it remains so for non-Europeans who set their sights on entering Europe.

The collection of papers in this volume clearly shows that social sorting will remain a central feature of contemporary society. It will be increasingly applied along borders of all kinds: social, individual, geographic and virtual. The development of surveillance technologies will be used to strengthen the power of the nation state. The borders of the state need no longer be confined to traditional points of entry which travellers, citizens, immigrants and other transient groups are accustomed to pass through – legally or illegally. Borders now exist elsewhere, so to speak, in places that traditionally belonged to sovereign states, but now have been transformed to enable governments to check across their geographic borders personal identity and monitor the movement of people before such movement actually takes place. In the age of 'war on terrorism', vulnerable groups, minorities and oppositional groups will be at the receiving end of this process of social sorting and profiling, which is bound to extract a toll in terms of human rights.

References

Albert, M. and Brock, L. (1996) 'Debordering the World of States: new spaces in international relations', *New Political Science*, 35:1, pp. 69–106.

Anderson, M. (1996) *Frontiers: Territory and State Formation in the Modern World* (Cambridge: Polity Press).

Bigo, D. (2001) 'The Möibus Ribbon of Internal and External Security(ies)', in M. Albert, D. Jacobson and Y. Lapid (eds) *Identities, Borders, Orders: Rethinking International Relations Theory* (Minneapolis: University of Minnesota Press), pp. 91–116.

Bigo, D. (2002) 'Security and Immigration: toward a critique of the governmentality of unease', *Alternatives*, 27, pp. 63–92.

Foucault, M. (1977) *Discipline and Punish: The Birth of the Prison*, A. Sheridan (trans) (New York: Vintage).

Haggerty, K.D. and Ericson, R.V. (2000) 'The Surveillant Assemblage', *British Journal of Sociology*, 51:4, pp. 605–22.

Lyon, D. (2001) *Surveillance Society: Monitoring Everyday Life* (Philadelphia: Open University Press).

Lyon D. (ed.) (2002) *Surveillance as Social Sorting: Privacy, Risk, and Digital Discrimination* (London: Routledge).

Lyon, D. (2003) *Surveillance after September 11th* (Oxford: Blackwell).

Mitchell, T. (1988) *Colonizing Egypt* (Cairo: American University of Cairo Press).

Muller, B.J. (forthcoming) '(Dis)Qualified Bodies: securitization, citizenship and "Identity Management"', *Citizenship Studies*, 8:3.

Salter, M.B. (2003) *Rights of Passage: The Passport in International Relations* (Boulder: Lynne Rienner).

Salter, M.B. (2004) 'And Yet It Moves: the global mobility regime', in L. Assassi, D. Wigan and K. van der Pijl (eds) *Global Regulation: Managing Crises after the Imperial Turn* (London: Palgrave), pp. 177–90.

Torpey, J. (2000) *The Invention of the Passport: Surveillance, Citizenship and the State* (New York: Cambridge University Press).

Zureik, E. with K. Hindle (2004) 'Governance, Security, Technology: the case of biometrics', *Studies in Political Economy*, 73: Spring-Summer, pp. 113–37.

Zureik, E. (2001) 'Constructing Palestine through Surveillance Practices', *British Journal of Middle Eastern Studies*, 28:2, pp. 205–27.

Chapter 2

Some conceptual issues in the study of borders and surveillance

Gary T. Marx

> *We are at any moment*
> *those who separate the connected*
> *or connect the separate.*
>
> Georg Simmel

> *A question well put is half answered.*
>
> William James

> *Because you're mine*
> *I walk the line.*
>
> Johnny Cash

The Canadian sociologist Everett Hughes advised that the study of society should begin at home.* In fact it should begin (and continue) wherever the observer is. In that regard the conference at which the papers in this volume were delivered can illustrate some border issues.

One that stands out is the common form of a temporal process of linked border crossings. Here the initial crossings of various personal borders are a prerequisite for some kind of permissive or restrictive action on the part of border guards (as broadly defined). This permits the subsequent crossing of organizational borders (which can, but need not, be linked with geographical borders) in the form of exiting and then entering.

*These reflections expand on earlier work available at www.garymarx.net, in particular Marx 1997a, 1997b, 2001, 2002, 2003.

Consider those of us who passed through one or more international borders in coming to Canada. We were permitted to cross into the physical and organizational Canadian border, but only under the prior condition of permitting a variety of our personal borders to be crossed – first by the country that we were permitted to exit, perhaps were in transit through, and then the country we entered.[1]

These personal border crossings included 'non-public' information (both that personally known by the subject but not immediately manifest to strangers, and information not even necessarily known by the subject). Take, for example, the biographical and biometric identity information encoded into a passport or visa and offered to (or 'taken' by)[2] an agent, and the disparate and disaggregated details of prior transactions and behaviour which are accessed, combined, cross-checked and compared against watch and risk profile lists.

This checking in turn can rend asunder knowledge inhibitors stemming from the logistical borders of fragmentation, incompatible formats and time. Consider the resurrection for decisional consumption of events long past (which in an earlier age could be easily concealed and were often beyond human memory) or in widely dispersed records and those in varied non-combinable formats. Note also how inspectors go beyond direct searches and through x-rays, electronic, chemical, canine and other scans pierce the protective border coverings of the unaided senses offered by our bodies, clothes, backpacks and suitcases. For some travellers the transversing of the body is a transgression.[3]

In these border crossings we see several central characteristics of contemporary surveillance – the breaking through previously protected information barriers/borders of the person often in a low-visibility or invisible fashion; the use and integration of multiple kinds of data (no border is an island); and the use of acontextual, non-local and abstract categories to construct profiles of, and decisions about, the individual.

As with video cameras applied equally to guards and prisoners or workers and managers, we see the reproduction or generalizability of these means as they are also applied to those licensed to cross the personal borders of travellers. Consider the use of drug tests, background investigations, biometric identification and video – including a recent proposal for cameras in airline cockpits, as applied to those in the transportation industry.

The articles in this volume emphasize the juridical and geographical national border. This form which can be so vital with respect to issues of citizenship, identity, economics, security and culture can be located within a broader conceptual space which permits comparisons across kinds of borders, and an emphasis on the links between borders.

At the broadest level border issues are central to the idea of any system, whether physical, cultural, social or psychological. Thinking about society as a system is, of course, fundamental to modern social theory (Park and Burgess 1921; Parsons 1956). Any notion of society involving a system of interdependent parts implies the ideas of internal and external borders and means of defining and regulating them. The parts are differentiated from each other, even as there are points of connection and exchange between them.

Many forms of surveillance can be usefully viewed as techniques of boundary maintenance. Surveillance serves to sustain borders through defining the grounds for exclusion and inclusion – whether to physical places, opportunities or moral categories. Differential treatment based on surveillance results is central to many forms.

Surveillants (whether at an airport, a welfare office, a credit card company, a highway, a mall or in a family) serve as gatekeepers, compliance inspectors, social-essence definers and guardians, assessing aspects of individuals to determine who they are, what categories they fit into and how they are to be treated.[4] Conversely, while it usually generates less attention as a policy issue (because it can more easily be framed as legally and often ethically wrong), surveillance is also a tool for undermining borders.

At a very general level there are likely some universal border structures or forms, regardless of specific content, that serve to define and protect organisms as well as groups. Borders that serve one group's interest (and are functional for it) may of course be challenged by those whose interests are not served and for whom the border is dysfunctional. The topic involves a fundamental natural and social process of border differentiation and creation/re-creation that has accelerated under modernization. We see a kind of boundary musical chairs, as actors and organizations strategically pursue their ends in ever-changing environments.

Changes in life conditions, social organization, cultural values and technology rearrange borders, generating various combinations of the new and the old. Borders may become ever more inclusive and generalized and simultaneously (in other forms) ever less inclusive and more specialized,[5] as well as becoming more permeable for some elements and less for others.[6] Depending on the point of view and the analytic component, surveillance may serve to maintain or undermine borders.

Beyond its broad usefulness in thinking about social behaviour and organization in any context, the concept of borders offers an organizing perspective for considering contemporary surveillance issues. When these are sociologically and socially significant and newsworthy, it is often because defining, crossing or failing to cross a border of some form is at issue.

I hypothesize that when individuals feel their personal borders are wrongly invaded (their privacy is violated) one or more of four conditions are present (Marx 1999): 1) A natural sense border protecting information is crossed (e.g. the presence of secret video or audio transmission devices); 2) A social border assumed to be protective of information is breached (e.g. violations of confidentiality); 3) The temporal and spatial borders separating various periods or aspects of one's life are violated (the matching and mining of diverse computer data sets); 4) The assumption that unless notice is given, interaction and communication are ephemeral and transitory like a river, and not to be recorded and shared with others for future use.

From the early stirrings of surveillance studies in the 1970s through to the end of the twentieth century, empirical research and moral concerns focused on the use of new computer technologies to break through personal borders, as well as their potential for bringing greater organizational accountability. Those concerned with privacy and civil liberties argued for tightening the newly vulnerable borders around personal information, and they met with some success. At the same time, fallout from the 1960s and Watergate led to increased pressure for greater organizational openness and transparency (e.g. the Freedom of Information Act). The technological and social changes related to economic globalization also meant the weakening of several forms of organizational borders, resulting in the freer flow of goods, information and persons.

Yet after 9/11 in some ways the above was reversed. We see less public concern over the invasion of privacy and less support for governmental and organizational openness. Pressures to cross personal borders in order to protect organizational and national borders have greatly increased. Many in government argue that the privacy and openness of recent decades, and the unrestricted use of new technologies such as encryption and the web, undermine national security. Contrary to the trend of recent decades, many social borders are now more difficult to cross – whether entering another country, a neighbourhood or a building, seeking immigrant or asylum status, or accessing information – while some individual borders are easier to cross as a result of new laws such as the Patriot Act.

This can confuse the righteously indignant researcher on the side of the angels. Is the social problem the difficulty of crossing the borders of the individual and the ease of crossing organizational borders, or the reverse? Of course there is not one social problem, and much depends on the context.

But however viewed, we need to attend to enduring as well as changing aspects. To this end I first suggest a framework and questions for analysing and seeing the connections (whether theoretical or literal) between various border structures and processes. I next offer examples of how recent developments in communications, surveillance and related technologies undermine and alter some of the physical, geographical, spatial, juridical and temporal borders that have traditionally defined the self, the body, the human, home, work and other institutions, communities, cities, regions and nation states as entities. Understanding these changes in borders ought to be a central project for social science.

Classifying borders

In dictionary terms a border is a boundary or an edge that separates elements within from those beyond it. I use the term border to encompass a family of overlapping concepts and meanings. I emphasize personal and social borders as they affect, and are affected by, new communication and surveillance technologies.

The border demarcation may be metaphorical, symbolic and largely definitional, as with the borders between good and evil, loyalty and disloyalty or art and kitsch. Or it may be more literal, material and tangible, as with the borders of a printed page, the walls of a prison or an expressionless face.

I am interested in the norms and physical/technical conditions involved in the discovery or protection/concealment of information, particularly as this involves the borders of the individual in relation to other individuals, as well as to organizations.[7] The area can also be analyzed by considering organizational borders and inter-organizational relations.

The topic may be usefully approached by studying the interplay of the cultural and the physical/material as both border barriers and border breakers. Border barriers are intended to serve as blockages in defining edges, and border breakers are intended to overcome these.

Borders as barriers can be understood as literal containers or excluders of persons, objects and information (e.g. as in a prison, a purse or an encrypted communication). Some of this is done using 'hard' physical factors[8] (e.g. closed doors, clothes, locked display cases, armour) and some using 'soft' normative factors ('don't ask, don't tell' rules, 'you can look, but don't touch', 'stop on red') and very often both (e.g. doors on restrooms and the expectation that 'ladies' and 'gentlemen' signage will be appropriately directive).[9]

Border breakers may also involve physical (e.g. explosives, night vision or decryption technology) or cultural factors (e.g. search warrants, self-disclosure and notice rules), as well as combinations (e.g. the voluntary[10] offering of information on customs declarations forms and electronic and chemical searches of persons and luggage at international borders).

A fundamental question is how agents and subjects of surveillance create borders around themselves and/or their opposition and, in game-like fashion, seek to transcend or undermine their opponent's borders. To pursue this we need a comparative and dynamic framework for thinking about types of barrier borders and barrier breakers and the questions they raise.

Knowledge advances through identifying variation in outcomes. Below I suggest some of the main forms of border variation. A next step is to analyse their causes, correlates and consequences. For ease of presentation these variables are discussed in either/or terms, although many are best seen as continua.

Table 2.1 combines the dimensions of the presence or absence of physical and cultural factors in the determination of borders. This yields four types helpful in considering the sociology of information. Cells 3 and 4, involving barriers to border crossings, are most applicable to technological surveillance issues. The cases in Cell 1 (absence of cultural or physical barriers) are likely characterized by greater trust, equality,

Table 2.1   Borders

cultural (normative) barrier to crossing	physical barrier to crossing	
	no (soft)	yes (hard)
no (open)	1. looking at a person speaking to you, city borders	2. sense limitations (darkness, distance)
yes (closed)	3. staring, backstage regions, privacy and confidentiality expectations,[12] religious and sacred areas[13]	4. convent, military base[11]

resource abundance and cooperative group and individual relations, and lessened hierarchy than borders with barriers. That pattern holds for the single barriers of Cells 2 and 3 relative to the cases in Cell 4, where we see both cultural and physical barriers.

Key issues here are the extent to which a border is naturally 'readable' and 'crossable' without special disclosure rules or technological means of access, or in contrast serves as a barrier. The barrier may be natural as with limits of the unaided senses or because a border (whether to movement or perception/comprehension) has been created.

The compulsion of disclosure norms and the frequently involuntary (for the subject) character of surveillance technology represent major social markers for understanding and evaluating the ethical and public policy aspects of personal information collection.

In the same fashion the use of borders to restrict access and information (sometimes as a result of initial personal border crossings to determine eligibility) are relevant to understanding current questions around the privatization of public space and access and new restrictive copyright rules. The latter block access to what, in their absence, would be otherwise available (e.g. the right to physically be in a given place, to access information without restrictions or to reverse engineer and modify software).

Contrast a bank visitor with a Halloween mask bearing a threatening note and a customer without a mask also making a withdrawal; calling from an unlisted (or listed) telephone number to phone numbers with and without Caller ID; a supervisor seeing or smelling employees smoking dope as against inferring dope smoking from a drug urine test; observing police behaviour on a public sidewalk versus in the back areas of a police station; or driving within, as against beyond, borderless EC countries. My discussion will focus on the border barrier cells (i.e. Cells 2, 3 and 4).

In 'The Mending Wall' Robert Frost (1975) writes:

> Before I built a wall, I'd ask to know
> What I was walling in or walling out,
> And to whom I was likely to give offence.
> Something there is that doesn't love a wall,
> That wants it down.

Implicit in the poem are some major questions about borders. In classifying border barrier phenomena and processes, I suggest asking a series of questions.

What is the purpose or immediate goal of the barrier from the standpoint of its owner/controller/responsible agent? By definition a border demarcates. But beyond its denotative function, a barrier can be intended to keep in, keep out or do both simultaneously and differentially, depending on the category. A fence around an electrical power facility is intended to exclude persons. Physical borders – whether high mountains, islands or limitations of the senses – also serve to exclude, as do sealed or confidential records. Countries that deny residents the right to travel freely (whether within or beyond their national territory) use borders to keep the population within. The walls of a prison are intended to keep prisoners within, and a sometimes wrathful public out.

Whether the purpose is to wall in or to wall out, we can ask what is included/held within or excluded/blocked? What is a border intended[14] to be open or closed to? A mobility metaphor is often appropriate with any consideration of the idea of a border. The question being, what elements (under what conditions) are kept in or out, or permitted/able to pass through, and how often and in what direction? Major forms here are persons, valuables, information, communication, animals, insects, germs, heat and cold, and chemicals.

Given the richness of physical and social reality, all barrier borders are partial and limited with respect to what they can include and exclude. A mapping of even the most basic elements that can be contained within the catchment areas of a border and those that may cross in one or both directions is far from simple. Thus cyclone fences inhibit the movement of persons across them, but not sights and sounds (or movement over or under them). A broadcasting booth protected by a window permits light[15] and the visual to go back and forth, while internal sound is kept within and external sound without. As a Los Angeles teenager, I recall watching films I was unable to hear while parked beyond the fenced Griffith Park Drive-in Theater.[16] Conversely, I recall hearing, but not seeing, concerts outside the Berkeley Greek Theater (rather than doing both from inside with an admission ticket). A cattle grate keeps bovines from going from one territory to another, while permitting persons and vehicles to go both ways at will. However, it has no impact on seeing, hearing or smelling what is happening on opposing sides.

What is the barrier's operative principle? What is it based on? How does it keep out and in? What is it that must be crossed/broken through in order to enter or leave or be within or beyond? The distinction between the cultural and the physical applies. Cultural restrictions involve barrier norms – manners, diplomacy and secrecy, privacy and confidentiality rules.

Physical barriers that restrict or block may be inanimate as with cliffs, walls, safes or clothes.[17] Solid doors – with and without locks – windows with 'blinds' or curtains, drawers and secret compartments are related examples.

More permeable borders may be 'voluntarily' maintained out of habit or to avoid sanctioning for wrongful crossing (e.g. fear of electric shock, land mines or setting off an alarm and other deterrents). More gentle forms such as a mall store that keeps teenagers away by playing classical music can also be noted.

An armed guard, guard dogs, geese trained to quack at intruders, and alligators in a moat (who threaten to eat unauthorized entrants) offer examples of sustaining borders through animate means. Skin can be the functional equivalent of a wall in preventing access to body conditions. The face can be a potential mask of inner feelings and attitudes. Animals mark territory with their scent, and skunks and squid use their resources to deter predators in creating a defensive perimeter.

We can also note borders of an ecological or logistical nature in which there is a separation/compartmentalization/segmentation of activities, or the dispersal and disaggregation of information. Thus the absence of a national ID card or universal identifier means that personal information in distinct databases cannot be immediately joined. There may be cognitive borders to communication, as with incomprehensible languages and incompatible codes.

Time is a distinctive form of information barrier. Here the physical and cultural may be combined, as when rules provide that records kept in a locked vault may not be released for a fixed period of time. Time may also protect information as a result of memory loss or record disappearance or degradation. Time shares with the senses the idea of a border between the known and the unknown. To the extent that the past has been experienced or known, it stands in the same relation to an unknown future as does the unseen lying beyond the power of the naked eye.

The senses

A final operative principle for borders beyond the physical, cultural, logistic, ecological and temporal lies in the zones within and beyond which the unaided senses work, and fail to work. Erving Goffman (1959: 106) implies this limitation in his definition of front and back stage regions as applied to group interaction. In suggesting that 'a [border] region may be defined as any place that is bounded to some degree by barriers to perception', he identifies a central way that borders can vary and is discussing the senses. I would broaden this definition to 'any place bounded to some degree by barriers to the senses'. This avoids narrowing the topic to just the sense of vision as implied by 'perception'.

For borders and surveillance a key element is access or inaccess as these involve the various senses.

The senses stand in special relation to other border factors since persons may be the object of a border (whether having things taken from or imposed upon them, or being kept in or out). Persons may be the carriers of a border as with those wearing location monitoring transmitters (e.g. children, paroles),[18] the boy encapsulated in a plastic bubble for medical purposes, or high and low caste Hindus.[19] Persons are also of course the vehicles for comprehending borders through their senses. Many forms of surveillance as border crossing tools and border enhancement tools rely on extending or constricting the senses (whether of the agents or subjects of surveillance and in varying combinations).[20]

Border barriers and breakers often aim at limiting or strengthening sense data. The former thus can involve the construction of barriers that block or limit the normal range of the unaided senses (soundproof rooms, encryption, masks, blindfolds, concussion grenades),[21] as well as impeded human physical mobility and access. Border breakers may seek to extend that range by magnifying the sense in question, or by offering new forms of data and means of transcending physical limitations.

The senses, while invariably connected to perception and cognition, can also be seen as a distinct border form. The senses of course are not a border that one can physically cross as when going between countries or places. Sense borders are different from those that block the mobility of persons or objects. Nor are they a conceptual border involving opposites as between the sacred and the profane or hot and cold. The senses involve cognitive or experiential borders between the known and the unknown, or the experienced and what can only be imagined. The ignorance associated with the 'beyond' of a sense border also differs from limits to cognition that stem from being unable to give meaning to data because they are not understood, or are unknown as a result of disaggregation or being hidden.

Borders of the senses occur naturally when their thresholds are reached. Thus the horizon's border offers a barrier to sight, as does darkness. The borders beyond which we cannot hear (or smell, or touch and taste) are logically equivalent, if involving much shorter distances than sight. The latter two even require immediate proximity to the stimulus. The territory included in our unaided senses is miniscule relative to what there is to be sensed.

Asking what is on the other side of a border or a frame is a related question.[22] How does what is within the border differ from what is beyond it? With the conceptual border, there is a logical opposition (if not always opposite) based on what is included or excluded from the category. Physical borders may separate places with different social definitions (e.g. a river as the marker between countries) or simply different physical attributes (e.g. a valley and mountains).

The elements distinguished by a border may be basically equivalent (other than for their differentiating factor) as with the river banks separated by flowing water,[23] a national or state border defined by latitude, or the two halves of a basketball court. Such symmetrical borders contrast with asymmetrical borders that separate fundamentally different elements (whether beyond, below or above). Consider what lies beyond the edge of a cliff, below the wire of a tight-rope walker, surrounds a submerged submarine, or the in- and out-of-bounds lines of an athletic field. Or consider buildings with a concierge, or gated communities and what lies beyond them, or the jagged and shifting lines of police using fire hoses aimed at crowds.

The finite crossing of a physical border, such as opening a sealed envelope or in hiding a video camera in a wall, creates transparency – the act of border crossing reveals what is on the other side. But sense borders stand in a different relation to their other side. Sense borders may be extended through technology (e.g. binoculars, telescopes, microscopes and sound transmitters).[24] However, those extensions simply push the opaque threshold beyond which one can no longer receive sense stimuli. The ratio of what is known to unknown is altered as the border is extended, but it is not obliterated.

We may also ask about directionality and frequency of border crossings. Where border crossings are permitted we may ask if they are uni- or bi-directional. Mann, Nolan and Wellman's (2000) work in trying to take pictures of surveillance agents (in the tradition of Garfinkle's [1967] breaching experiments) illustrates the one-way nature of much surveillance and the question of how, and by whom, a social border is created.

A related factor is whether the transition across borders is sudden or gradual. The border change may be immediate and discontinuous, as with the edge of a cliff or a town wall. Or the border may be slow and continuous (even as a qualitative difference eventually appears), as with day and night and ecological regions that fade into each other.

Gradual transitions may be marked by in-between areas and intermediate buffer zones traditionally known in geopolitical contexts as 'no-man's-land' (which did not make them woman's lands). Contrast the direct division between entities as when leaving the US and entering Canada or Mexico with the demilitarized zone separating North and South Korea and equivalent contested areas.

Such interstitial border areas (while partly designed as conflict-minimization means) are particularly likely to be contentious, as those on opposing sides claim the interstitial area as their own, or one they are entitled to control and use to pursue their own ends. As we will note, this contention goes far beyond traditional issues of geography to the location and meaning of borders between the person and others under the stimulus of new surveillance technologies.

We may ask if the border is relatively fixed involving geo-coordinates and stationary barriers, or shifting and fluid. Consider, for example, the relatively fixed borders of an inland home as against a property line determined by tide levels or a bluff constantly eroded by wind, rain and waves. Diplomatic immunity and international planes and ships involve borders that move with the diplomat and vehicle, as do mobile homes. While Foucault noted how scientific measurement led to lines around presumed normalcy, many devices are fluid and their cut-off points specific to the situation and issue (e.g. the advisory note attached to credit score reports that there is no passing or failing grade).

When Frost writes 'something there is that doesn't love a wall' he implies both natural processes of erosion and the more purposive activity of insects, animals and hunters in undermining borders. Barrier borders are always partial and, to varying degrees, leaky. Many surveillance technologies rely on border seepage.[25] The logistical and economic limits on total monitoring (or perfect borders), the interpretive and contextual nature of many human situations, system complexity and inter-connectedness, and the vulnerability of those engaged in border work to be compromised frequently provide room for the inappropriate border crossings (whether involving legal or merely social violations).

In addition, new surveillance technologies give a momentous boost to crossing several forms of traditional borders. They call attention to contentious interstitial areas whose meaning is defined through political struggle. They also help create new types of border.

Border changes

Old borders never die.
They just get re-arranged.
General Douglas McDialectic

In one form of intact border we see rearrangement in the individuals who pass through them. With role transitions, persons continually cross social and cultural borders. The normative borders remain around categories, but role occupants move on. The game is roughly the same, but the players are different. Consider the move in childhood from being a non-swimmer restricted to the shallow end, to being able to cross the line into the deep water reserved for swimmers, not to mention the transitions from childhood to adulthood and beyond (and the gradations there at ages 18, 21, 25, 65, etc.), and the border crossings of immigrants, migrants and tourists.[26] There is also variation in the individuals passing through ticket-controlled perimeters on different days (e.g. sporting and musical events). Consider too, the less common transitions in role and identity entrances and exits – whether entering or leaving a school, marriage or religious order, or undergoing a sex-change operation.

Another kind of change involves the borders themselves. Closer to contemporary questions we see the link between surveillance and borders and how technology may change borders. Central topics here are how the agents and subjects of surveillance create, apply, sustain, challenge and change borders under conditions of the new surveillance.

Georg Simmel (1994: 5) has written that 'the bridge symbolizes the extension of our volitional sphere into space'. In the same way new border-creating and -breaking technologies extend our volitional sphere into areas far beyond space, including the senses, bodies, selves and time.[27]

Recent developments in communications, surveillance and related technologies in some ways undermine and alter traditional physical, geographical, spatial, juridical and temporal borders, making them more vulnerable to crossing, and, partly in response, new borders appear.

New forms and borders whose meaning is unclear or contested are appearing at an accelerated rate. New technologies that overflow and change the meaning of traditional borders may create disputed interstitial areas.[28]

Consider changes involving the borders of the person and personal information.[29] In the past, walls, darkness, distance, time and skin were boundaries that protected personal information and helped define the self. Information about the self resided with the individual and those who knew him or her. The number of records on an individual was limited. But now, with so many new ways of collecting personal data and the growth of data banks, we see the rise of a shadow self based on images in distant, often networked, computers.

New ways of defining the self have greatly expanded. We become not only the sum of our own biographies, but part of broader social types believed to have the potential to behave in certain ways. Individuals are defined relative to quantitative scales generated from enormous amounts of data.

Traditional borders blocked information about the self from flowing too freely to others without the individual's knowledge or will. This limitation enhanced the value of personal information to the individual, who could use it as a resource, doling it out as was appropriate. The boundaries of the body/self also served to keep out unwanted influences and information.

But with recent technical developments, the self may be less protected from covert intrusions and manipulations. Technologies being developed that seek to infer meaning from personal involuntary emanations such as brain waves and scents suggest the question of who such data belong to. Consider the case of a California man with a rare blood disease whose virus was cloned in an effort to help treat others. His claim that he had a property interest in the cell line that was subsequently developed was rejected by the Court. Determining identity from DNA 'prints' left on a drinking glass or by how a person walks can also be noted. Where does the person stop once elements associated with the person are expressed? With visual image, especially if it is used for commercial purposes, the individual has a property right. Should that apply to other forms?

Related examples can be seen when previously unavailable information protected by limitations of the senses are accessed and given meaning through technological supports. Night-vision technology takes what had been existentially private (regardless of whether it is in a legally protected private or public place) and makes it visible. Urine, hair and sweat analyses are used to infer drug-use patterns. The effort to read subtle facial expressions, voice tremors, handwriting and heat patterns around the eyes as clues to the person also seek to profit from porous borders.

Various forms of electronic and chemical scan are used to infer the presence of contraband by 'seeing' through closed objects such as a suitcase or clothes. Consider also unseen cameras with zoom lenses that look beyond their location in a private mall to a 'public' street, or a 'public' street camera that reveals the interior of a 'private' shop or home. A nice example of how heretofore meaningless personal data associated with a legally private place comes to a public place and is suddenly given meaning through a new technology can be seen in thermal imaging. Here heat from inside a house can be picked up by a device 'outside', revealing the outline of interior areas.

In crossing borders the above efforts take from the person and/or their possessions. But technological border crossings may also impose upon the person and, in so doing, often create contentious marginal zones in search of legal and social definition.

Consider a bakery pumping its smells onto the street, a factory pumping scents through its heating system, a department store spraying its 'perfume of the day', or the intrusive cellphone talking in a public place. These examples create and call attention to buffer areas traditionally free of such stimuli. Telemarketing and spam fit here. Auditory and visual subliminal messages may involuntarily and subtly cross personal borders of perception, just as tear gas, light or acoustic microwave crowd control means may not so subtly cross personal borders.[30]

A related border blurring involves the line between the human and the non-human, and the living and the machine. We are increasingly seeing humans with artificial parts, and research is well underway on artificial skin and blood. Computer chips have reportedly been implanted in chimpanzees, and a variety of implants have been proposed for humans. Cyborgs are not just science fiction. We see robots designed to behave as humans and efforts to have humans become more efficient by modelling their actions after machines. The ease with which we divided the human from the non-human and the organic from the inorganic is challenged.

Changes in institutional, organizational and place borders

The personal border changes noted above are a strand of a broader tapestry of blurred borders that also involve organizations. The lesser clarity regarding the separation of individuals and groups from each other, and from their environments, has counterparts within institutions and organizations. New communications and surveillance technologies (along with new crises, threats and opportunities) are also blurring and rearranging organizational structures and goals.[31] In some ways it becomes more difficult to draw clean clear lines separating the centre from the periphery, the rural from the urban, the national from the international, and the private from the public (whether involving material or intellectual property).

In the case of formal social control organizations, for example, we see if not outright merging, at least fogging up of the traditional lines between national and international authority, foreign and domestic police, military and police, and intelligence gathering and criminal prosecution. With increased internationalization and globalization of crime, terror and social control (McDonald 1997; Deflem 2002; Sheptycki 2003), the meaning of national borders and foreign and domestic actions is less clear. The links now made between dealing in contraband (drugs, weapons) and terror weakens the traditional distinction between crime and political activities. The previous separation of the military from domestic police, and intelligence from operational units, is also weakened by new legislation and new forms of cooperation.[32] The emphasis on prevention blurs the line between intelligence and crime-fighting activities, freedom of speech and association and crime, and weakens the tradition of a predicate before invasive surveillance is undertaken.

Consider also the boundaries of home and work. For an increasing number of people the traditional boundaries between work and home are blurred (in one way they are even restored to aspects of the pre-industrial age). With telecommuting, we see an increase in the number of people working at home. As well, fast-track employees with beepers, cellular phones, computers with modems, and fax machines are expected to be constantly available for work no matter where they are. In addition, company rules such as those against smoking or using drugs are applied to off-duty, as well as on-duty, behaviour. The workplace becomes everywhere the worker is. At the same time, with childcare facilities, health centres, lounges and recreational and commissary facilities, workplaces become more like homes.

The use of electronic monitoring to incarcerate people in their homes breaks and creates borders in another form. Since the development of modern rights, the home has represented a sanctuary and a refuge, relatively inviolate in defining one of the lines between the public and the private. But with electronic monitoring, the home can become de-privatized for both offenders and members of their families. The latter may also be seen and overheard on the video and audio means that frequently accompany home-confinement programs.[33]

We also see the weakening of selective borders of domesticity with respect to an increase in the hard and remote wiring and sensoring (and potentially censoring as well) of the home. Here the membranes that bring inputs into the home for entertainment, telephone and computer communication, electric power and heat, as well as various security sensors, send back records of internal activity to distant centres.

Developments in communication and surveillance tools over the last several centuries (and markedly accelerated in recent decades) fundamentally alter temporal lines. The ephemeral past is not what it used to be. With modern technologies, elements of the past can be preserved and offered up for visual and auditory consumption. Temporally bounded events move from a flowing river to a stagnant pool. This goes beyond filming of a birth, a wedding or a battle, to surfacing and preserving elements of the past that were previously unavailable, such as images of a growing embryo or a brain wave pattern in response to a given stimulus.

The growth of computer records offers a different type of preservation and access. In extending our ability to know the future (particularly on a probable basis), we see the weakening or even breaking of yet another border. Traditionally, many elements of the future were open-ended. This supported American optimism and a belief that with hard work or good luck things might get better. DNA analysis or expert systems that yield predictive profiles based on the analysis of large numbers of cases claim to offer windows into a determined future.

Another weakened temporal border involves the lag between the occurrence of an event and communication about it. Such time frames have been greatly shortened as the immediate past and the present almost merge and the temporal buffer offered by slower, more restricted means of communication is reduced. There is less time for judgement and greater pressure for instant action in our 24-hour globally connected informational world. For people who are 'on call' regardless of the time or where they are, the borders between action and inaction, on- and off-duty, and public and private that were available with the 'natural' rhythms of day and night, weekends and holidays and distance are shattered.[34]

Resistance and efforts to create new borders

Of course these efforts to change traditional borders occur in a dynamic environment. In Western liberal democracies the advantages of technological border-breaking developments are often short-lived and contain ironic vulnerabilities. Border creation and border crossing involve a dynamic adversarial social dance of strategic moves and counter-moves and should be studied as a conflict interaction process.

Elsewhere (Marx 2003) I identify eleven behavioural techniques intended to subvert the collection of information based on crossing personal borders. While my emphasis is on crossing personal borders, many of these tactics are relevant to other forms of border as well. Here I note several forms particularly relevant to the topic at hand.

For discovery moves (known as surveillance detection in the intelligence trade), the goal is to find out if surveillance is in operation and where it is. Examples of discovery moves include locating a hidden border-breaking device through the use of bug, tape and video camera detection devices.

Avoidance moves may follow the discovery that surveillance is present and involve self-regulation. The subject's behaviour varies depending on whether or not surveillance has been found to be in operation. For example, drivers slow down when their anti-radar 'fuzz buster' warns them that police radar is in use.

With piggyback moves the surveillance is directly faced rather than avoided. A border control is evaded, or information protected, by accompanying or being attached to a legitimate subject or object. For example, systems requiring an access card can sometimes be thwarted by walking or, in the case of a parking structure, driving quickly, behind a person with legitimate access.[35]

Blocking and masking call explicit attention to the communicative aspects of surveillance. Surveillors desire to read the signals given off by their subjects. With blocking, subjects seek to physically block access to the communication or, if they are unable or unwilling to do that, to render it (or aspects of it such as the identity, appearance or location of the communicator) unusable. The Faraday cage, which encapsulates space in metal or a metallic net, blocks electronic transmissions. A simpler version is the shoplifter who uses a large shopping bag with a familiar logo within which is concealed a second bag lined with aluminium or duct tape. Wearing a Halloween mask and writing in invisible ink are familiar children's games with adult counterparts. A 'photo flash deflector' fluid which blocks the photographing of a licence plate became available soon after systems for monitoring red-light runners appeared. Some 'fuzz busters' send white noise back to a police radar gun, producing a blank reading. The encryption of communications is another example. Electronic surveillance may easily intercept a message, but it is meaningless absent decryption.

Masking involves blocking in that the original information is shielded, but it goes beyond it to involve deception[36] with respect to the identity, status and/or location/locatability of the person or material of surveillance interest. Such actions include efforts to disguise identity, whether involving wigs, dyed hair, elevator shoes, padded clothing, plastic surgery or fake documents. Remote computer entries, whether taking or sending information, by using another's identification and password are a nice example of masking.

The goal of breaking moves is to render the surveillance device inoperable, often by stopping a border-breaking or -defining device. For example, Radio Frequency Identification (RFID) chips can be fried in a microwave, and a video monitor immobilized by spray painting the lens or aiming a laser pointer at it. A male guard dog may be neutralized with a tranquillizer dart, mace, poisoned food or a female dog in heat.

Terminus

In conclusion, I have suggested questions and concepts that may, consistent with the opening epigraph from Simmel, help connect the separate and separate the connected with respect to border phenomena. The prism of the border offers a way to order and reflect upon questions of surveillance, communication, privacy, accountability and social change.

It is tempting to see a linear pattern with the knowledge of science and technology leading to the breaking of ever more borders that seemed impassable and immutable to previous generations.[37] Yet we are hardly at the age of the end of borders. The pushing back of borders and frontiers does not mean they disappear given their functionality, social and cultural supports and the richness and complexity of an onion-skinned universe. It is just as reasonable to note the discovery and invention of new borders and the pushing further back (or ahead) of older ones in a continuing process. We see continuity in the progressive erosion of borders, but also in the creation of new borders. What changes is content, not form.

Developments in communications and surveillance create new forms and destroy, rearrange and alter some of the physical, geographical, spatial, juridical and temporal borders that have traditionally defined and protected the integrity of individuals and groups.

When surveillance topics are controversial it is often because defining, creating, crossing or failing to cross a border of some form is at issue. Policy issues in a wide array of contexts often revolve around the appropriateness of crossing, or failing to cross, personal and organizational borders and the wise and unwise use of border barriers. Concepts such as those offered above can identify questions and variations. A next step is to study correlates, consequences and causes of this. Studies of the structures and dynamics through which agents and subjects of surveillance strategically create border barriers and border breakers around themselves and/or their opposition ought to be a central topic for social inquiry.

Notes

1 Note also borders between and within countries. Being inside a country once a plane or train arrives need not ensure leaving the controlled confines of a disembarkation centre. Consider the film *Terminal* in which an arriving visitor is told, 'Welcome (almost) to the US international travel lounge which you are free to be in.' He is not, however, 'free' to be out of it.

Non-citizens face additional monitoring and limitations, if within a floating, materially invisible normative border (e.g. prohibitions on working or on free movement).

2 What is 'given' and 'taken' corresponds broadly to voluntary (consensual) as against coercive means, however difficult drawing this line often is (e.g. 'an offer that can't be refused').

3 Note the controversy over the 'pat downs' of female air travellers. On my last trip to a Canadian conference in Vancouver, after I left the train for the controlled place of the station, the man in front of me attracted the attention of a customs dog and was quietly taken inside for further questioning and a more intensive possession, and likely body cavity search.

4 This excludes much of the surveillance work of intelligence agents, voyeurs, paparazzi, blackmailers, documentarians, strategic planners and researchers in which the surveillance is its own end or is used for publicity. In Marx (forthcoming A) I discuss a number of surveillance roles and goals. The goals of the above actors stand in contrast to the social sorting and categorization examples found in Lyon (2003) and Gandy (1993).

5 Thus we see new global and regional political, economic and cultural units such as the European Union and the North American Free Trade Agreement. Yet we also see a dialectical move towards smaller, less inclusive units as in Eastern Europe, the former Soviet Union and parts of Africa. Note also Great Britain where Scottish, Irish, Welsh and Kentish identities are in some ways more prominent, or moves to split Italy and California into southern and northern units. Consider also new hybrid units such as those based on Kurdish identity crossing several countries, as well as the gradual emergence in the geographical and cultural borderlands between the United States and Mexico as a third way. The further weakening of the historical connection between physical proximity, temporality and social relations made possible by cyberspace breaks and creates new borders as well.

6 Andreas (2000), for example, notes how the United States–Mexico border has become formally much more permeable for the flow of goods but less permeable for the flow of undocumented immigrants and drugs.

7 I suggest that information about persons be seen as involving a series of concentric circles moving from the outermost, which includes individual information, to private information to sensitive/intimate information to unique identification to core identification. I identify ten broad types of descriptive information and 18 analytic dimensions that can be used to characterize them (Marx forthcoming B).

8 These of course vary in their degree of strength from hardened steel barriers to minor restraints (e.g. most railroad crossings or ropes guiding customers in a line).

9 Such arrangements of course seek to simplify the social and physical world and ignore the issue of persons with a mixed male-female identity/ physiology. One sensitive drug-testing agency asked such a person whether they wanted to be observed in sample production by a male or female and was told 'it doesn't matter'. Small children of course often cross such borders at will, as may those experiencing great urgency.

10 Voluntary refers to whether or not the individual chooses to fully reveal. Legally there is no choice, even if there is practically (absent being singled out for an intensive search).

11 Here the border to be crossed involves both the physical passage and who can become a member.

12 The border here involves the confines of the confidential relationship within which the shared information is kept.

13 A British General said the shrine in Fallujah, Iraq is protected by 'an invisible shield'.

14 In the case of natural physical borders we need to ask about consequences rather than intentions. However, intention may be considered when humans fail to take altering action such as building a bridge or moving a mountain.

15 There are of course kinds of light. Sun screens and expensive dark glasses promise to let in one kind of light and not another. One-way mirrors permit seeing out but not in.

16 After the ticket booth closed for the last midnight showing it was possible to back in the exit and steal the sound as well. A few years later that could be done only at the cost of destroying one's tyres, given the development of slanted spikes in the ground that permitted exiting but not entering. The latter mechanism, along with turnstiles that go one or both ways, is a nice illustration of directional flow built into a border-control mechanism.

17 Clothes may hide scars, tattoos and appearance-altering devices.

18 There is great variation in the goals and context for using these and related forms. Contrast the moving border associated with those under court injunction to stay away from a particular person such as a former spouse, to those sentenced to house arrest, to cellphones that indicate location when 911 is dialled.

19 The borders determining issues of ritual pollution such as being in another's shadow, touching higher status persons and their objects, or looking directly at the ruler might usefully be contrasted with those involving literal pollution or contamination (the isolation of those with contagious diseases or the sanitary zones of a hospital or manufacturing facility).

20 These tools in turn fit within broader efforts to engineer social control by affecting the actions of controllers, targets, potential victims and their environments (Marx 1995).

21 Note also more permanent actions such as the reported blinding of some of the builders of the Pyramids and the medieval cutting out of tongues of non-literate persons as a means of ensuring their silence. We see the opposite with sense-enhancement means which, when voluntarily used, cross (via extending) the sense borders of the user. However, when sense data are imposed upon the person (e.g. smells, sound or images) a border of a different sort is crossed. Technologies that strengthen the senses may in turn be used to cross the personal borders of another person against his or her will.

The concept of borders, particularly when we consider persons in interaction, is expansive and illusive and dependent on the component in question and whose, or which, perspective is adopted (the sender or receiver of stimuli, the controller or the controlled, potential victim or perpetrator). Borders are hopelessly interwoven and reciprocal, like the parts of an Escher drawing. This speaks to the topic's ironic and paradoxical qualities. However, conceptual unpacking permits some disentanglement, at least for purposes of analysis.

22 Consider also the mysterious and magical phenomena that mythology suggests lie beyond the borders – barbarians and the uncivilized, dangerous creatures, temptation, damnation and pollution, and less often, salvation, angels, heavenly delights and utopia. Apart from the inchoate 'beyond', note the sense of foreboding and uncertainty associated with interstitial borderlands. Being beyond the formal control of the established order within the border, these are in many ways often messier and more dangerous, if more dynamic and energized.

More generally this is also the case for regions of cultural conflict where diverse peoples meet – whether at crossroads, frontiers, ports or borderlands. Tolerance may be greater and rule-violating behaviour more common because of the weakness of a central authority and lesser consensus on the rules. Such places may also be incubators of social change given lesser traditionalism and the sparks of cultural confrontation.

As Rosaldo (1993) observes, understanding border regions can offer insight into broader cultures. Here, as sources of insight, border areas share something with the cracks and ruptures in the social order appearing with natural and social disasters.

23 Of course, in conjunction with other borders these can matter enormously – consider the two sides of the Ohio River which for slaves meant the difference between slavery and freedom, depending if they were on the Kentucky or Ohio side.

24 The thresholds of the senses are somewhat individual, varying from those who in varying degrees are blind or deaf to those with acute senses (e.g. the astounding vision of baseball great Ted Williams or the greater hearing ability of many of those who are blind, as with Ray Charles).

25 A dog need not enter a vehicle to search it for explosives since the scent escapes from the metal walls of the vehicle. Speech from inside a room creates vibrations on windows which can be remotely 'read' by outsiders. Consider the related difficulties in border definition and control seen with pollution, whether airborne pollutants from smokestacks, industrial waste emptied into a river going downstream, or when sewage pumped into the ocean from Victoria, Canada or Tijuana, Mexico makes its way to the western waters of the USA. Surfing in Coronado, California, a few miles from the Mexican border, sometimes has its drawbacks.

26 While it is of a different order, a life cycle model of various forms of birth, maturity and death can also be applied to organizations – from empires to

scholarly and artistic fields to family units. Both entropy and innovation are factors here.

27 However, these may be one-way or bi-directional bridges. Who the 'our volitional sphere' refers to and what interests are served should always be analysed.

28 This is also the case with new land use patterns such as shopping malls, entertainment worlds and large apartment, university, hospital and corporate complexes that blur lines that had been clearer as between the public and the private. While privately owned, they are dependent on steady flows of people in and out. The ratio of public to private spaces has been altered so that the amount of public physical space, as traditionally defined, appears to be declining. In addition, what had formerly been public, or at least ignored, space (such as empty lots) is increasingly built upon and the rapid growth of gated communities and access-controlled buildings further alters conventional borders.

29 This draws from and expands on Marx (1997b).

30 Since the 1970s Russian experimenters have claimed to have techniques to control rioters and dissidents, demoralize or disable opponents and enhance performance through what is termed 'acoustic psycho-correction'. This is done with computerized acoustic devices said to be capable of implanting thoughts in people's minds which are intended to alter behaviour, without their awareness of the source. Here come the Manchurian candidates.

31 We also see border blurring among distinct objects such as telephones, computers and televisions which are merging, as well as the merging of what had been distinct formats and types such as sound, image, print and data. Issues of simulation and the blurring of lines between copies and originals also fit here.

Beyond empirical changes that need to be culturally framed, some of the blurring involves lack of definitional singularity. For example, note the various dimensions (e.g. property, access, information) that may be present when the terms 'public' and 'private' are used (Marx 2001). Understanding the range of empirical and causal connections between physical borders and social and cultural conceptualization of borders is vital for understanding. Nippert-Eng (1995) creatively explores aspects of this in studying boundary negotiations between home and work.

The physical and the cultural borders are also joined in language with expressions such as 'over the top', 'out of bounds', 'off base' and 'beyond the pale'. In the latter case, a pale is part of a fence. The expression, however, refers to social distance from a normative standard, not physical distance from the fence.

32 Of course, more is going on here than the impact of technology. In some cases blurred borders are clearly a functional means to get around organizational restrictions. Note the US federal government turning to the use of data gathered and analysed by private agencies as a means of avoiding privacy and related legislation (O'Harrow 2005).

33   In another poem, 'The Hired Hand', Robert Frost writes, 'Home is the place that when you have to go there, they have to take you in'. The proliferation of electronic borders may require us to update this, at least for some persons, to 'Home is the place that when you want to leave, they have to keep you in'.

34   It took many days for news of Napoleon's defeat to reach France, and some battles were fought after the Civil War was ended because combatants had not heard the news.

35   An important context for this form is entrance and exit controls. The fact that the door or gate must remain open long enough to permit legitimate entry may offer a window for illegitimate entry. While not quite the leakage noted elsewhere, this nicely illustrates the ironic vulnerability of control systems in which there is exchange across borders. The need to open creates the possibility for illegitimate as well as legitimate entrance and egress.

36   Deception offers challenges to border conceptualization. The border here involves manipulating perceptions to make it appear that an illusory border is literal (e.g. the Potemkin village, the seeming firm ground above an animal trap, signs warning that video surveillance is present when it isn't). Deception may also be used to misinform with respect to what it is that is on the other side of a border – note cans of 'shaving cream' and other consumer goods sold as containers for valuables or a picture hung over a wall safe. The 'honey traps' (sexual lures) of covert police work and flypaper seek to draw their subjects in via temptation, in the former case to break through informational borders of the suspect and in the latter to create a border with no exit.

37   Consider Copernicus and Galileo for breaking the conventional border between earth and heaven, and Darwin for that between the human and animal, as well as technologies that blur the line between the human and the machine and those overcoming traditional physical limitations permitting space travel, microscopic and telescopic data, and new sense-extending means of communication.

References

Andreas, P. (2000) *Border Games* (Ithaca: Cornell University Press).

Deflem, M. (2002) *Policing World Society* (New York: Oxford University Press).

Frost, R. (1975) *The Poetry of Robert Frost* (New York: H. Holt and Co.).

Gandy, O. (1993) *The Panoptic Sort* (Boulder, CO: Westview).

Garfinkle, H. (1967) *Studies in Ethnomethodology* (Cambridge: Polity).

Goffman, E. (1959) *The Presentation of Self in Everyday Life* (Garden City, NY: Doubleday).

Lyon, D. (2003) *Surveillance as Social Sorting* (London: Routledge).

Mann, S., Nolan, J. and Wellman, B. (2000) 'Sousveillance: inventing and using wearable computing devices for data collection in surveillance environments', *Surveillance and Society*, 3, pp. 321–55.

Marx, G. (1995) 'The Engineering of Social Control: The Search for the Silver Bullet', in J. Hagan and R. Peterson (eds) *Crime and Inequality* (Stanford: Stanford University Press), pp. 245–56.

Marx, G. (1997a) 'The Declining Significance of Traditional Borders and the Appearance of New Borders in an Age of High Technology', in P. Droege (ed.) *Intelligent Environments* (North-Holland: Elsevier Science), pp. 484–94.

Marx, G. (1997b) 'Social Control Across Borders', in W. McDonald (ed.) *Crime and Law Enforcement in the Global Village* (Cincinnati: Anderson Publishing), pp. 23–39.

Marx, G. (1999) 'Ethics for the New Surveillance', in C. Bennett and R. Grant (eds) *Visions of Privacy: Policy Choices for the Digital Age* (Toronto: University of Toronto Press), pp. 39–67.

Marx, G. (2001) 'Murky Conceptual Waters: the public and the private', *Ethics and Information Technology*, 3:3, pp. 157–69.

Marx, G. (2003) 'A Tack in the Shoe: neutralizing and resisting the new surveillance', *Journal of Social Issues*, 59, pp. 369–90.

Marx, G. (Forthcoming A) *Windows into the Soul: Surveillance and Society in an Age of High Technology* (Chicago: University of Chicago Press).

Marx, G. (Forthcoming B) 'Varieties of Personal Information as Influences on Attitudes Toward Surveillance', in R. Ericson and K. Haggerty (eds) *The New Politics of Surveillance and Visibility* (Toronto: University of Toronto Press).

McDonald, W. (ed.) (1997) *Crime and Law Enforcement in the Global Village* (Cincinnati: Anderson Publishing).

Nippert-Eng, C. (1995) *Home and Work* (Chicago: University of Chicago Press).

O'Harrow, R. (2005) *No Place to Hide* (New York: Free Press).

Park, R. and Burgess, E. (1921) *Introduction to the Science of Sociology* (Chicago: University of Chicago Press).

Parsons, T. (1956) *The Social System* (Glencoe: Free Press).

Rosaldo, R. (1993) *Culture and Truth: The Remaking of Social Analysis* (Boston: Beacon Press).

Sheptycki, J. (2003) *In Search of Transnational Policing* (Aldershot: Dartmouth Publishing).

Simmel, G. (1994) *Bridge and Door: Theory, Culture, and Society* (Thousand Oaks: Sage).

Chapter 3

At the threshold of security: a theory of international borders

Mark B. Salter

This chapter questions the foundations for a general theory of borders, which could be categorized in terms of permeability according to state capacity, state intentions and the character of the mobile subject. Rather than use macro-theories of migration, this model arises from a concern with the micro-politics of border control, illustrated by an individualistic focus. Starting from the site of the airport, the anthropological model of the 'rite of passage' is applied to modern borders – separating crossings into pre-liminal, liminal, and post-liminal rites – which are shaped by architecture, the confessionary complex and hyper-documentation. The interface between state policies and discourses of border security and the practise or capacity of state policing is much under-theorized and under-studied. These questions have taken on an accelerated salience since 9/11. I would argue that there has been no deep-structural change to the process of crossing borders since the terror attacks. But, the amount of public attention and policy scrutiny has increased.

Borders are always contested by social practices and in some sense arbitrary in their evolution and policing. A central aim of most national border narratives is to obscure the arbitrary and contingent nature of borders and to fix the play of meanings of the community bounded by these incomplete and unstable boundaries. Balibar (2002: 78–9) contributes an extremely useful series of concepts to illustrate the contemporary meanings of borders. He describes borders as over-determined, polysemic and heterogenous. The political border always coincides with other kinds of borders, be they cultural, economic, linguistic, historical and so on. Borders are always experienced differently by different social classes, as Dalby expresses: 'The crucial point, however, is that boundaries play very different roles for people and for images, commodities and financial flows, dependent on which larger framework is invoked as the overarching spatial architectural of politics' (1999: 135). And borders are never homogenous in their materiality, effects or functionality across the space of them.

We might point to a number of functions of the border: both to repress (police powers) and to constitute (constructive).

Table 3.1 What does the Border Control?

Legal	Sovereign	Economic	Language	Identity	Culture
Citizenship	Territory	Currency	Of interrogation	Us/them	Space
Law	Int'l law	Customs/ taxes	Of government	Inside/ outside	Time
Bureaucracy		Regulations		Nationalism	

These dual operations constitute insiders and outsiders. In the case of international borders, the territorial separation of state jurisdictions is constitutive of the world system. In addition to historical studies of the evolution of state borders, a number of scholars investigate the degree to which state border functions persist in the globalized world. We can point to a large number of studies that analyse European borders, fewer that examine American borders, and very few that go beyond the core of the world economy. Within international relations, only Zacher (2001) has looked at the persistence of borders – though not border functions – on a global scale.

I have suggested elsewhere that the permissive or discriminatory function of borders varies considerably by mobile population and state capacity. In particular, anthropological studies of thresholds and rites of passage can contribute to our analysis of the international border. The border examination is a rite of passage for international travellers. Following from anthropologist van Gennep, the territorial passage is divided into three specific rites: pre-liminal rites (the rites of separation from a previous world); liminal or threshold rites (rites of transition); and post-liminal rites (rites and ceremonies of incorporation into the new world) (1960: 21). In classical or pre-modern civilizations, communities often had neutral space between them, on which to hold negotiations, conduct battles, or hold markets – the 'original' inter-national, interstitial space of world politics. Borders themselves are over-determined by social, political, cultural, ethnic and linguistic barriers. The transition between spaces, which van Gennep describes as taking place within the neutral zone, is now more often a matter of policing than exclusion. When one petitions to enter a state, the traveller abdicates all rights (except basic human rights, I would argue). The application of sovereign power at the border is absolute; travellers possess only basic human rights guaranteed by international conventions and dramatically circumscribed nationally derived rights. The border represents the limit of the political community – the territorial incarnation of the inside/outside boundary (Walker 1993: 127). 'Until that threshold is crossed, the person is outside the covenant with its privileges and benefits; but when it is crossed, or passed, the person is a partaker of all that is within' (Trumbull 1896: 266). This circumscribed position as petitioner is well-illustrated by anthropological theory. Girard discusses the individual 'in passage' – in the transitory state between one space and another. The passenger 'is regarded in the same light as a criminal or as a victim of an epidemic: his mere physical presence increases the risk of violence' (Girard 1977: 281). He continues to describe the community's reaction to the individual in transition: 'isolate the victim … forbid all contact between him and the healthy members of the community; he must be placed in quarantine' (282). To the degree that modern politics, commerce and society depend on the easy movement of individuals, the state must clearly balance this unpredictability and thus insecurity with freedom and mobility.

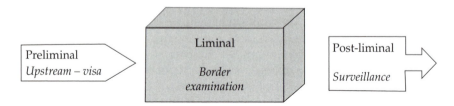

Figure 3.1   Border as Rite of Passage

Rites of territorial passage are rites of social passage. They attempt to provide some stability and predictability to a fundamentally disruptive change (such as adolescent/adult, single/married, childless/child, familiar/strange, etc). The entry of a stranger into the community is plainly a dangerous and unpredictable act. However, as Girard (1977) illustrates, 'with regular repetition and a pattern of success, these rites are gradually transformed into simple tests or trials, become increasingly "symbolic" and formalistic' (284). The world has faced a radical reminding of the unpredictability which the border rites of passage were meant to contain. Faced with the radical undecideability and subsequent risk of the 'alien' or 'foreigner', government agents are struggling to introduce new rites of passage that will somehow contain the contagious violence inherent in the terror threat.

Yet, we should not under-estimate the importance of the rituals of obedience, confession and discretion that are embodied at the border post. We proffer our passport – that request by our sovereign to another – that we may enter. By responding to the inspector's questions, we recognize the validity of the sovereign to demand of us truth, which we provide. The sovereign bids us enter, and with it an implicit promise to abide by that sovereign authority. Without the implicit confessionary complex, that psychic rite of passage wherein we disclose our intentions to the agent of the sovereign, the border cannot fulfill its discretionary function – excluding the dangerous and admitting the safe. However, that discretionary function itself relies on individual acts of discretion as each state agent stands in for the sovereign. Contemporary rites of passage involve not just examination and confession, but also information and risk management – the truth of the confession is double-checked by the examiner and the technology available. This crucial moment of decision sets up this project.

Bodies, biopower and borders

Conventional political accounts of migration focus on masses of moving populations – broad demographic and social trends – or the public policy process by which those populations are constrained or enabled. This account turns traditional analysis on its head and asks: What if we were to put the individual at the centre of our analysis? This is not to adopt a method wherein the life-experience of an individual stands in for any representative social group. It is important not to fill the position of the individual in this analysis as a universal, white, property-owning, male citizen (or any other figure). Rather, our aim is to put an empty marker in the place of the individual and track how different force fields empower or limit the individual's progress through the global mobility regime.

In this model, we point to a number of factors affecting the mobile individual: construction of the traveller through social scripts; material body characteristics, which often suggest particular scripts and are a subject of biometrics and documentation; linguistic ability and the implicit compliance with the confessionary examination at the border; the facilities or constraints imbued by class position; admission or exclusion at the border within a framework of international rights and responsibilities, which is dependent on technologies of risk assessment and the application of discretion under the shadow of failure and catastrophe; state capacity for intelligence gathering, information management and risk assessment; state policing powers; and finally, surveillance of the individual before, during and after the border moment.

In a typical journey, an individual will face several points of decision or discretion: legal, social and financial ability to leave home (passport, agency, ticket); financial and bureaucratic ability to travel internationally (visa, ticket); linguistic and social ability to enter the target country (examination, confession, discretion); and finally, the ability to leave that country again. Traditional narratives of migration describe the macro-process in terms of 'push' and 'pull' factors that induce or deter populations from moving. Scholars discuss economic, political and humanitarian motives for international movement (hope for a better future, fear of harm, etc.) (Brettell and Hollifield 2000). The abstraction of the 'push/pull' model of migration or the policy-oriented analysis of specific border cases helps downplay the role of social scripts and agency in migration. However, this model of migration downplays the crucial role that state policies and state agents have in facilitating or restricting mobility. Governments are key players in this narrative, by establishing barriers and inducements to specific kinds of movements – harsh refugee adjudication procedures, fast tracks for entrepreneurial investors, and so on. By placing the individual – the body of the individual – in the centre of the analysis, we see that both macro- and micro-politics of power structure the permeability of state borders.

This analysis in no way detracts from the ability of the state to repress or to exclude, but puts forward the idea that the state's ability to construct and to include should play an equal role in study. As Foucault suggests, we must be attendant not only to the power to prohibit or to regulate, but also to the power to create and to normalize. In addition to the ability of the state to admit or exclude travellers, state agents – such as visa, passport and immigration officials, not to mention police and intelligence officers – have the capacity and responsibility to define travellers as desirable or undesirable, safe or risky, healthy or diseased, etc., definitions which have profound effects on the freedom of those individuals. In doing this, we must be mindful that the ability to construct and to repress are not democratic, and involve the application of power (both repressive and constructive) which may take the form of knowledge, material or class position, as well as physical violence.

This contrapuntal position draws on the tension between empiricism and constructivism: working from the material circumstances of global mobility, but admitting that these circumstances are the result of political discourses that are not reducible to physical factors. Following Bigo's criticism of post-structural theory, following the work of Said and others, this prompts us to include the category of experience – without making this category foundational or irreducible – in our analysis of global mobility regime (Bigo 2002). The focus on micro-politics, rather than macro-politics, illustrates the importance of the politics of scale. As Adey suggests, 'little research has been completed on the microscale movements that occur in border zones and airports. This lack of enquiry is somewhat paradoxical given that the control of international mobilities that cross through airports and border zones are effectively managed, filtered and screened within these sites' (2004b: 1365).

This individualistic orientation is prompted by three concerns: normative, theoretical and empirical. While policy analysis provides an important empirical superstructure for this project, we have invested in an empathetic project in which we keep firmly in our view that these restrictions and regulations are important and fundamental in structuring the possible lives of millions of travellers. Rather than discuss the lack of international agreement on a TRIPS visa (which would allow all professionals with particular skills the ability to travel without restriction), this kind of analysis will investigate the ways in which the mobility gradient changes with skill level, not in a bilateral sense but within a much wider ambit. This individualist orientation refocuses our attention on the micro-politics of border control.

While state policy represents a *primus inter pares* of sources, we are mindful of the role of discretion by individual policers in enforcing the abstract restrictions of policy. The research in public administration of front-line officials confirms and elaborates anecdotal evidence that general policies are always subject to interpretation – indeed, that front-line flexibility is necessary for any large-scale exclusion system to function (Bouchard and Carroll 2002). The Office of the Inspector General investigations also illustrated the importance of individual confession and examination in crossing borders. This is not to privilege the terrorist as the most important of travellers, but rather to suggest that the age of terror has reoriented the anxieties of state officials. To supplement the diplomatic history of foreign policy implementation, we need a technocratic or governmental history of border policy and policing (Salter 2003).

We can classify the axes of free movement in four categories: legal, economic, social and bureaucratic.

Global transportation grids have displaced points of entry (POE) from the border to within the heart of the country. Domestic, national space is understood as unevenly vulnerable – in contrast to the unvariegated safe space of modern geopolitics. While this smooth safety was undone by the

Table 3.2

Legal	Economic	Social	Bureaucratic
Citizenship	Travel	Agency	Examination
Passport	Ticket	Desirability	Confession
Visa	Visa/guarantee	Risk	Discretion

Inter-Continental Ballistic Missile and the triumph of speed over distance, the end of the Cold War resurrected the nineteenth-century mood of complacent invulnerability. From the macro-politics of inside/outside, we see the emergence of a micro-politics of surveillance nets and vulnerable nodes. Thus, we have seen a sea change in our notion of territoriality, wherein the anxiety which was previously centred on the border has been projected onto a set of internal security measures (such as airport security and mall surveillance).

While these international border functions exist at all POEs, the international airport best illustrates the organization of state repressive and constructive power to discriminate between safe and undesirable travellers and thus to facilitate or hinder international mobility.

Airports as transient institutions

The traditional tools of Foucauldian institutional analysis illustrate the distinction between 'complete' and 'transitory' institutions. Foucault discusses the school, the workhouse, the psychiatric clinic and the prison as complete institutions, in that they attempt to fix and control the inhabitants of those institutions through incarceration, enclosure and discipline (1977). The architecture, rules and structuring of behaviour are designed either to harness the biopower inherent in those labouring bodies or to regulate the pathological body into normal conduct. Foucault analyses the architecture, rules and operating procedures, the inter-relationships between knowledge and power, and how these power/knowledge networks both create subjects and repress behaviours. Each of these institutions is designed for staticity – the regulation of limited movement through repetition. The airport is designed for movement – the regulation of mass movement and the discrimination of desirable and undesirable travellers. At the airport, the border is collapsed spatially – there is no 'foreign' airport space, only the interstitial space of the gate area – beyond exit control, not yet in transit, and before entry control.

The crucial threshold between inside and outside is the displaced international border, the arrivals hall. Using van Gennep's model of the threshold rite, we can parse the airport into three distinct spheres: preliminal rites, liminal rites, post-liminal rites. I would highlight three aspects of the airport's control matrix: preliminal rites are structured by airport architecture, liminal rites are dependent on the confessionary complex; post-liminal rites, or the re-integration of the subject into the new space, are dependent on hyper-documentation. Architecture, confession and hyper-documentation are all mutually reinforcing mechanisms of control – shoring and supporting the sovereign power of the state to compel subjects to docility and obedience.

Preliminal – architecture

Similar kinds of social institutions are designed for transitory control through spatio-knowledge management: freeways, shopping malls, emergency rooms. In each case, the maintenance of safe and efficient flows is central to the use of the space. Freeways, malls and hospitals fail if agents do not move through the space. Airports are complex institutions which striate mobility and access. From the ground-level control of baggage, technical and support staff, to the separate levels of arrival and departure and the distinction between domestic and international flights, airports are designed to survey, discriminate and control mobile bodies. A key technology of control is surveillance – by which passengers are knowingly monitored by security personnel. Adey goes as far as to argue that 'the airport is now a surveillance machine – an assemblage where webs of technology and information combine' (2004b: 1375). Building on his excellent work, I hope to introduce some kind of spatial analysis to bear on the structure of airport spaces.

In this, I follow the work of sociologists and human geographers in charting the power imbued to social spaces. Lyon powerfully argues that current methods of surveillance and social organization have led to an increase in 'social sorting' in which hierarchies of class, social position and race are increasingly instantiated in modern spaces. He argues 'the leading trend, in most sectors, is towards classificatory, pre-emptive surveillance, which tries to simulate and anticipate likely behaviors' (2001: 104). Rites of passage are a form of social sorting – they regulate who may be admitted into the community, and under what conditions.

The space between the gate and the arrivals hall is a genuine interstitial space of politics: you are physically in a country which has not yet admitted you, not yet claimed sovereignty over you, and not yet accepted your obedience. And consequently anomalies arise, such as Merhan Karimi Nasseri who was 'stuck' in Charles de Gaulle airport for over ten years because his papers were not in order, or a family that lived at Cairo

International Airport for several weeks.[1] Preliminal rites are preparatory – they declare the past, and the intention to enter another space. In modern times, one may point to the application and receipt of a visa, the ordering of the passport and the completion of an arrival card (customs, immigration, arrival declaration) as preliminal rites, which must be concluded before arrival at the liminal space (CBSA 2003a). The Canadian Customs Declaration card, which is to be filled out on the plane before landing, 'was designed, in part, to replace certain questions customs officers ask travellers at the primary inspection line' (CBSA 2003b). By completing this form, travellers are already disclosing information in preparation for the actual examination. The preliminal rite of paramount importance is the transport from airplane to arrivals hall – in which travellers self-organize into citizens, foreigners, refugees. To wait in the wrong line is to present one's self dishonestly before the examiner in the first instance – or to proclaim ignorance of the language of interrogation (Derrida 2000). In the arrivals hall itself, the fundamental question of admission – 'do you belong' – is answered by a traveller's organization of him/herself in space. Travellers sort themselves into categories of belonging: citizens who claim the right to return to their country (Article 13 [2], Universal Declaration of Human Rights [UDHR]); refugees who claim the right of asylum (Article 14, UDHR); or foreigners (who may claim no right to enter a foreign country under the UDHR – there is a right to freedom of movement and a right to exit, but no corresponding right of entry). This self-sorting also takes place with regard to privileged travellers, such as the American INSPASS program which exchanges an extensive background check and extended biometric data-gathering with a shortened examination and wait. Others also monitor whether travellers 'belong' to a particular space (Curry 2004). For the most part, however, the preliminal rite at the border is one of self-sorting.

Liminal – confessionary complex

Foucault is extremely useful in examining the ways in which the individual comes to police him/herself as part of the machinery of airport security. He discusses the growth of the confessionary complex, by which state power is used not only to restrict certain actions, but also to impel individuals to disclose the truth about themselves – even when that truth is damning (1994: 81). The confessionary complex is at the heart of the airport's security regime. When a traveller petitions to enter a state, he/she abdicates all national rights (except basic human rights, I would argue); the application of sovereign power at the border is absolute. The first act of obedience before the law is self-disclosing the truth of our intentions (Derrida 2000: 27). Even the space of examination is established like a confessional: the border agent behind the glass asks of your past, your future intentions, examines your passport, and then grants absolution or further investigation. In Foucault's terms, the modern subject is controlled not simply through repression of certain desires, but through a structure in which 'unconditional obedience, uninterrupted examination, and exhaustive confession form an ensemble [which] appears as an indispensable component of the government of men by each other' (1994: 84). Institutions such as the courts of law, medicine, the psychiatric clinic or the classroom are imbued with a structure by which the subjects of those institutions are conditioned to confess their deeds, thoughts and capabilities to those in authority according to an externally defined norm of innocent, sane or attentive. In contrast to torture, confinement or the violent manipulation of individuals found in other systems, modern institutions function through discipline: the creation of obedient and self-policing subjects (Foucault 1977: 193). Even in the transit space of the airport, mobile individuals are trained to obey an underlying logic of control.

The confessionary dynamic is illustrated by the ubiquitous 'no joking' rule which is posted at most airports. In the words of the Canadian Air Transport Security Authority 'you should never joke or make "small talk" about bombs, firearms or other weapons while going through pre-board screening' (CATSA 2004). Small talk and jokes are dangerous because they express untruths for effect – either amusement or a sense of easing social tension. But airport examiners rely on the anxiety of the passenger and themselves to effect the dynamic of obedience and confession in the airport. Like doctors, judges, teachers and other authority figures, we must all tell the truth to airport security personnel – not just the truth from a certain point of view, but the whole, entire, self-policing truth. It is ironic that these examiners of our bags, our documents, and our intentions – whose chief responsibility is discerning serious threats from safe travellers – are portrayed as being unable to take or interpret a joke or small talk. Though their power is limited to policing, these regulations against joking and small talk train travellers to self-police their speech and behaviour to present a low-risk profile towards the authority figure. In particular, the confessionary complex depends on the self-policing of individuals: the 'aim of the examination is performed with the help of a ... mechanism of shame that makes one blush at expressing any bad thought' (Foucault 1994: 84). Just as the architecture and concomitant surveillance lead to the social sorting of safe and risky travellers, so too do airport examination polices train docile travellers.

The ability of a border official to read the intentions of any particular traveller is severely limited. Initial or primary inspections take between 30 and 120 seconds. In that time, officials must verify the authenticity of the document, input the data from the passport and visa, and gauge the intention of the traveller (Gilboy 1991: 578–80). Immigration inspectors face enormous bureaucratic pressure to handle an immense caseload, and are often sanctioned if they refer too many travellers to secondary examination (though this norm may have changed since 9/11). Border officers rely on profiles that allow them to sort passengers into 'those who are safe, those about whom more needs to be known, and those who are not to be trusted' (Curry 2004: 477). Curry and Gilboy both investigate how profiles – which are socially constructed stereotypes – share an arm's length relationship to data. The method adopted in this construction of profiles is risk management: the allocation of resources to the probable target, and the quick approval of the vast majority of cases which are predicted to be unproblematic. As I have argued elsewhere, there is a structural problem with this type of risk management (Salter 2004).

Bouchard and Carroll's study of discretion provides us with a conceptual framework for distinguishing between the policy as written and the policy as enforced (2002: 239–57). They argue that agent discretion provides vital flexibility and interpretation in the immigration system, while simultaneously undermining the integrity of that system. Administrative justice simultaneously requires discretion to allow for special circumstances and is undermined by discretion which prevents equal treatment. The assessment of risk requires discretion because not all necessary information can be known – the crux of risk is ignorance. But risk itself is also increased by the making of uninformed decisions. This fundamental uncertainty at the moment of policing renders mobility a constant and irreducible danger. As with any regime that rests on obedience, there remains the opportunity for resistance and secret intentions. As is illustrated by the 9/11 terrorists, some individuals place themselves in a state of war with the state and do not feel the impulsion towards confession. Even in the face of sustained inquisition, a state may not be able to determine a terrorist's intentions. Richard Reid was interrogated by French police on two consecutive days for nearly seven hours but still boarded a United Airlines flight with explosives in his shoe. While there has been greater allowance made after 9/11 for inspection, the underlying structure remains the same: only The Shadow knows what evil lurks in the heart of men. Part of the target's resistance against the target is lying to the agents of state. The confessional complex is undone and reversed. Each act of resistance is a victory. A system that depends on confession cannot comprehend, police or control anti-systemic, revolutionary individuals (Hoffman 2003). I would also argue that the smooth operation of discretion relies on the confessional complex which is an essential supplement to the surveillance state. The necessary cynicism of the border official is twinned with the necessary anxiety of the traveller to create a space of interrogation and confession which creates the likeness of control without actual coercion (or covert coercion). As in the arrivals hall, the moment of examination is coupled by an examination of our papers.

Post-liminal – hyper-documentation

Linking the mobile body to stable or reliable information is a crucial technique of risk management. The mobile body of the traveller must be linked to information which reveals intentions – risk factors – which the individual him/herself will not reveal. There is a kind of hyper-documentation at work here, by which I mean that each piece of data is linked to other data, and ultimately to a risk profile: body-biometrics-file-profile. The notion of hyper-documentation also indicates the speed of communication by which information is abstracted into data and then compared to a risk profile. Adey suggests that biometrics abstract mobile individuals into objects which can be tracked and sorted (2004a: 507). As Bennett (2005) and Koslowski (2004) have contended, a key factor to this social sorting is the exchange of information between agencies.

Giving your passport to the immigration officer – having that information checked against databases – effectively signals your integration into the machinery of the modern state. You become data – an instance of a profile, a case, a file number. Without doubt, this may be an acceptable price to pay for admission into the territory of that state. My point here is solely that the submission of one's self in terms of information is still a political act of obedience – the data trail of your entry will remain etched in the memory of the state long after you have been forgotten.

We might point to three dynamics of this border control mechanism: the weaknesses of biometrics, the reliance on technological fixes to an inherently psycho-governmental problem, and the failure of risk management as a strategy for security. In short, states are faced with a dilemma in the post-9/11 world: a totalitarian strategy to increase their surveillance of domestic (and international) populations so that they might 'know' more; or the bifurcation of world regions and world populations into safe and dangerous in a way that completely replicates the nineteenth-century imperial model of the colonial world and reverses any modern movement towards freedom of mobility. Borders in either case become mechanisms of state control – for either those on the inside or those on the outside.

This description of airport architecture, the confessionary complex and hyper-documentation indicate the extent to which state capacity, state policy and the characteristics of the mobile subject may radically change the permeability of a state border.

State capacity: the emperor's new border policy

We are familiar with the fable of the emperor's new clothes. An emperor is convinced by his tailors that they possess a fabric which is so refined that only the brilliant and virtuous may even see it. At enormous cost, they fashion a suit for the emperor, who proudly wears it during a parade. Citizens, courtiers and the emperor all discuss the absent cloth in order to prove that they are brilliant and virtuous – until a child (seemingly innocent of guile or insecurity) laughs at the emperor's nakedness. Much contemporary analysis of border security amounts to a tallying of the emperor's accounts.

A crucial part of the discussion of border security must be state capacity. Can any state – or any particular individual or group of states – guarantee border security? I would suggest there are three areas of state capacity which highlight the question of security: information and intelligence, examination and confession, and policing. Can state actors gather, guarantee and diffuse intelligence about all potential travellers? Can the state examine travellers with an expectation of exhorting a true confession? Can the state effectively police its borders and its POE?

In addition to pointing to some articles (Bigo 2002; Walters 2002; Salter 2004) that do investigate this question seriously in the European context and some work (Andreas 2003; Flynn 2004) on American borders, there is a real paucity of research on border policing capacity. The interface between state policies and discourses of border security and the practise or capacity of state policing is much under-theorized and under-studied. I would argue that there has been no deep-structural change to the process of crossing borders since the terror attacks of 9/11, but the amount of public attention and policy scrutiny has increased.

Theories of borders

To establish a model – or substructure – of modern rites of border passage, the three dimensions of state capacity, state policy and the characteristics of the mobile subject are determinative. Symbolically, borders function in a similar way to demarcate the boundaries of community and authority. However, the life-worlds of international borders differ radically based on superstructure, structure and agent. In the past, these dimensions have been examined in the aggregate. This chapter has suggested that: a) we need to (re)place analytical focus on the individual; b) such an individualist methodology yields different and interesting results from macro-analysis of migration or public policy; and c) greater research needs to be done into the interface between state capacity and state policy.

Notes

1 The Hollywood version of this story, *The Terminal*, starring Tom Hanks, is far less tragic than the reality.

References

Adey, P. (2004a) 'Secured and Sorted Mobilities: examples from the airport', *Surveillance and Society*, 1:4, pp. 500–19.

Adey, P. (2004b) 'Surveillance at the Airport: surveilling mobility/mobilizing surveillance', *Environment and Planning A*, 36, pp. 1365–80.

Andreas, P. (2003) 'Redrawing the Line: borders and security in the twenty-first century', *International Security*, 28:2, pp. 78–111.

Balibar, E. (2002) 'What is a Border?', in *Politics and the Other Scene* (New York: Verso), pp. 75–86.

Bennett, C.J. (2005) 'What Happens When You Book an Airline Ticket (Revisited): The Computer Assisted Passenger Profiling System and the Globalization of Personal Data' in E. Zureik and M.B. Salter (eds) *Global Policing and Surveillance: Borders, Identity, Security* (Cullompton: Willan).

Bigo, D. (2001) 'The Möibus Ribbon of Internal and External Security(ies)', in M. Albert, D. Jacobson and Y. Lapid (eds) *Identities, Borders, Orders: Rethinking International Relations Theory* (Minneapolis: University of Minnesota Press), pp. 91–116.

Bigo, D. (2002) 'Security and Immigration: toward a critique of the governmentality of unease', *Alternatives*, 27, pp. 63–92.

Bouchard, G. and Carroll, B.W. (2002) 'Policy-Making and Administrative Discretion: the case of immigration in Canada', *Canadian Public Administration*, 45:1, pp. 239–57.

Brettell, C.B. and Hollifield, J.F. (2000) 'Migration Theory: talking across disciplines', in C.B. Brettell and J.F. Hollifield (eds) *Migration Theory: Talking Across Disciplines* (New York: Routledge), pp. 1–26.

Canadian Air Transport Security Authority (CATSA) (2004) 'Frequently Asked Questions'. Available at: http://www.catsa-acsta.gc.ca/english/help_aide/faq.htm (accessed on 19 July 2004).

Canadian Border Services Agency (2003a) 'E311 (03) Customs Declaration Card'. Available at: http://www.cbsa-asfc.gc.ca/E/pbg/cf/e311/README.html (accessed on 19 July 2004).

Canadian Border Services Agency (2003b) 'Memorandum D-2-5-7: E311 Customs Declaration Card and Multilingual Leaflet CE311, Translation of the Customs Declaration Card'. Available at: http://www.cbsa-asfc.gc.ca/E/pub/cm/d2-5-7/d2-5-7-e.html (accessed on 19 July 2004).

Curry, M.R. (2004) 'The Profiler's Question and the Treacherous Traveler: Narratives of Belonging in Commercial Aviation', *Surveillance and Society*, 1:4, pp. 475–99.

Dalby, S. (1999) 'Globilisation or Global Apartheid? Boundaries and Knowledge in Postmodern Times', in D. Newman (ed.) *Boundaries, Territory and Postmodernity*, (Portland: Frank Cass), pp. 132–50.

Derrida, J. (2000) 'Foreign Question', in J. Derrida and A. Dufoumantelle (eds) *Of Hospitality*, translated by R. Bowlby (Stanford: Stanford University Press), pp. 3–73.

Flynn, S.E. (2004) *America the Vulnerable: How Our Government Is Failing to Protect Us from Terrorism* (New York: HarperCollins).

Foucault, M. (1977) *Discipline and Punish: The Birth of the Prison*, translated by A. Sheridan (New York: Vintage).

Foucault, M. (1994) 'On the Government of the Living,' in P. Rabinow (ed.) *Ethics: Subjectivity and Truth. Essential Works of Foucault 1954–1984* (New York: New Press), pp. 81–5.

Gilboy, J.A. (1991) 'Deciding Who Gets In: decisionmaking by immigration inspectors', *Law and Society Review*, 25, pp. 578–80.

Girard, R. (1977) *Violence and the Sacred*, translated by P. Gregory (Baltimore: Johns Hopkins Press).

Hoffman, B. (2003) 'The Logic of Suicide Terrorism', *The Atlantic Monthly*, 291:5, pp. 40–47.

Koslowski, R. (2004) 'International Cooperation on Electronic Advanced Passenger Information Transfer and Passport Biometrics', presented at the International Studies Association Meeting, Montreal, 17–20 March 2004.

Langewiesche, W. (2004) *The Outlaw Sea: A World of Freedom, Chaos, and Crime* (New York: North Point Press).

Lyon, D. (2001) *Surveillance Society: Monitoring Everyday Life* (Philadelphia: Open University Press).

Salter, M.B. (2003) *Rights of Passage: The passport in international relations* (Boulder: Lynne Rienner).

Salter, M.B. (2004) 'Passports, Security, Mobility: how smart can the border be?', *International Studies Perspectives*, 5:1, pp. 71–91.

Trumbull, H.C. (1896) *The Threshold Covenant or the Beginning of Religious Rights* (Edinburgh: T&T Clark).

van Gennep, A. (1960) *The Rites of Passage*, translated by M.B. Vizedom and G.L. Caffee (Chicago: University of Chicago Press).

Walker, R.B.J. (1993) *Inside/outside: International Relations as Political Theory* (Cambridge: Cambridge University Press).

Walters, W. (2002) 'Deportation, Expulsion, and the International Police of Aliens' *Citizenship Studies*, 6, pp. 265–92.

Zacher, Mark (2001) 'The Territorial Integrity Norm: international boundaries and the use of force' *International Organizations*, 55:2, pp. 215–50.

Chapter 4

Borders, migration and economic integration: towards a new political economy of borders

Hélène Pellerin

Borders have received renewed scholarly attention in recent years. This certainly shows that changes brought about by globalization did not eliminate borders, contrary to what many analysts have suggested in the early 1990s (Ohmae 1993; O'Brien 1992). Borders seem to become a privileged place of regulation, as we follow the assessments of intelligence services, police and some politicians. In the scholarly texts, borders and security are increasingly linked together, in an attempt to demystify their social construction (Waever *et al.* 1993; Huysmans 2000; Anderson 1997; Balibar 2004). These analyses often neglect the economic dimension of borders, perhaps surprisingly since the increasing tightening of borders occurs in large part in regions where economic integration is moving ahead, notably in North America and the European Union. The relationship between the border of economic integration and the border of security needs to be addressed. The argument pursued here will argue that these two analytical logics are linked into what can be called a re-territorialization of economic space, in the context of globalization.

A political economy analysis, drawing also from social and critical geography, will be used to explore this link, focusing on the restructuring of the economic space, as well as on power relations involved in the practices of borders. The first section will present recent developments in North America and the European Union, indicating that borders become central for implementing reforms. Next will be an analysis of borders as places and processes of recording and expressing power relations.

1. The centrality of borders in North America and the European Union

In the two regions, border policies had been adopted already in the 1990s, in the context of economic integration on the one hand, and the search for greater security and control measures on the other. With the 1997 Amsterdam Treaty, the European Union promoted the creation of a space of freedom, security and justice, also called the Schengen space.[1] The constitution of this space was designed to promote economic liberalization, particularly the greater mobility of capital and labour within the confines of the Schengen Agreement, by eliminating border controls among member states. At the same time, external controls, between Schengenland and the peripheries, were to be reinforced, notably through the harmonization of controls, coordination of intelligence and police forces. The security controls constituted the counterpart of the liberalization of internal frontiers.

In North America, borders have also seen a sustained, if not an increasing, interest in recent years. Between Canada and the United States, the border is first seen as a place of exchange for trade. The World Trade Center attacks revealed the continuity of measures already started in the 1990s, but this time on enhanced security measures. The fear of terrorist threats and economic pressures from businesses on both sides of the border focused on the need to link security concerns with economic liberalization. The Mexican–American border received historically a very different kind of attention. Since the mid-twentieth century, the border between the United States and Mexico was the focus of efforts to limit the flow of Mexican migrants to the American south. Later on, the war on drugs added another perception of risk to the United States, coming from its southern borders. The events of 11 September 2001 impeded the development of a new dialogue about the American–Mexican border.

2. Interpreting border policies

Borders have not been theorized extensively in the social sciences. This can be explained, in large part, by the 'territorial trap' (Agnew 1994) that characterizes at least the discipline of international relations. National territory is a fixed, permanent and ahistorical feature of world order according to many theories. Consequently, the national space and borders have become fundamental features of the state. Borders are conceived as one instance of the affirmation of the state's sovereignty on society and in relation to the inter-state system. From such a perspective, the strengthening of border controls is interpreted as the rational reaction to growing threats represented by a 'leaking' or perforated border (Rudolph 2002).

Traditional Marxist analyses have also considered the borders as a natural feature of the capitalist state, used to control and divide the world labour force. The border, in that sense, contributes to creating what the natural factor endowment could not provide, that is differences in the supply and in the quality of the factors of production. By imposing restrictions on the access, on the judicial status and on the movement of people, border controls make more vulnerable some categories of workers. The precarious status of migrants has generally negative consequences on their negotiating power, and might even have a deleterious effect on the labour market as a whole, a sort of reserve army of labour constantly renewed and made precarious by new restrictions (Portes and Walton 1981; Burawoy 1976).

The renewal in the study of borders of recent years questioned its immutable character, partially thanks to changes in the spatial configuration of power and economic activities in the globalization context, and partially thanks to critical thinking about institutions. These new studies look at borders as the construction of a space or as the exercise of power. From one of these perspectives, a constructivist one, borders represent an act of authority, real or symbolic, which serves to consolidate the state's power in domains where its capacities are questioned, but where they can be re-actualized (Bigo 2002; Crépeau and Carlier 1999; Andreas 2000; Foucher 1998). Such analyses allow a look at borders as instruments of state power, particularly over people (Nevins 2001), but often by assuming a single and unified state logic. This is not unlike many studies in human geography, where borders are constructions not just of states, but also of communities (Gottman 1952). Borders are imagined divisions, constructed over time with physical or symbolic signs. The image of borders as being constructed through myths, historical narratives and experiences is becoming a central feature of many citizenship studies (Balibar 2004). In political science, however, borders' functions are not solely symbolic. Bigo, for instance, showed the number of bureaucratic agencies involved in constructing borders and border policies (Bigo 2003).

These analyses identified some of the important processes and modalities of control that are growing in numbers, as well as the social processes whereby symbolic borderlines shift, change or stay the same in human history. But the complexity stops short of addressing the economic dynamics that are partly constitutive of borders and border functions.

In economic analyses, space as distance, rather than borders, has been an explanatory factor of internal and international dynamics (Schwartz

1994). Borders led to the possibility of an international division of labour on a global scale, that is, a specialization based on the relative abundance and scarcity of goods, capital and people. Borders came to be seen as a node to be used as a regulatory tool, in the global circulation of production factors. Both neoclassical and Marxist economists have rested their analyses on this conception of borders as a characteristic of a fragmented world economy. For neoclassical economists, such a feature of the world economy is a given and constitutes the dynamics of economic growth; unequal opportunities are the engine of innovation and expansion. For Marxists, and neo-Marxists, borders are used deliberately by the capitalist state to maintain or to exacerbate unequal treatments of the international proletariat.

Although inequality exists and states have often used – and still use – restrictive policies in order to make precarious a particular group of foreigners (Portes and Walton 1981; Burawoy 1976), these analyses take the forms and functions of borders for granted, without probing into their transformation throughout history. The border is thus conceived as a line of demarcation, protecting the internal from the external environment. Secondly, borders are seen mostly in their function of exclusion and of restrictions of people. While this explanation was convincing in an economic context where labour-intensive industries were the engine of growth in the industrialized world, with a potency to marginalize the status of a large number of workers, it is less central today.

A political economy analysis of borders should take the border as a constructed space, that is, a space where different social forces, each with specific economic and political interests, meet and interact. The border should be seen as simultaneously dividing and connecting the internal and the external realms of politics and economic activities. As a social construction therefore, the border is a political process reflecting the power relations present in specific regions and historical periods (Anderson 1997). In the context of globalization and the spatial restructuring of the economy, borders become important nexus where new flows and forms of cooperation are designed and implemented.

A starting point is to recognise that borders can play a variety of functions, similar to what Raffestin had identified: differentiation, connection, regulation and translation of a political will (O'Dowd and Wilson 1996). The second step is to recognize that borders are processes with specific power relations; a border, like many other places, is a social space (Massey 1992; Harvey 1989; Lefebvre 1974). Conceiving the border as a social space problematizes the automatic link with the state or with some economic sectors, and opens up the realm of social actors and forces involved in the practice of borders. As a social space, borders produce power relations; at the same time, they are the site of power relations.

Borrowing from Allen (1999), three theoretical propositions can be formulated to analyse borders as social processes fulfilling several functions. First, the border can be conceived as marking a difference, which is then translated by practices of inclusion and of exclusion. The second form of power is the ability to create space with some coherence and meaning. This is the differentiation which has long been explored in scholarly work. The second proposition sees the border as creating a space, not only by delineating what is inside, but also by emphasizing what deserves to be differentiated from the outside. Finally, the border is also an actor, constituting power. It becomes not only a place, but also a specific way of exerting power. Through borders, specific techniques are used that define processes of control and new power relations that emerge. These propositions will be explored through the description of European and North American border practices of recent years.

3. Border issues in Europe and in North America

A) Border as differentiation

The function of differentiation is important when analysing borders, not only because it accounts for major world inequalities and exclusions, but also for the opportunities that it thus creates for business. Borders are also a space for the exchange of products, and spaces of circulation for policy making and business strategies. Charles-Albert Michalet showed very clearly in the 1970s the importance of differentiation for business expansion internationally, both in terms of trade and in terms of production strategies (Michalet 1976). Borders are legal posts that demarcate wage differentials, taxation, social and environmental policies, as well as interest rates. These differences become institutionalized with borders. In order to play this role, borders have to be both restrictive and permissive, they have to be places of connections and places of exchange and of regulations.

The border is used to differentiate between legal and social systems, and the practice of differentiation carries with it various forms of exclusion. 'Fortress Europe' has often been used, since the Maastricht Treaty of 1992, to refer to the policies of the European Union towards foreigners, particularly non-EU nationals. Exclusion targets currently two categories of foreigners: asylum claimants and illegal migrants. The Dublin Convention of 1990 was meant to address the first group. By forbidding the possibility of making multiple asylum claims, by adopting an information exchange system among member countries, and by identifying one state responsible to study the claim, the Convention sought to limit the number of asylum claimants who would stay in Europe prior to their hearing. Regarding the undocumented migrants, the European Union has upgraded police cooperation, notably through the Schengen Information Systems I and II. With these measures, many controls are taking place at the border or destined to be used at the border: the issuing and checking of visas; sanctions by airline companies; and the use of surveillance technologies such as infrared cameras, movement or heat detectors.

Restrictions towards foreigners have had the effect of levelling community policies and member states' policies towards foreigners in the European space. To that effect, a programme for administrative cooperation for external frontiers, visas, asylum and immigration (ARGO) was put in place in 2002, accompanied by a programme for police and judicial cooperation (AGIS). To this one should add the Schengen Information System, which has existed since 1995 and facilitates intelligence cooperation among police forces of the member states. This facilitated the criminalization of migrants, while it also led to a partial shift of the costs of controlling illegal migration to countries of origin and of transit.

Access to European Union labour markets became more selective, geared towards attracting the most qualified workers. Borders are an important instrument for this selection process; they constitute a regulator of labour markets. Through the issuing of temporary labour contracts, reinstated in the 1990s in Europe, after 20 years of restrictions, greater selection of foreigners into the European Union space was possible. The exclusivist tendency of the European Union also applies to regions, and the function of differentiation is very important, especially at the outskirts of the EU, at its hard borders which separate the European Union from East European countries, Turkey and the Mahgreb. The cooperation agreements between the EU and these countries contain clauses selecting and restricting trade in goods, and the movement of people. For instance, there were attempts to combat organized crime and increased controls on migrants from third countries. Security measures at the borders involved the adoption of converging policies regarding asylum, visas and police and judicial frameworks. For the ten countries that became members of the EU on 1 May 2004, many limits will remain, from no access for some agricultural products, to restrictions on the mobility of people that can vary from four to seven years in some cases.

The borders in North America also reflect a trend towards restriction and differentiation, but with very different realities depending on whether it refers to the northern or southern border of the United States. The southern border, between the United States and Mexico, has long been the object of police surveillance, serving to control both undocumented migrants and drugs. The North American Free Trade Agreement (NAFTA) did not change that situation, not only because international migration was not part of the agreement, but also because it maintained wage and social differentials that were the original conditions for economic integration in the first place. NAFTA institutionalized, in some ways, the economic and social inequalities between the United States and Mexico. A bilateral commission on migration questions was created that served to facilitate police cooperation in the fight against illegal migration (Miller 2000), thus consolidating the border as a place of controls, with limitations on the mobility of nationals from Mexico. In the 1990s, the United States made a major offensive, with measures of great visibility such as the construction of a wall between San Diego and Tijuana (Andreas 2003). Mexico also initiated a series of measures in the early 2000s for reinforcing its border controls at the frontier with Guatemala (Flynn 2002), in an attempt to raise the perimeter dividing North from Central America.

The border between Canada and the United States knows a different dynamic of differentiation. In the past at least, it was not so much exclusion that characterized border practices, but rather collaboration and the creation of border zones: industrial border zones for agricultural products on the west coast, and industrial products in the centre-east of the border. The Canadian–American border thus served for a long time more as a point for trade and tourism. The NEXUS programme (for fast track) and EXPRES (rapid and safe expedition) were put in place in the 1990s to facilitate and even accelerate the movement of goods and people among two of the three trade-agreement partners. The Border Accord of 1995 sought to promote international trade, facilitate the movement of people, reduce costs for governments and users, and increase protection against drug trafficking and illegal migration (Coalition 2001; Pellerin 2004). But since the mid-1990s, border cooperation increasingly focused on securing the border, in response to both terrorist threats and economic strategies to make the border more efficient. This cooperation resulted in the Smart Border Accord between Canada and the United States. It favoured the coordination of intelligence services and the rapprochement of asylum policies. Greater cooperation between the two countries in combating illegal migration was also underlined in a 2001 Declaration, which led to an agreement on safe third country status in December 2002. The September 2001 attacks in the United States prompted more direct talks of a common Security Perimeter, particularly between Canada and the United States. There emerged more coordination of border managements, with regard to security measures in particular;

a list of safe third countries for rejected asylum claims was produced; joint teams of custom officials were constituted in some ports; and there were initiatives for the joint exercise of fighting terrorism (Government of Canada 2003). All of these measures concurred in making the border tighter, and making the North American region more distinct from the rest.

The border as marker of differences seems to have both distinct and similar features in North America and in the European Union. In North America, internal borders remain an important feature of economic expansion and integration, which is less the case for the European Union. The reason for this difference stems from the model of economic integration that is pursued. The North American model seeks to exploit economic differentials built in a fragmented political framework, but in an integrated market network, whereas in the European Union one important objective has been, since the Single Market, to create a common economic space, backed by institutions and legislations. Yet, the events of the last 20 years have seen a rapprochement between the two regions. They have increasingly emphasized the importance of strong, hard, external borders, both for security and for competitive reasons.

B) Borders as regulators and organizers of the internal space

Human factors are important in understanding political geography, and in shaping space. And if borders are political processes, this means that they do not only operate on existing or given distinctiveness, they can also create them. Borders are a point of comparison, or points that mark the in from the out. By doing this, borders are both a demarcating line and a defining instrument of what is included and what is excluded. In other words, borders define as much the line as the content of the space being demarcated.

Defining the inclusive space translates into a debate over the nature of place, of various models of spatial organizations. Two models seem to be opposed: the territorial model and the global or network model of firms (Cox 1996; Amin and Thrift 1997; Palan 2003). In this context, it comes as no surprise that border regulations are at the centre of important debates between more outwardly and more inwardly social forces, notably around regulations of migration, tax havens and trade in services. Yet the opposition between global and territorial logics is more conceptual than real. As Harvey put it, global does not mean non-territorial, as places of fixity territorially located still exist and are required for economic expansion to unfold (Harvey 1989). With economic integration, the regional space becomes a place of fixity for capital accumulation. This often requires the smoothing out of some differences within the region. And borders constitute an important instrument for doing so. Border is a central legal object, as it is often the point of departure of legislations having internal and external implications. The delimitation of a space through the erection or consolidation of borders is a process that is as important as the content of regulations being developed and implemented. The exercise of marking is thus not just a technical matter. In fact, the delimitation of borders directly contributes to defining the content, insofar as it must impose the parameters of regulation.

Border regulations tend to impact physically much more beyond the borderline, because border regulations are expansionist. They tend to involve more domains than transborder phenomena. An example of this is the European area of freedom, security and justice, being created by Justice and Home Affairs of the European Union. The project was to create a space where security and justice would be developed to accompany and to foster the economic space already in place. As one observer signalled, it was not security as such that was the objective, but rather a space of security; in other words, the ability to constitute a cooperative framework that would cover the whole space of the European Union (Chevallier-Govers 2003).

The nature of border regulations is extensive also because the marking of the border between the internal and the external requires the progressive harmonization of those units that are now combined. In the European Union and North America, the progressive harmonization proceeds in a context where the paramount objective is economic liberalization and competition. Yet some differences remain that are perhaps of degree rather than substantive. The judicial framework produced by Justice and Home Affairs aimed to develop a European justice system that could supervise police and surveillance activities. Such development is generally acclaimed, with good reason, since it should provide counterbalance mechanisms to the powers of police and other security agencies. But the judicial framework put in place also serves to regulate the economic and social activities at the European level. From pension systems to labour markets, to education systems, a whole series of domains is now affected, in order to create a more coherent internal judicial order. It should be emphasized, however, that such harmonization did not lead to complete convergence of legal orders, historical and political reasons forbid, only to the reduction of political and judicial insecurities which generate transaction costs and uncertainty between member states (Riemen 2001). Some commentators have seen in this dynamic the successful attempt to assert the domination of liberal economic objectives, by restructuring and eliminating barriers to economic growth such as union participation in decision making and other social obligations (Panitch and Gindin 2004).

The focus on border regulations did not bring about so much convergence in North America. Many differences had been diluted over years of integrating production activities among the three countries. NAFTA added economic rules for trade and investment facilitation among the three member countries. And the reinforcement of police controls around the borders in the 1980s and 1990s has added some legal thickness to the regional space being created. Canada and the United States signed several agreements on legal cooperation to deal with transborder crimes and police investigations. The Canadian–US forum on the fight against trafficking, telemarketing and money laundering, instituted in 1997, is also a good example of the significance of borders in creating incentives to cooperate, and to develop a more coherent legal and police space (Solicitor General of Canada 2002; US Department of Justice 1995). And the domains covered spill over strictly transborder phenomena and activities. As the Commissioner of the RCMP was suggesting, a common management of borders implies a common vision, with shared priorities and objectives, not simply the adoption of similar tactics (Zaccardelli 2002). The content of the common legal order being created in North America, similar to what happens in the European Union, is shaped by trade liberalization and competition. The common border between Canada and the United States has become a smart border, which means that it combines security and commercial interests of firms. Security and economic efficiency and competition become indivisible (Coalition 2001). The influence of business interests is no stranger to this development. Following the attacks in the United States in 2001, a coalition of the main Canadian businesses (Canadian Chamber of Commerce, Business Council for National Issues, Canadian Federation of Independent Businesses, and the Canadian–American Alliance for Trade Border) have produced a report suggesting a solution that would provide for a secure and prosperous economic space (Coalition 2001). Such a plan involved decentralizing border management, and multiplying points of control and surveillance throughout already existing trade corridors. In spatial terms, this involves the displacement of borders, inward as well as outward, to places where controls can be done more efficiently. Hence the Canadian Council of Chief Executives proposed the reinvention of borders. From this perspective, borders in North America should be zones of cooperation over the continent, with greater surveillance on the perimeter of North America (CCCE 2003). The same cannot be said of the southern border between the United States and Mexico, at least for the important border points between San Diego and Tijuana, or between El Paso and Ciudad Juarez. It is slightly different between Laredo and Nuevo Laredo, where more trade occurs. These specificities might change if the project of Puebla-Panama finally takes off.

C) Border as a space of power

Power is not simply the attribute of an actor or the imposition of one's will onto another; it is also constitutive. Power, in other words, is acquired through action. This Foucauldian view of power, transplanted into a spatial framework, gives a social dimension to space, which can no longer be seen as simply the environment in which social relations unfold.

Power is acquired through its exercise at the border or in relationship to borders. Border regulations often rely on old and traditional mechanisms of authority – the army and treaties – but also on new means – police and private agencies to which some regulating functions or product have been assigned. These new agents benefit from border regulations (private companies and services, and security officials). These three facets of power in space will be explored more empirically in two case studies.

Police services, for one, are central in the new border management, what Didier Bigo calls the archipelagos of security professionals (Bigo 2003). Militaries, customs officers, police forces and intelligence services have all increased their functions since the mid-1990s, both in Europe and in North America. Their areas of expertise have been widening to include not only drug offences but also white collar crimes, anti-trust practices and migration.

The growing power of police forces in the European Union, together with the growing influence of the Ministry of Justice and Interior, has often led to the withdrawal of ministries of health, labour and social affairs (Bigo 2003). In North America too one can find this tendency, although in a less acute form. The United States centralized its security service on the creation of the Department of Homeland Security, combining what was, until then, the services of eight large departments. Although it is too early to tell, this centralization might give greater power to security services in implementing a strategy for internal protection. In Canada, resistance is stronger, but recent reforms and new policies adopted in the aftermath of the 11 September 2001 attacks, notably an anti-terrorist bill and a law on public security, have strengthened the power of police and intelligence forces (Gouvernement du Canada 2002).

At least two other forces are involved at borders: private agencies now responsible for the security and surveillance that states delegated to them, and organized criminal groups. Regarding the first category, there are two types of agents involved: companies directly involved in the transborder activities, such as airline companies or travel agencies, and high technology enterprises that offer surveillance and control products, such as infrared technologies. Airline companies have seen their functions of border controls increased over the last ten years, yet it is not clear how much power they managed to gain from these activities. High technology enterprises did not have power over border activities five years ago. But recently, these companies have been able to gain power over the processes of control at the border, and were even involved in the design of a security perimeter around North America, which would not only control people and goods, but also the protection of data and systems (Purdy 2002).

Criminal organizations have increased their power, paradoxically perhaps, in the context of greater transborder surveillance and regulations. The *coyotes* at the American–Mexican border for instance, increased their influence and power. The logic goes as follows: the use of smugglers increases as the difficulties arise for crossing the border illegally. And the more they are used, the more influence they gain, if not in relation to states, at least to potential migrants (Andreas 2000). Furthermore, since risks are high for these organizations, they tend to diversify their smuggling activities: people, and various kinds of illicit merchandises. Both North America and the European Union are important sites for the activities of transborder criminal organizations. This makes the border a potentially very lucrative place, and thus it represents an important stake for these organizations, as much as for states. And these agencies are not there simply to challenge the state, even less the existence of borders. It is the existence of borders that makes them powerful. Their power stems from their ability to capitalize on restrictions and differences at the border, a power that they can exercise against states, but also to seek profits.

Conclusion

Contemporary issues of borders have surfaced in the industrialized world, in the context of globalization and of increasing migration flows, xenophobic reactions and popular dissatisfactions towards political institutions. It is important, in this context, to examine carefully what is at stake around borders. Too often, studies of borders focus on only one dimension of the issue, either on social reactions, on the political power of the state, or on the economic gains of business.

The analysis offered here suggests that these various issues involve a series of agencies, but also a series of processes of power relations that need to be looked at carefully. In North America and in Europe, thanks to the strength of neo-liberalism, issues of borders are heavily influenced by the power of business to create a specific regulatory space that often contradicts that of states, or perhaps that of communities. In this context, the restrictive aspect of borders is only part of the problem, the other issues being the opening of borders, and the shaping of the regional space according to business priorities.

Reactions to border issues in this context involve both a move towards restrictive measures, suggested by conservative forces, and a different kind of openness in the creation of regional places that are both socially grounded and respectful of diversity. Europe and North America might have different models to propose, but the challenge for progressive forces is to foster greater thinking and action in making this possible.

Note

1   Following the Schengen Agreement, which came into force in 1999. It includes 13 member states of the European Union; Ireland and the UK decided to exclude themselves from it, as well as two other European states, not members of the EU (Iceland and Norway).

References

Agnew, J. (1994) 'The Territorial Trap: the geographical assumptions of international relations theory', *Review of International Political Economy*, 1:1.

Allen, J. (1999) 'Spatial Assemblages of Power: From Domination to Empowerment', in D. Massey, J. Allen and P. Sarre (eds) *Human Geography Today* (Cambridge: Polity Press), pp. 194–218.

Amin, A. and Thrift, N. (1997) 'Globalization, Socio-economic, Territoriality', in R. Lee and J. Wills (eds) *Geographies of Economics* (London: Arnold), pp. 147–57.

Anderson, M. (1997) 'Les frontières: un débat contemporain', *Cultures & Conflits*, 26–27: Fall.

Andreas, P. (2003) 'Contrôles frontaliers en Amérique du Nord à la suite du 11 septembre 2001', in M. Fortmann, A. Macleod and S. Roussel (eds) *Vers des Périmètres de Sécurité? La Gestion des Espaces Continentaux en Amérique du Nord et en Europe* (Montréal: Athéna).

Andreas, P. (2000) *Border Games: Policing the U.S.–Mexico Divide* (Ithaca: Cornell University Press).

Balibar, E. (2004) *We, the People of Europe? Reflections on Transnational Citizenship* (Princeton: Princeton University Press).

Bigo, D. (2003) 'Les archipels des professionnels de l'(in)sécurité', in M. Fortmann, A. Macleod and S. Roussel (eds) *Vers des Périmètres de Sécurité? La Gestion des Espaces Continentaux en Amérique du Nord et en Europe* (Montréal: Athéna).

Bigo, D. (2002) 'Security and Immigration: toward a critique of the governmentality of unease', *Alternatives*, 27: Supplément, pp. 63–92.

Burawoy, M. (1976) 'The Functions and Reproduction of Migrant Labor: comparative material from Southern Africa and the United States', *American Journal of Sociology*, 81:5, pp. 1050–87.

CCCE (2003) 'Security and prosperity. Toward a new Canadian US partnership in North America. Profile of the North American Security and Prosperity Initiative.' Available at: http://www.ceocouncil.ca (last accessed May 2003).

Chevallier-Govers, C. (2003) 'Le concept de sécurité intérieure et l'Union européenne', in J.-C. Froment, J.J. Gleizal and M. Kaluszynski (eds) *Les États à l'Épreuve de la Sécurité* (Grenoble: Presses Universitaires de Grenoble).

Coalition for Secure and Trade-Efficient Borders (2001) *Rethinking our Borders: A Plan for Actions* (Ottawa: Coalition for Secure and Trade-Efficient Borders).

Cox, R.W. (1996) 'Production and Security', in R.W. Cox and T.J. Sinclair (eds) *Approaches to World Order* (Cambridge: Cambridge University Press), pp. 276–95.

Crépeau, F. (2003) 'Contrôles migratoires aux frontiers européennes: l'accélération sécuritaire', in M. Fortmann, A. Macleod and S. Roussel (eds) *Vers des Périmètres de Sécurité? La Gestion des Espaces continentaux en Amérique du Nord et en Europe* (Montréal: Athéna).

Crépeau, F. and Carlier, J.-Y. (1999) 'Intégration régionale et politique migratoire: Le modèle européen entre cooperation et comunautarisation', *Journal du Droit International*, 4, pp. 261–85.

Flynn, M. (2002) 'Donde Està La Frontera?', *Bulletin of the Atomic Scientists*, 58:4, pp. 24–35.

Foucher, M. (1998) 'The Geopolitics of European Frontiers', in M. Anderson and E. Bort (eds) *The Frontiers of Europe* (London: Pinter), pp. 235–50.

Gottman, J. (1952) *La Politique des États et leur Géographie* (Paris: Armand Colin).

Government of Canada, Department of Foreign Affairs and International Trade (2003) 'Declaration on safe and smart border'. Available at: http://www.dfait-maeci.qc.ca (last accessed March 2003).

Gouvernement du Canada, Ministère du Transport (2002) 'News release. Public safety Act 2002'. Available at: http://www.tc.c.ca/mediaroom/releases/nat/2002/02_gc001e.1 (last accessed April 2002).

Harvey, D. (1989) *The Condition of Postmodernity* (Cambridge: Blackwell).

Huysmans, J. (2000) 'The European Union and the Securitization of Migration', *Journal of Common Market Studies*, 38:5, pp. 751–77.

Lefebvre, H. (1974) *La Production de l'Espace* (Paris: Editions Anthropos).

Massey, D. (1992) 'Politics and spare time', *New Left Review* 196, Nov–Dec 1992, pp. 65–84.

Michalet, C.A. (1976) *Le capitalisme mondial* (Paris: PUF).

Miller, M.J. (2000) 'International Migration in Post-Cold War International Relations', in B. Ghosh (ed.) *Managing Migration: Time for a New International Regime?* (Oxford: Oxford University Press), pp. 27–47.

Nevins, J. (2001) 'Searching for Security: boundary and immigration enforcement in an age of intensifying globalization', *Social Justice*, 28:2, pp. 132–48.

O'Dowd, L. and Wilson, T.M. (eds) (1996) *Borders, Nations and States: Frontiers of Sovereignty in the New Europe* (Aldershot: Ashgate).

Ohmae, K. (1993) 'The Rise of the Region State', *Foreign Affairs*, Spring, pp. 78-87.

O'Brien, R. (1992) *Global Financial Integration: The End of Geography* (London: Royal Institute of International Affairs).

Palan, R. (2003) *The Offshore World: Sovereign Markets, Virtual Places, and Nomad Millionaires* (Ithaca: Cornell University Press).

Panitch, L. and Gindin, S. (2004) 'American Imperialism and Eurocapitalism: the making of neoliberal globalization', *Studies in Political Economy*, 71/72, pp. 7–38.

Pellerin, H. (2004) 'Intégration économique et sécurité: Nouveaux facteurs déterminants de la gestion de la migration internationale', *Choix*, 10:3, pp. 1–30.

Portes, A. and Walton, J. (1981) *Labor, Class and the International System* (New York: Academic Press).

Purdy, J. (2002) Presentation at the Annual Conference of the Canadian Association for Security and Intelligence Studies, Ottawa, September 2002.

Riemen, O. (2001) 'European private international law, the European Community and its emerging Area of Freedom, Security and Justice', *Common Market Law Review*, 38, pp. 53–86.

Rudolph, C. (2002) 'Security and the political economy of international migration'. Available at: http://www.cionet.org/eps/ruc02.pdf (last accessed November 2002).

Schwartz, H.M. (1994) *States Versus Markets: History, Geography, and the Development of the International Political Economy* (New York: St Martin's Press).

Solicitor General of Canada (2002) 'Cross border crime and security: Canada–United States cooperation. Frequently Asked Questions'. Available at: http://www.sgc.gc.ca (last accessed April 2002).

US Department of Justice (1995) 'New Antitrust Cooperation Agreement Signed Between United States and Canada', August 1995. Available at: http://www.usdoj.gov/opa/pr/rie_90/August95/428.txt.html (last accessed April 2002).

Waever, O., Buzan, B. and Kelstrup, M. (1993) *Identity, Migration and the New Security Agenda in Europe* (New York: St Martin's Press).

Zaccardelli, J. (2002) 'Intelligence, security and the integration of law enforcement', keynote speech of the annual Conference of the Canadian Association for Security and Intelligence Studies, Ottawa, September 2002.

Chapter 5

The border is everywhere: ID cards, surveillance and the other

David Lyon

Introduction

'The border is everywhere' is a phrase sometimes used to express the experience of racialized 'others' within the territory of a given nation state. You don't have to be trying to cross through a physical border checkpoint to sense that you are an alien, a non-citizen, someone who does not belong. But there is another sense in which the border is everywhere. Although national ID card systems have many purposes, one of them is to enable authorities to distinguish, clearly and automatically, between those who do and those who do not belong as full members of the nation state. This paper is mainly about this second sense in which the 'border is everywhere' – it is both portable (the plastic card) and virtual (the database). In terms of membership with the majority within the border, the card system helps to sort insiders from outsiders. No doubt ID cards also exacerbate the sense of being 'other', but that is not the main focus of this chapter.

National ID card schemes are being debated in several countries around the world – though in Canada the debate was stillborn – and in some places they are already being implemented. Such ID cards, that keep track of citizens mainly inside the borders of the nation state, mark a major step forward in the surveillance capacities of any nation state. From paper-based identification records with limited personal details used for extraordinary purposes (such as policing), the new proposed

ID is 'smart' in that it is linked with networked searchable databases (both public and private), uses biometrics, and is likely to be used for a range of activities well beyond any policing or administrative function for which such cards are currently used. From time to time the gradual evolution of socio-technical systems experiences a sudden spurt, and the establishment of a national ID in the UK (or anywhere) is a case in point.

As well as outlining the ways in which the proposed ID represents a quantum leap in 'scientific' identification processes, this paper also looks critically at several issues. One is the limitations of such systems, particularly their dependence on dubious biometric technologies. Another is the issue of 'function creep' in which subsequent novel uses are devised for existing technical systems, which are added to the original panoply of functions. A third is to consider the experiences of other countries that have cards or are introducing them – Hong Kong, Malaysia, Japan, China – along with countries that have yet to make clear decisions about national ID card systems or have thus far resisted them – such as Australia, Canada, South Korea and the USA. Different cultural and political situations mean that each nation has different reasons for establishing ID cards, reasons that relate to who is defined as 'other' for purposes of immigration control.

Important questions of privacy and civil liberties such as freedom of movement are raised, but it is also important to see such significant shifts in surveillance (in this case ID cards) as augmenting the ability of nation states to engage more directly in 'social sorting'. That is to say, in the twenty-first century, as nation states find themselves with diminishing power over some entities (such as corporations), they tend to reinforce their interest in 'law and order' and 'social safety' in which surveillance features prominently. What appears to be a system that augments the capacity of nation states to identify citizens for administrative and policing purposes turns out also to facilitate extensive social, economic and political categorization within emerging processes of control and governance. Those who are defined as 'other' within such systems are most likely to experience negative discrimination as a result.

The main argument of this paper is that the current establishment of smart ID cards is highly significant for surveillance. Whereas earlier forms of state surveillance relied to an extent on both identification and, in some countries, actual ID cards, this still did not spell a tight and highly informed administrative relation between citizen and state. The earlier phases of rationalization that applied bureaucratic forms of governance that helped constitute modern nation states as such were subject to both legal and technical limits that militated against the totalitarian tendencies built into any such advances. Even though they were claiming a monopoly of means of identification – over familial practices or religious organizations, for example – the effect was mitigated by restricted capacity.

Today's database and biometric ID card systems ratchet up the surveillance capacities of ID cards in several respects. They are being introduced in an international climate of media-amplified fear and suspicion; they adopt a means of automated classification that removes this process further from discretion and compassion; they introduce a further level to the virtual border of the nation state, in which decisions made about 'citizens' and 'others' are remote and removed from geographical borders; and they depend on personal data gleaned not only from administrative and law-enforcement sources but also from cooperation with private databases. A comparative look at 'other nations' (in this case nations other than the UK) shows that the 'nation's others' are, as has too often been the case, most at risk.

Modern horrors come home: ID cards for the UK

An ID card proposal, introducing a national registry and a multi-purpose card for all citizens by 2013, began its passage through the UK Parliament from November 2004, but its progress was delayed by the May 2005 election. What Jon Agar (2001) entertainingly describes as a 'modern horror' – identity cards in Britain – is proposed for a country that has resisted their introduction for a long time. While much media rhetoric surrounds the cards themselves – 'Do you want to have police officers demanding to see your card?' – it is important to note that there are two issues: the cards and the national registry.

Cards are markers of membership and distinguish those eligible for the benefits of being British. But the surveillance issue, the way the state scrutinizes society as a means of governance, is not so much the multi-purpose cards as the national registry. The unique identifiers on the cards act as the 'phone number' or the google keyword that connects the card-holder with the stored record. Searchable databases are the key item in any twenty-first-century surveillance system, where surveillance is understood as focused attention to personal data for the purpose of influence, management or control, and where this is facilitated by electronic infrastructures.

The UK system is intended to achieve three ends: immigration control, fraud control and anti-terrorism. As an 'entitlement' system it is an outcome of 'e-government' initiatives, giving citizens automated access to public services. As a 'governance' system it is designed to keep track of the daily lives of citizens, checking eligibility for services and benefits and enabling more efficient policing. Either way, it represents a major movement in securing a monopoly of the means of identification. However, its public acceptability depends on neither of these but rather on the 'anti-terror' function which, ironically, is the one benefit it cannot deliver. Interestingly, the 'modern horror' for the British included a largely fictitious character – the bigamist – that earlier schemes would allegedly root out. Is today's equivalent the 'terrorist'?

Understanding identity cards: rationalization and the modern state

Identity cards are a product of modernity. More specifically, they emerged as a means of rationalization within the nation states that invented themselves during the nineteenth century, starting in Europe. One aspect of this rationalization was the effort to determine who was and who was not a member of a given nation state. In order to connect someone with a bureaucratic record of membership, some form of document was needed, and two specific ones began to appear, first in France: the passport and the identity card. The passport, as John Torpey has clearly shown, became a primary means of 'regulating the means of movement' and of distinguishing between 'nationals' and 'foreigners', particularly at border points (Torpey 2000). Identity cards, on the other hand, straddle two domains. They relate to movement but also to entitlement. They are as much about the 'means of identification' as the 'means of movement'.

In this section identity cards are explored, briefly, as products of the modern nation state's quest for rational organization and administration. Before discussing this, a link with the next section is worth remarking. From earliest days, the attempt to establish identity card systems was frequently associated with the desire to be 'scientific' in the classification of 'insiders' and 'outsiders'. This may be seen, again, in the case of France, where 'Bertillonage' – anthropometric scales for measuring body dimensions – was legally introduced for internal passes in 1912 (Kaluszynski 2001; see also Piazza 2004). These also related to 'racial' characteristics, designed to maintain the purity of French nationality, and were used especially for criminals and marginal groups, notably 'gypsies'.

Two points may be made here. One, rationalization often has recourse to science and technology, and in the later twentieth century, with the promise offered by computerization, this tendency took on a new lease of life which would be realized in the 'smart' ID cards currently being rolled out or debated. Two, the means of classification touches most heavily on the areas of marginality or movement – when the membership of certain persons is moot or when they move around according to a logic of their own. But however 'scientific' the means, it must be recalled that standardization, centralization and the imposition of national identity was always associated with the desire for cultural homogeneity (Calhoun 1997). These are themes to which we return below.

What are identity cards? This deceptively simple question raises a host of complex issues and the best answers begin historically. Identity cards appeared as visible markers of membership within the early nation states of the nineteenth and twentieth centuries. But as Torpey rightly observes, they also immediately 'confront us with a documentary "gray zone"' (Torpey 2000: 165) because their remit lies between the regulation of movement (like passports) and the entitlement to benefits of membership (such as healthcare, voting rights or welfare). If passports deal primarily with movement in and out of the territory governed by the nation state, ID cards refer above all to activities carried out within the nation state's boundaries. Passports are a reminder of the territorial aspect of the nation state, while ID cards point towards the membership aspect (even though these are far from exclusive distinctions).

Sociologically, ID cards may be considered in relation to two inter-related processes; the ways in which the nation state is constituted as such, and the ways that 'identities' are established. Each must be understood in terms of power relations. As Torpey argues, the 'monopolization of the means of movement' represented especially by passports indicates the state's drive to develop the 'capacity to "embrace" their own citizens in order to extract from them the resources they need to reproduce themselves over time' (2000: 2). This is in fact one of the key ways in which nation states, beginning after the French Revolution, became such, and, by extension, continue to be such. This affirms the state's control over territories where it has jurisdiction, and thus over those considered its citizens. The ID card establishes the identity of citizens (and in some cases would-be citizens), distinguishing them from others; assists administrative efficiency; and ensures that benefits are received by those who bear the card.

Because the 'establishment of identity' involves a classification which imposes 'identity', this process always involves interpretation and sometimes struggle or conflict. As Ian Hacking notes, the classification of individuals is central to modern bureaucratic and rationalized strategies of government and control (Hacking 1990) and thus may be subject to resistance. After all, says Torpey, ID cards are intrinsically illiberal in the sense that they presume the bearers' guilt when called upon to identify themselves. The state seems to assume that people will lie about who they are and that therefore durable identities are needed to guarantee the ongoing political, economic and administrative aims of that state. Thus '... documents authorizing movement and establishing identity discourage people from choosing identities inconsistent with those validated by the state' (Torpey 2000: 166). As Richard Jenkins helpfully puts it: 'Identification is something *over* which struggles take place and *with* which stratagems are advanced – it is means and ends in politics – and at stake is the classification of populations as well as the classification of individuals' (Jenkins 2004: 23).

The struggles and stratagems of identification systems have been evident throughout their history, starting in France (see Piazza 2004a) and – often in an attempt to remain distinct from that country! – continuing in the UK (see Lyon 1993). As we shall see below, such struggles and stratagems occur in different ways in different countries, depending on their cultural distinctions and political histories. But the simple paper-based documents relating to manual file storage and retrieval that characterized the establishment of stable identities from early modern times (see Higgs 2001) are now rapidly giving way to quite different systems. Although the drive towards finding a 'scientific' basis for securing identities has also been evident from the start, rationalization is now seen in the technological means sought. Such schemes take the monopolization of the means of identity to another level altogether.

Smart ID cards: surveillance society and safety state

In the twenty-first century, proposals are proliferating to set up new smart ID systems, or to upgrade old ones. It would be a mistake to see this upsurge merely in terms of the current international obsession with 'anti-terrorist' techniques, although the aftermath of 9/11 certainly has had a powerful effect in galvanizing and catalysing such developments (Lyon 2003a). National identification schemes have been used or proposed for some time, mainly for handling routine administrative transactions between government agencies and citizens, with the rationale of cost savings, convenience and to reduce fraud. But the post-9/11 security drive has helped to provide a previously absent urgency to the search for viable ID systems, and momentum appears to be picking up, internationally.

First, though, it must be remarked that new ID systems relate to already existing processes that are discussed here: bureaucratic rationalization and computerization, most recently expressed in 'e-government' initiatives; growing mobility rates which mean that more people are on the move and marginal groups are harder to trace; and the changing role of the state in the wake of deregulation of trade and the withdrawal from economic management, which magnifies its 'law, order and security' function. ID cards are also intended as an 'anti-cybercrime' measure, where 'identity theft' has been cited as a major growth area for domestic offences. One could argue that each of these factors points towards the possibility of reinforcing identification regimes, and that 9/11 offers the rationale for accelerated implementation.

If one takes the British ID card case as an example, each of these factors is evident. The initial 2004 press release from the Home Office included statements by David Blunkett, Home Secretary, which indicate this clearly (the following quotations are taken from this document; Home Office 2004). The idea that government is re-tooling itself for the twenty-first century is plainly stated. Citizens will be enabled to 'play a full role in our increasingly global and technologically complex world', and the scheme will 'place the UK at the forefront of a world-wide drive by industrialized nations to produce biometric identity and travel documents'. People will be able to 'live their everyday lives more easily, giving them a watertight proof of identity for use in daily transactions and travel'. Access to government services will be facilitated, it is said, and along with this, better ways of preventing access to those with no entitlement. This is part of a long-term UK goal of moving towards e-government, and it also reflects growing mobility rates and ease of travel, especially between EU countries.

The 'challenges of the twenty-first century' which ID cards address are equally clearly of the 'law, order and security' variety: 'ID cards will help tackle the type of serious and organized crime which depend on being able to use false identities – terrorism, drug trafficking, money laundering, fraud through ID theft, and illegal working and immigration.' The document makes much of the threat of 'recent events' – a dark hint at 9/11 presumably – and of ID fraud which apparently costs the UK £1.3 billion per year. These challenges are best met, it is claimed, by biometrics devices built into the card system. Referring again to a world-wide 'drive to increase document security with biometrics', the UK press release acknowledges the shift now taking place. 'Taking people at face value' and 'trusting them to be who they say they are' is taken for granted in a free and open society, says Blunkett, but now the opportunity must be taken to 'move beyond this' to 'new biometric technology which allows for a completely new level of verifying identity'.

Much has been made in recent decades of the rise of 'risk' as a central social and political phenomenon. While the first major risks were thought of as environmental, stemming from irresponsible industrial practices (Beck 1992), the category of risk has since been extended to cover a variety of situations and processes including, notoriously, 'terrorism'. Since 9/11 especially, 'security' has become a predominant political preoccupation, dominating the 2004 US presidential election and much else besides. While this notion of 'security' has much to do with the 'terrorist' threat, it is important to note the continuity with what was already emerging within the so-called risk society. As Ericson and Haggerty put it neatly, 'In risk society, governance is directed at the provision of security' (1997: 85). Of course, by 'governance' they refer to other agencies as well as the state, but the state still plays a very significant role in governance. The nation state is now centrally concerned with the provision of security (which has in turn become an economic category as well – the 'security industry'). ID cards fall fully into this kind of risk society analysis.

As Ericson and Haggerty also observe, the 'yearning for security drives the insatiable quest for more and better knowledge of risk' (1997: 85). This is where surveillance comes into the picture. Ericson and Haggerty write primarily about police surveillance but the analysis they engage may be extended elsewhere with profit. Risk knowledge is gleaned through surveillance practices, which today means, above all, the use of information technologies. To meet the demand for enhanced security, surveillance measures of the most advanced kinds are called for. In the present case, a national database and biometric measures offer the means to support a national ID card. And this is not without its own attendant risks, as Zureik and Hindle (2004) show. Their argument leads to the conclusion that biometrics is likely to increase population 'management and control' and to put particular pressure on 'poor, marginal, and vulnerable people' (2004: 134). We look at this further below.

For the present, the message of the British government is clear: security is at risk on several levels, and the role of the state is to ratchet up security measures to meet the challenge. Leadership in new technology is vital, to provide citizens with the latest, best and world-travel compatible means of identification, which simultaneously allows access to government services and denies it to pretenders. ID cards with biometrics is the key, which necessitates a new national database. Thus the surveillance society and the safety state (Raab 2005) go hand in hand.

ID cards: including and excluding the state's citizens

Modern states have successfully monopolized the 'legitimate means of movement' (Torpey 2000) using documents such as passports and ID

73

cards to distinguish between citizens – 'nationals' – and others, and to regulate their movements. This is in part what constitutes states as they embrace their own citizens so that they can extract from them resources needed to reproduce themselves. What began in Western Europe and the USA has been extended to cover all modern states, although this has been intensified at particular times, such as during war. The so-called war on terror consequent on 9/11 is having similar effects, even though the 'war' is of a different character from previous ones that generated interest in ID cards.

People have become dependent on states for an 'identity' – or, rather, identification – which both enables and inhibits movement within a given territory and across borders. The 'identity' that includes also excludes those who do not meet the criteria of citizenship. In an era of networked databases, pressure exists to find multiple-purpose cards that combine, for example, national IDs with passports. National communities may be imagined (Anderson 1991) but they are also dependent on codified ID documents. Cultural identities should not be confused with national identifications, even though they relate to each other in varying degrees of tension (see Jenkins 2004). Several factors make current projects somewhat different from earlier ones.

One is that they are dependent on electronic information infrastructures that support a variety of functions through access to networked databases. Secondly, this takes further the already existing integration of state with commercial data and connects conventional national interests in personal identity with consumer ones. Thirdly, not only are state and economy linked by means of the new systems, but so are internal-external issues of movement regulation. Indeed, the introduction of 'internal' IDs is likely to be closely tied to the 'external' IDs of passports. In the UK case, the new ID card is associated in the first instance with passport and driver's licence renewals.[1] The consequent globalization of personal data takes further the challenge to conventional political distinctions between domestic/international, territorial/non-territorial and inside/outside.

The fact that contemporary surveillance is heavily dependent on networked searchable databases means that an automated system is permitted to do the work of categorizing populations, distinguishing between 'insiders' and 'outsiders'. In the case of ID cards, as I have suggested, it is the database that is likely to have the largest long-term impact even though the cards themselves are the lightning rod for the emotional and political charge. This is because the database permits 'pre-emptive' surveillance, a fact that was first underscored by Gary Marx (1988) in his use of the phrase 'categorical suspicion'. Such anticipatory activity may already be seen in the criminal investigation sphere, but may easily be transposed to an anti-terror key. As Malcolm Feely and Jonathan Simon say, the approach seeks 'techniques for identifying, classifying, and managing groups sorted by levels of dangerousness' (Feely and Simon 1994).

In the case of ID cards, 'levels of dangerousness' is only one issue to be confronted. Cards are intended to sort for likelihood of committing fraud, both financial and in self-representation, as well as for entitlement to benefits and services. The difficulty here is that for the purpose – anti-terrorism – that gives the ID cards debate its timing and its apparent acceptability, the efficacy of smart cards is moot to say the least. Even the most advanced biometrics depends on having a clear threat profile, and even with this, the cards can still be tampered with by determined people. Equally, advanced biometric cards still have to be based on some other documentary identification in the first place, pushing upstream to the humble birth certificate, which in most cases is far from forgery proof (see Stalder and Lyon 2003).

If the aim of introducing ID card systems is to counter terror – and in the USA the debate is almost exclusively couched in these terms – then distinguishing between those who may pose a threat and those who do not is paramount. Amitai Etzioni has recently begun to promote the cause of ID cards, or of strengthening *de facto* IDs such as drivers' licences (Etzioni 2004). He has found himself opposing the 'privacy lobby' which, he claims, often pushes the most emotional buttons it can find. He says that privacy advocates are wrong to suggest that ID cards would lull citizens into a false sense of (technology-dependent) security, that privacy would be violated more with ID cards, and, most importantly for our purposes, that minorities would be discriminated against more readily.

Space forbids a full treatment of these arguments, but a central objection to each of them is that they ignore the broader context. First, high technology surveillance is being promoted by high technology companies and governments (often working in collusion, see ACLU 2004), to the virtual exclusion of low-tech, labour-intensive alternatives. The balance is tilting decisively towards reliance on algorithmic methods. Second, it is hard to believe that supposedly more reliable methods of identification would reduce privacy violations, given that any smart ID system is dependent on an array of databases, public and private, and that data-mining is a key means of discovering personal data associated with a given identity. Third, the idea that consistent ID documents would reduce racial and other minority discrimination is very doubtful indeed in a world where media-amplified fear and suspicion are commonplace and where the consequent need for 'security' has become a primary political goal.

New ID cards, touted as a key means of ensuring a reliable means of identifying the *bona fide* citizens of a given state, are both less than ideal of this stated purpose and are likely to have other attendant effects which are socially retrograde. This differs from place to place, of course, and it is instructive to discover what difference culture and history make in the adoption of ID card systems. Many Europeans have had paper-based ID systems for a long time, and countries in East and South East Asia have adopted electronic database ID systems more recently. Each experience is different and produces varying effects.

The experience of others I: other nations

Whenever a nation state initiates a process leading to the adoption of a new ID card system it tends to be seen as an internal event that seeks precedent or past experience as a guide. Yet with increasingly similar means of identification being sought, and for similar purposes, it seems appropriate to examine the experience of several different nation states. In addition, certain nations or federations – such as the USA or EU – put pressure on others to conform to standards, which again suggests that understanding both similarity and difference of approaches would be advisable. It is not only the monopolization of the means of violence (Giddens 1985, 1990) that has given modern states their chief *raison d'être* and is now challenged in globalizing situations. Just as national security in a military sense now depends on multi-lateral cooperation (Held 2004: 9), so too in the realm of movement across borders, including the securing of stable identities, cooperation is also required as never before. The means of movement and of authorized identification are central to this.

Over the past two decades several multi-purpose smart card IDs have been proposed, trialled, rejected or implemented. Those in operation tend to be in fairly authoritarian states such as Malaysia and Thailand, and perhaps a little less so, Hong Kong. Each of these uses a national database and includes biometrics (thumb prints) in the card. Those being implemented, in India or China, are also fairly authoritarian by the standards for Western Europe and North America, but not enough is known about the details of their prototype systems to make comment. In countries that went through earlier phases of modernization – Japan, South Korea – there have been major controversies about their emergence. The Koreans rejected a card; the Japanese experienced a huge wave of (ongoing) civil disobedience over theirs (see Lyon and Wood forthcoming). It should be remembered that although many European countries – including Italy and Finland – already have ID cards, few have implemented upgrades that would turn them into fully fledged smart card systems. If the British plan goes ahead, it will be by far the most advanced.

In the USA and Canada no official national ID card system has ever been established but this is not for want of trying. Several proposals have been made and in 2005 it appears that the USA may initiate at least a *de facto* card before Canada does. The Intelligence Reform Bill, passed by the Senate in December 2004 (Anon 2004) calls for an overhaul of the driver's licence system that would be tantamount to making a national ID. But in Canada, what appeared to be building towards a serious proposal in 2003 came to nothing. A Department of Immigration report, based in part, interestingly, on a fact-finding visit to several European countries, led to its dismissal before the 'national debate' initiated by the minister responsible, Denis Coderre, had ever begun in earnest (McClintock 2004). True, an upgraded immigration document, the Permanent Resident Card, was established in 2003, but this has a very specific purpose and is a very small change compared with a national ID.

In the USA there has been much talk about ID cards since 9/11 but no official plan has finally been announced. After the flurry of interest following the offer by Oracle's Larry Ellison to provide 'free' software for a proposed national ID, the public discussion of the issue has been fairly quiet. As the most common *de facto* ID in the USA is the driver's licence, however, it is likely that an upgraded version of that document may well become the centrepiece of an ID system, or something closely resembling one. The plan, during 2002–03, was to create a federal system linking all the existing state systems and to include a biometric identifier in the new card. The American Association of Motor Vehicle Administrators is working with Homeland Security to this end. Each state would still run its licence system but using standardized data and security features (O'Harrow 2001). At the time of writing this enhanced driver's licence proposal is still the most likely scenario for a *de facto* ID card.

The experience of others II: nations' others

The comparative study of ID card systems suggests that the key question relates to who are the 'others' that the nation state in question would like to exclude or regulate. It is the entry of 'others' into the territory of the nation state with which passports deal, and their presence within the borders of that territory, in the long or short term, for which ID cards are sought. For many countries, the implicit agenda is how to demonstrate that they are prepared for potential 'terrorist' attacks. In this case, the experience of the USA, where, as the official report on 9/11 shows, several of the attackers used false documents, is the example to avoid. How far other countries are also keen to avoid the civil-rights abuses that have followed in the wake of the American development of a culture of suspicion is unclear (see Lyon 2003). But the longer-term agenda behind the establishment of ID cards must not be forgotten, and although this varies from country to country, a constant factor is immigration control.

The use of passports, it seems, is insufficient. A means is sought, particularly for regulating residence and access to government services and benefits, of verifying identities in terms of citizenship. Immigration control is an explicit aim of the British ID card proposal. Although one key complaint of both the UK Information Commissioner and the House of Commons Home Affairs Committee is the lack of clarity of purpose about the proposed ID card system, it is clear that preventing illegal immigration and illegal working is among the top government priorities (House of Commons 2004: 25). Although the Commission for Racial Equality has accepted that the use of ID cards could ensure fairer treatment of asylum seekers and other new immigrants, it is also argued that this will only be the case if proper controls are exerted over wider factors such as the hiring policies and practices of firms.

Other countries with ID card systems also have strong incentives to sort between legitimate and illegitimate workers and residents. Hong Kong wishes to limit Chinese mainlanders; Malaysia has long tried to regulate Indonesian migration; Germany has ambivalent attitudes towards *gastarbeiters*, especially those from the former Yugoslavia and from Turkey; the USA makes ever more strenuous efforts to keep illegal work-seeking Mexicans from crossing the border; Japan is concerned about Korean workers in its midst; and so on. In a world where many obstacles have been removed to free movement and to working in foreign contexts – especially in the EU – it is interesting to note that particular groups are still proscribed, for a variety of reasons.

Another issue, which may help to reveal negative dimensions of new ID card systems, is the use of biometrics. Such practices are not themselves new, of course. Earlier in the twentieth century the American administration attempted to use fingerprinting on Chinese immigrants, which must count as one of the first attempts to use 'biometrics' on a minority population for ID purposes (Cole 2001). But it is interesting to note which countries actually use some kind of biometrics within their existing ID card systems. They include Cambodia, Egypt, Israel,

Malaysia, Nigeria, Pakistan, Peru, Russia, Spain and Thailand (PI 2004). If the UK were to succeed in implementing its proposed card, it would be joining a list of nations, none of which is taken to be exemplary in its pursuit of racial and ethnic equality. However, lacking studies of the consequences of biometric IDs for minority groups in those countries, it is impossible to judge whether or not this is a significant factor.

To return, finally, to the events that have given ID card proposals a new lease of life in the early twenty-first century – 9/11 and its aftermath – it is clear that, even without ID cards, much injustice has been experienced by certain minority groups through widespread processes of 'racial profiling'. The stated effort to exclude such profiling from anti-terrorist activity may actually be betrayed by reliance on 'silver bullet' technology in the post-9/11 era. Biometrics, as Clive Norris has argued (Norris and Armstrong 1999) and as Jeffrey Rosen reminds us, though it may have originated with Bertillon, was championed by Francis Galton, the father of eugenics (Rosen 2004: 125). Rosen argues that, as with Galton's work, technologies of hierarchy masquerade as technologies of equality. While crude racial profiling may ostensibly be avoided, 'instead of eliminating the evils of stereotyping and discrimination, the technologies of classification extend them across American society as a whole' (Rosen 2004: 126).

Conclusion

It may be that the advent of smart ID cards makes affected populations vulnerable to increased 'invasions of privacy' or a snooping 'Big Brother'. Equally, those may be justified who fear gratuitous restrictions on the free movement of citizens following the introduction of new ID cards. But neither of these necessarily takes into account the working of the national registry database that facilitates digital discrimination and social sorting. It is this, along with the use of biometrics, which is exposed and debated in this paper. I have suggested that in ratcheting up the technological elements of the state's monopoly over the means of identification, not only are the opportunities for misuse and abuse multiplied – routine use is also questionable.

As national ID card systems are adopted, the nation state's implicit definition of the 'other' will be built into an automated system for determining who is and who is not a member, thus reducing dependence on face-to-face accounts of individual identity. So the border will increasingly be everywhere, in at least two senses. First, the smart ID card is a portable means of identification – surveillance is literally borne by those who are its subjects – and yet the identity revealed there may well be doubted or disputed by the bearer. This is because it originates in the networked databases to which the card is virtually connected, whose categories may be clear, but may also be opaque or, worse, stereotypical. Identity and identification are – especially for minorities – in a kind of dialectical relation of struggle and compromise. Which brings us to the second sense of cards serving to bring the border everywhere – the experience of otherness becomes steadily more ubiquitous, no longer limited to physical borders.

The question of whether or not a society accepts the major step up to a smart ID system relates to how far that society wishes to go in effectively rejecting or at least suspecting personal narratives in favour of the database of identification. That database, composed as it is by myriad small personal details, concatenated through data-mining and other advanced techniques, extends processes used commercially to constitute consumers, to constitute *bona fide* citizens. And it thus raises questions about the paradox of cosmopolitanism, where nation states are in complex and intricate institutional relationships, depending on networked new technologies, but where citizens still find their loyalties and commitments in relation to tradition, locality, ethnicity and, in some circumstances, nation.

This also raises large questions about the politics of information. Who decides on the categories of suspicion and of opportunity? How far are citizens involved in this process, and at what level? What ethical scrutiny is there of these categories? And lastly, how accountable are the managers of these massive new systems on which the life-chances of so many are dependent? When the border is everywhere, answers to these questions are the more urgently needed.

Note

1 This is interesting because it ties in with a further feature of ID card history – the incentives offered for acceptance. In the UK case, the Second World War ID was required for food rationing (see Agar 2001). Today, the new IDs are tied to other 'necessary' functions – driving and foreign travel.

References

ACLU (American Civil Liberties Union) (2004) *The Surveillance Industrial Complex* August 2004. Available at: http://www.aclu.org/SafeandFree/SafeandFree.cfm?ID=16224&c=207

Agar, J. (2001) 'Modern Horrors: British Identity and Identity Cards', in J. Caplan and J. Torpey (eds) *Documenting Individual Identity: The Development of State Practices in the Modern World* (Princeton: Princeton University Press), pp. 101–20.

Anderson, B. (1991) *Imagined Communities: Reflections on the Origins and Spread of Nationalism* (London and New York: Verso).

Anon (2004) 'Senate OKs intelligence overhaul bill' *CNN.com*, Friday 10 December 2004. Available at: http://www.cnn.com/2004/ALLPOLITICS/12/08/intelligence.bill/

Beck, U. (1992) *Risk Society* (London: Sage).

Calhoun, C. (1997) *Nationalism* (Buckingham: Open University Press).

Cole, S. (2001) *Suspect Identities: A History of Fingerprinting and Criminal Identification* (Cambridge: Harvard University Press).

Ericson, R. and Haggerty, K. (1997) *Policing the Risk Society* (Toronto: University of Toronto Press).

Etzioni, A. (2004) 'It's not just a driver's license anymore: It's a de facto national ID. We should make it secure', *The Washington Post*, Sunday 16 May 2004, B3.

Feely, M. and Simon, J. (1994) 'Actuarial Justice: The Emerging New Criminal Law', in D. Nelken (ed.) *The Futures of Criminology* (London: Sage), pp. 173–201.

Giddens, A. (1990) *The Consequences of Modernity* (Cambridge: Polity Press).

Giddens, A. (1985) *The Nation State and Violence* (Cambridge: Polity Press).

Hacking, I. (1990) *The Taming of Chance* (Cambridge: Cambridge University Press).

Held, D. (2004) 'Becoming Cosmopolitan: The Dimensions and Challenges of Globalization', in Peter Heslam (ed.) *Globalization and the Good* (London: SPCK), pp. 3–15.

Higgs, E. (2001) 'The Rise of the Information State: the development of central state surveillance of the citizen in England 1500–2000', *Journal of Historical Sociology*, 14:2, pp. 175–97.

Home Office (2004) 'David Blunkett: National ID card scheme is the key to the UK's future', 26 April 2004. Available at: www.homeoffice.gov.uk/n_story.asp?item_id=918

House of Commons (Home Affairs Committee) (2004) *Identity Cards Volume 1*, 20 July 2004. Available at: http://www.publications.parliament.uk/pa/cm200304/cmselect/cmhaff/130/13002.htm

Jenkins, R. (2004) *Social Identity* (London and New York: Routledge).

Kaluszynski, M. (2001) 'Republican Identity: Bertillonage as Government Technique', in J. Caplan and J. Torpey (eds) (2001) *Documenting Individual Identity: The Development of State Practices in the Modern World* (Princeton: Princeton University Press), pp. 123–38.

Lyon, D. and Wood, D. (forthcoming) 'Surveillance in Japan, before and after September 11', under submission to *Urban Studies.*

Lyon, D. (ed.) (2003) *Surveillance as Social Sorting: Privacy, Risk, and Digital Discrimination* (London and New York: Routledge).

Lyon, D. (2003a) *Surveillance after September 11* (Cambridge UK and Malden MA: Polity Press).

Lyon, D. (1993) 'British Identity Cards: "the unpalatable logic" of European integration?' *The Political Quarterly*, 62:3, pp. 377–85.

Marx, G. (1988) *Undercover: Police Surveillance in America* (Berkeley: University of California Press).

McClintock, M. (2004) 'ID card plan fails grade', *Calgary Sun*, Friday 9 April 2004.

Norris, C. and Armstrong, G. (1999) *Towards the Maximum Surveillance Society: The Rise of CCTV* (Oxford: Berg).

O'Harrow, R. (2001) 'States devising plan for high tech national identification cards', *The Washington Post*, Saturday 3 November 2001, A10.

PI (Privacy International) (2004) *Mistaken Identity: Exploring the Relationship Between National Identity Cards and the Prevention of Terrorism*. Available at: www.privacyinternational.org/

Piazza, P. (2004) 'Septembre 1921: la première "carte d'identité" de français', *Geneses*, March, pp. 76–89.

Piazza, P. (2004a) *Histoire de la Carte Nationale d'identité* (Paris: Odile Jacob).

Raab, C. (2005) 'Towards the safety state?' Inaugural lecture at the University of Edinburgh, Scotland.

Rosen, J. (2004) *The Naked Crowd: Reclaiming Security and Freedom in an Anxious Age* (New York: Random House).

Stalder, F. and Lyon, D. (2003) 'Electronic Identity Cards and Social Classification', in D. Lyon (ed.) *Surveillance as Social Sorting: Privacy, Risk, and Digital Discrimination* (London and New York: Routledge), pp. 77–93.

Torpey, J. (2000) *The Invention of the Passport: Surveillance, Citizenship, and the State* (Cambridge and New York: Cambridge University Press).

Zureik, E. and Hindle, K. (2004) 'Governance, Security and Technology: the case of biometrics', *Studies in Political Economy*, 73, Spring–Summer, pp. 113–37.

This paper was originally prepared for a seminar at the Institute for Advanced Study in the Humanities, University of Edinburgh, Scotland during a visiting fellowship there in 2004. This revised version was prepared for the Surveillance Project research workshop on Borders and State Surveillance, at Queen's University, August 2004.

Chapter 6

Borders, bodies and biometrics: towards identity management

Benjamin J. Muller

'Borders' of engagement: security, liberty, identity

Borders have always been integral to discourses of international security and world politics. Predictions of a borderless world and a dustbin of history overflowing with the stalwarts of modernity were quickly recognized to be little more than the over-zealous *Zeitgeist* born of a post-1989 hangover (see Ohmae 1999; Fukuyama 1992; Friedman 1999; Beilharz *et al.* 1992; Salter 2002). The state and indeed international frontiers have proven to be far more resilient than such commentaries predicted. As the process of European integration once again found its feet, the rhetoric of freer movement and the eradication of borders only vaguely cloaked dominant preoccupations with constructing a 'Fortress Europe' (Walters 2002; Donnan and Wilson 1999; Borneman 1998; Pieterse 1991). In fact, even before the events of 11 September 2001, some analysts argued for the critical importance of 'identities, borders, orders' as an integral triad in contemporary international relations theory (Albert *et al.* 2001; Wilson and Donnan 1998). The politics of identities, borders and orders *has* nonetheless changed. Notably, the hours and days immediately following the horrific events of September 11 reminded us that sacrificing the unfettered movement of capital, goods and services at the altar of security was no option; a long-term solution for 'managing' identities, borders and orders was essential (Carr 2002; Andreas and Biersteker 2003). As if it were privy to some prophecy, the biometrics industry seemed immediately ubiquitous, claiming to provide all the right answers for the 'new' challenges of the global security environment.

Focusing on physical (or physiological) characteristics, or 'the body', as the unique identifier/verifier of individuals, biometric technologies provide a means for 'measurement'. As the body becomes password (Davis 1997), one's retina or iris, or even the angle of one's nose, is converted through algorithms into a binary code, for the purpose of verification or identification (Muller 2004; Zureik 2004). Not unlike debates surrounding the ever burgeoning field(s) of biotechnology, even the most ardent advocates of biometrics concede the need for public consultation and debate. However, what is the nature of this debate? In many cases, the field of biotechnology has witnessed some rather contrived discussions that have done little to grapple with deeply ethical and political concerns, and focused instead on questions of market management and the role/ rights of the consumer.[1] In many instances, deeper cultural and political considerations are only entertained in the 'consumer space', lest one is forced to take on the uncomfortable mantle of late-modern Luddism, and all its unsavoury consequences (Leiss 2004). Moreover, the production of political space by discourses of biotechnology, or in this case, biometrics, has important consequences for political engagement/resistance, and the contemporary politics of security and identity.

What then is the political space of biometrics? What are the limits/ possibilities of political and ethical engagement with the (impending) introduction of biometric technologies? What is the relationship between security, liberty and identity in the context of 'biometric security'? More to the point, how does one actually define 'biometric security'? In hopes of coming to terms with the politics of biometrics, I reflect on a number of these questions here. Focusing on various texts, or what could be described as 'implementation manuals', as well as the report on the biometrics forum hosted by Citizenship and Immigration Canada in October 2003, I consider how the political space of biometrics is framed. Closer scrutiny of many of the aforementioned questions begins to paint a picture of the politics of biometrics that has very little to do with the politics of borders and bodies, and much more with the management of the database. In fact, much of the debate over the relationship (and sacrifices) among security, liberty and identity are framed in the context of the dataset. As a result, I reflect on the political space of biometrics as the space of the database, and consider the resulting implications for the politics of security and identity.

Persistently revisiting the relationship among notions of security, liberty and identity as the dominant 'borders' of engagement, I reflect on the ways in which the politics of biometrics are (re)presented within the 'body' of biometrics literature. Focusing on 'implementation manuals', I expose the extent to which these texts 'produce' a politics of biometrics, overtly framing/limiting the space of political and ethical engagement. Then, focusing on the report on the forum hosted by Citizenship and Immigration Canada on 'Biometrics: Implications and Applications for Citizenship and Immigration', I engage the possible (ab)uses of biometrics and the importance of what I call the 'inevitability crisis' to the politics of biometrics. The paper concludes with some reflections on 'biometric security', and its implications on wider notions of (international) security.

'Bodies' of literature

What is initially striking about the 'biometrics literature' – and here I am referring to what are best described as 'manuals' produced by industry analysts – is an incredible lack of irony. The challenges of post-September 11 global (in)security and the unshakeable problem of identity theft/fraud are forwarded as challenges or rather problems that biometrics is only too capable of 'resolving'. The titles of these manuals are telling in and of themselves: *Biometrics: Identity Assurance in the Information Age* (Woodward Jr. *et al.* 2003); *Army Biometric Applications: Identifying and Addressing Sociocultural Concerns* (Woodward Jr. *et al.* 2001); *Biometrics: Facing Up to Terrorism* (Woodward Jr. 2001); *Implementing Biometric Security*, with the by-line *'timely, practical, reliable'* (Chirillo and Blaul 2003).

Biometrics are certainly timely. The amalgamation of public and private concerns over 'securing identity' – and here one might also consider the increasing reliance on 'military contractors' for *security*, which I discuss later (see Singer 2003; Davis 2000; Silverstein 2000) – has served to reinforce the 'need' for the sorts of solutions the biometrics industry believes it can provide. If timely, then the question of practicality would appear moot, leaving questions of reliability as the singular site of debate and contestation; hence, Charles Mann's preoccupation with 'smart failure' (Mann 2002). I return to this point of 'timeliness' more explicitly when discussing the Citizenship and Immigration Canada biometrics forum, under the heading of the 'inevitability crisis'. At this point, it is worthwhile interrogating the extent to which the biometrics literature produces the political space of biometrics.

Discourse and the political space of biometrics

According to Jim George, 'a discourse makes "real" that which *it* prescribes as meaningful' (George 1994: 30). I wish to avoid a long retracted discussion on the merits, relevance and challenge of 'discourse', as this is adequately addressed elsewhere (Caldas-Coulthard and Coulthard 1996; George 1994; Howarth *et al.* 2000). Furthermore, as the role of discourse(s) in social science literature is far from revolutionary in the early twenty-first century, one would expect to hear few reservations, directed only at the most 'post-post' forms of discourse analysis from the most positivistic corners of the discipline; as a result, I fail to see the need to engage in any sort of sub-disciplinary jousting here. Much like the constructivist point that maintains 'reality' is socially constructed, the suggestion that discourse is important in *producing* realities elicits little more than yawning acceptance except in the darkest recesses of the peculiar discipline of international relations (on constitutive role of theory see also Booth 1997; Smith 2004).

The most important articulation of discourse for the discussion presented here is, as Bradley Klein puts it: 'A discourse, then, is not a way of learning "about" something out there in the "real world"; it is rather, a way of producing that something as real, as identifiable, classifiable, knowable, and therefore, meaningful' (Klein quoted in George 1994: 30; see Klein 1994). In this way, I examine the manuals on biometrics, and later the forum report, reflecting on how a 'politics of biometrics' is produced. What is the political space of biometrics? And, what are the constitutive limits of political and ethical engagement in this political space? This 'production of political space' by the biometrics literature is done rather un-ironically, merely signifying the depth (or lack thereof) of its own reflexivity and commitment to the power of discourse. The way in which the limits of the politics of biometrics are produced is most obvious in practice, such as the biometrics forum held by Citizenship and Immigration Canada. However, the industry-produced literature is influential, and as such deserves attention.

Biometrics literature

While arguably timely, practical and reliable, the three basic factors influencing the adoption of biometrics according to the industry itself are: security, convenience and cost (Woodward Jr. *et al.* 2003: xxiv). In the wake of the events of 11 September 2001 and the subsequent 'war(s) on terror', the overwhelming preoccupation with 'security' has reduced other considerations; this point is further highlighted in the context of the biometrics forum. One of the important considerations here is the ongoing erosion of the separation between public and private. While relevant to changing notions of privacy in modern surveillance societies (Bennett and Grant 1999; Lyon 2001, 2003), the blurred distinction between public and private is particularly essential in terms of the (in)security of identities and spaces, or 'borders and bodies'. The current Iraq War is the exemplar here, as 'private military contractors' are now the second-largest contributor to coalition forces after the US (Wilson 2004). This private army of 'bodyguards' is charged with protecting contractors and industrialists involved in the reconstruction of Iraq, as well as certain locations of the Coalition Provisional Authority (Wilson 2004). Other than highlighting the increasing reliance on the privatized military industry for contemporary warfare and security, this example demonstrates the changing nature of 'security' itself. As the motivation for the war in Iraq remains mired in controversy, the significance of resource wealth is never far off the radar, and the immediate actions of coalition forces and the International Monetary Fund/World Bank towards the Ministry of Oil in Iraq has done little to quell such controversies (see Ali 2002). To suggest then that Iraq (in)security is both a public and private concern is not necessarily surprising, but the involvement of private contractors in 'securing' Iraq might create interesting nuances. Similarly, in the field of biometrics the (in)security of identity is both a public and private preoccupation. The rising problem of identity theft/fraud coupled with the obsession over 'securing the inside' *vis-à-vis* varying constructions of 'homeland security', speaks to the joint public–private interest in 'securing identity' for the security of both the state space and the consumer space.

These brief reflections on the relationship between the erosion of distinct public and private spaces, and their increasingly shared interests, in terms of the (in)security of identity and space/place, is an important first step in coming to terms with the politics of biometrics. To understand and subsequently engage in the politics of biometrics is to come to terms with what the Iraq example demonstrates: the increasing unfeasibility of separating public interests from private interests. As a private industry, a secure consumer space and state space – dependent of course on the perceived insecurity of these spaces and the bodies within them – is in the best interests of the biometrics industry. In terms of counterterrorism, Lon Troyer refers to this phenomenon in the following manner:

> A simulacral reenactment and coordination of public, corporate, and private spaces, the field of observation is translated into the space of integrated databases and searched for figures, moments, and acts that stand out from the homogeneous surface noise of human traffic ... To stand out is to be at risk; to become undifferentiated from the mass of other lives translated into the binary language of electronic encoding

becomes the goal in the age of Total Information Awareness. (Troyer 2003: 271)

Much like the role of private military contractors in Iraq, the eroding separation between public and private and the close connection between security and insecurity playing out in the space of the database are constitutive characteristics of the politics of biometrics, which the industry literature unsurprisingly fails to point out. However, it periodically alludes to this political space of the database, (un)consciously limiting the politics of resistance to the maligned spaces of the physical body.

In *Army Biometric Applications: Identifying and Addressing Sociocultural Concerns*, John D. Woodward Jr. and others point out that as surprising as it may seem, biometrics has its critics. The authors begin their discussion on the sociocultural concerns associated with biometrics, examining how they differ from other identification methods, focusing on questions of informational privacy, physical privacy and religious objections (Woodward Jr. *et al.* 2001: 21–2). Texts or manuals on biometrics do not, however, always explicitly address what they see to be important sociocultural or political concerns. For example, in *Implementing Biometric Security*, although Chirillo and Blaul's very first sentence of the text is: 'As unfortunate as it may be, the events of September 11, 2001, forever changed our lives' (Chirillo and Blaul 2003: vii), the authors spend no time dealing explicitly with the 'political' aspects of biometrics. In contrast, the Woodward Jr., Orlans and Higgins text, *Biometrics: Identity Assurance in the Information Age*, also takes the events of 11 September 2001 as a critical point of departure (Woodward Jr. *et al.* 2003: xxiv), but devotes a substantial portion to examining 'Privacy, Policy, and Legal Concerns Raised by Biometrics' (Woodward Jr. *et al.* 2003: 195–279). The Woodward Jr. *et al.* collection *Army Biometric Applications: Identifying and Addressing Sociocultural Concerns* represents what is arguably the most overt preoccupation with such matters, and the clearest example of the effective role of the text in producing a politics of biometrics.

According to Woodward Jr. *et al.*, the key sociocultural concerns associated with biometrics fall into three main categories: 1) informational privacy; 2) physical privacy; 3) religious objections (Woodward Jr. *et al.* 2001: 23). In their other text, *Biometrics: Identity Assurance in the Information Age*, Woodward Jr. *et al.* raise a similar set of concerns, focusing on privacy, policy and legality (Woodward Jr. *et al.* 2003: 195–279). Although the texts willingly entertain a specific and rather narrow set of concerns with biometrics, predictably the authors argue in favour of biometrics, highlighting the way in which it is legal and privacy-enhancing and demonstrates human diversity and individuality in practice, rather than a sacrifice of individuality for (securing) the state (Woodward Jr. *et al.* 2003: 198, 209–10). In another testament to the un-ironic tone, Woodward Jr. *et al.*

point out, 'biometrics could refocus the way Americans look at the brave new world of personal information' (2003: 198). This new way of looking at personal information is to look at the political space of biometrics as the space of the dataset. In the case of privacy, legality and broader sociocultural concerns, the site of contestation is the database itself, preoccupied with maintaining the integrity of the binary code, not the 'integrity' of the body. As a result, the sorts of issues that arise all assume the timeliness and practicality of biometrics, and indeed the way in which identity, security and liberty are already altered.

Notably the argument regarding privacy – or liberty – suggests, 'biometrics is privacy's friend because, for example, it can be used to help protect information integrity and deter identity theft' (Woodward Jr. *et al.* 2003: 199). Consequently, biometrics quickly resolves the seeming rivalry between liberty and security: it is in fact securing the database that facilitates liberty/privacy. Specifically, the database is protected from misuse/abuse of information; the problem of 'functional creep', where information is later used for purposes other than those originally intended; and tracking, or the 'Big Brother' fear, where anonymity and autonomy can no longer be maintained (Woodward Jr. *et al.* 2001: 23–6). These concerns fall into the category of 'informational privacy', where the (in)security of the database is directly related to, and not divergent from, the concerns of liberty/privacy. The effort devoted to informational privacy/security in all texts on biometrics, compared with the minimal (or even nonexistent) reflections devoted to issues of 'physical privacy', hints at the extent to which the space of the database is congruous with the political space of biometrics.[2]

In the only examination of 'physical privacy' found in the consulted texts, Woodward Jr. *et al.* list three core characteristics: stigmatization, actual harm and hygiene (Woodward Jr. *et al.* 2001: 23–6). Stigmatization is quickly maligned by linking it directly with wider sociocultural norms (which can of course be changed in the 'brave new world of personal information'). A most interesting aspect of physical privacy, however brief, is the issue of 'actual harm'. The biometrics industry and its advocates who urge citizens unfamiliar with biometric technologies to consult Hollywood films for a better grasp of these technologies, seem unaware of the centrality of 'actual harm' in both popular culture's representations of biometrics and the lived experiences of those engaging in resistance against biometrics. In an attempt to familiarize readers with biometric technologies, Chirillo and Blaul suggest:

If you've ever watched high-tech spy movies, you've most likely seen biometric technology. Several movies have depicted biometric technologies based on one or more of the following unique identifiers:

face, fingerprint, handprint, iris, retina, signature, and voice. (2003: 1)

Some advocates of biometrics have indicated that such strategies are problematic, indicating an awareness of the central role of 'actual harm' in most Hollywood representations of biometrics. As Australia's Immigration Minister Amanda Vanstone confessed in 2004, 'I don't think I have ever heard of a movie being made that's demonstrated where biometrics have in fact saved people from improper persecution' (*Herald Sun* 2004). The (ab)use of biometrics in films often involves 'actual harm', such as Tom Cruise's character in *Minority Report*, who is forced to carry his own eyeball in a plastic bag after a clandestine botched medical procedure. As the body is password, the appendage – in this instance, the eye – is required for authorization. Woodward Jr. *et al.* seem concerned with 'actual harm' only insofar as it might lead to deceiving biometric systems: 'Others may be concerned that a dismembered limb could be stolen and used to "fool" a system' (2001: 27). Such comments only serve to reinforce the industry's representation of the political space of biometrics as the space of the database, rather than the space of the body. Physical harm, hygiene and stigmatization are summarily dismissed as little more than peripheral reservations with biometrics. One might consider to what extent this move pushes the politics of resistance to these maligned spaces, as resistance becomes futile in the highly restricted space of the dataset. I reflect briefly on this later in the paper (see Muller 2004).

The body of biometrics literature to which I refer goes to great lengths to present both the possibilities (and risks, however minimal) of biometric technologies. In doing so, this literature serves to construct the political space of biometrics. Not overtly stating what is or is not 'political' about biometrics, the literature raises what it says are *the* sociocultural, policy and legal concerns associated with these technologies. The (in)security of the database is forwarded as the space of biometrics politics: here privacy/liberty are 'secured', but this is premised on a rather narrow account of liberty and privacy. Again, this move is not lost on the biometrics literature. Rather than engaging privacy or liberty in the abstract or general sense, privacy is broken down to informational privacy and physical privacy. Clearly, in the physical sense there is little privacy and minimal liberty, yet the space of the database remains secured. Questions of physical privacy/liberty are rapidly dismissed, yet would appear to be the precise space of resistance, but this is another matter. Reflecting on what a politics of biometrics might look like, the texts of biometrics themselves appear to begin 'after' the body, where liberty, identity and (in)security are entertained in the space of the database rather than in the space of the physical body. This production of a particular political space of biometrics in which there is little room for resistance was exposed further in the Citizenship and Immigration Canada forum on biometrics held in October 2003.

Biometrics: (ab)use and the 'inevitability crisis'

At the very outset of the report on the Citizenship and Immigration Canada forum on biometrics, the common need for biometrics by both public and private sectors is raised as a critical starting point (CIC 2003: 2). In the introduction to the report, a number of key points and conclusions are raised, notably echoing the framing of the political space of biometrics found in the literature. In particular, the dichotomy between security and privacy is deemed false. Reinforcing the extent to which the politics of biometrics is congruent with the space of the dataset, the report notes that:

> By the end of the Forum, many if not most participants and presenters agreed that although there may be challenges with the use of biometrics in some contexts, there is nothing either inherently privacy-enhancing or privacy-limiting about the use of biometrics. Biometrics must therefore be looked at in the context of specific applications and their related *data management* environment. (CIC 2003: 5; emphasis added)

The report's introduction goes on to stress the importance of managing data in order to ensure accuracy and avoid abuse (CIC 2003: 6). Finally, the introduction plainly states that 'the status quo is not sustainable', hinting at the inevitable use of biometric technologies which is expressed more explicitly later in the report and recurs throughout (CIC 2003: 5).

Denis Coderre, the then Minister of Citizenship and Immigration, focuses on the inevitability of biometrics, suggesting that 'the biometrics train has left the station' (CIC 2003: 11). Although Mr Coderre highlights the amalgamation of public and private needs, notably identity theft/fraud and security, freedom and privacy, an 'inevitability crisis' seems persistent throughout the report. Echoing the commitment in the biometrics literature to framing the political space of biometrics as the space of the database, the biometrics forum report focuses on questions of information management. In the context of public policy analysis, the report cautions of a problem in the introduction, but nonetheless falls prey to it: 'It is important to make sure that policy imperatives are driving the development of technology and not technology driving policy' (CIC 2003: 5). As the space of the database is produced as the political space of biometrics, it would seem that questions associated with policy implementation precede considerations over agenda setting and problem definition. From both public and private perspectives, the general issue is 'terrorism' and addressing the (in)security of borders and identities. However, these are general issues, and depending on subsequent problem definition, the appropriateness of biometrics as a sufficient (re)solution is not altogether clear. Much like the oft-cited example of 'homelessness', if the problem is defined as a lack of housing, rather than insufficient employment, or substance abuse, the sort of policy solution will be quite incapable of coping with other associated problems. In the case of terrorism, if the problem is a lack of sufficient information, rather than overt state-sponsored stigmatization of particular individuals, or the preservation of certain rights and privileges to specific individuals and the subsequent exclusion of others from these sets of rights and privileges, the appropriate policy response would again be markedly different. As the title of the forum report suggests, the preoccupation is with the implications and applications of biometrics – questions of implementation – while prior questions of problem definition are assumed, further reinforcing the inevitability crisis of biometrics. As one of the forum participants, Gerry Van Kessel, notes: 'The question is not whether to adopt biometrics as it is too late to turn back the tide of biometric technology; rather the issue now is how to manage its applications' (CIC 2003: 21). The second point to the inevitability crisis which characterizes the biometrics forum report is the preoccupation with the space of the database, echoing the biometrics literature itself.

Throughout the biometrics forum report, many of the invited experts – and it should be noted that the question of 'invitations' was a controversial point in and of itself[3] – focus on the space of the database. The keynote speaker, Dr Colin Soutar, focuses on issues of management, security (encryption) and identification/verification. When asked about the role of biometric technology in the war on terror, Dr Soutar is quick to once again return to the space of the database, suggesting that aside from deterrence and prevention of identity fraud, in the space of the database privileges and access can be revoked quickly to those considered to be threats or risks to security (and identity) (CIC 2003: 16). When considered in the international context, Martin Giles from the UK Home Office speaks of the very concept of identity, suggesting that territoriality is an insufficient aspect of identity since it is not unique. In contrast, the physical characteristics of the human body converted to binary codes produce a unique and distinctive identity (CIC 2003: 17). Citing streamlined security clearance, fraud reduction and the prevention of 'multiple identities', Giles extols the virtues of biometrics in maintaining and 'securing' identity. The question of biometrics politics and the space of the database reaches it zenith in the European Commission Directorate General Gillian Russell's discussion of EURODAC, the European Union-wide biometric database for tracking asylum requests (CIC 2003: 19). Russell notes the importance of privacy and security, but again, such concerns are framed in the space of the database.

Finally, Gerry Van Kessel – who, as the earlier quoted passage demonstrates, expresses the inevitability crisis as starkly as Denis Coderre's metaphor of the biometrics train already having left the station (CIC 2003: 21) – was also asked to consider the abuse of biometrics. In particular, Van Kessel was asked to consider the history of the (ab)use of technologies that 'exacerbate inequalities' (CIC 2003: 24; also see Muller 2004). Again remaining close to the space of the database, the response suggested that securing access (to information, spaces/places, etc.) to 'legitimate people' and minimizing abuse is the underlying principle of biometrics in the first place.

Reflections on security and identity

In the biometrics literature referred to here, and the recent forum report on the implications and applications of biometrics, the space of the database is consistently reinforced as the space of biometrics politics. In both instances, the separation between public and private erodes, if not altogether withers away, in the space of biometrics. A post-September 11 obsession with 'securing identity' has, through the political space of biometrics, helped produce identity as physical characteristics translated into binary codes. Not only is the line between public and private eroded, but the interests of security and identity also become congruous. In this context, considerations of privacy, liberty and freedom fail to be juxtaposed to the concerns of '(in)secure identity', and are instead subsumed as principle motivation for this securitizing move. As a recent Canadian Press article suggests, secure identity is becoming integral to a nation's status as a 'First World Nation' (Bronskill 2004). Here the question of exclusion in the politics of biometrics is framed more widely than the simple exclusion of particular rights, privileges and individuals, but also (in)secure identity as a criteria in the hierarchy of nations.

The ramifications of the particular (co)construction of the space of the database as the political space of biometrics not only conflates security and identity, but also ends up (re)producing identity in this space of the database. As such, (secure) identity becomes a physical characteristic translated into binary code. Questions of privacy, freedom and liberty are then also transposed to this space of the database, where the management and integrity of information, and subsequent streamlined (freer) movement address these concerns in the secured space of the database. As noted in the biometrics forum report, the perceived dichotomy between security and privacy/liberty does in fact prove to be false, as the (secure) space of the database (read: biometrics politics) reads the securing – and subsequent (re)production – of identity as the direct resolution of questions of liberty, security and identity. The implication of this move is to push the politics of resistance outside of the space of the database, which, as the political space of biometrics, tends to malign questions of the physical body and force resistance to the space of bodily manipulation (physical harm).

Acknowledgements

I wish to thank all the participants at the State Borders and Border Policing workshop at Queen's University, Kingston, ON, 20–22 August 2004, for their helpful comments on this paper, with special thanks to Mark Salter and Elia Zureik for their comments and their efforts as workshop organizers. Also, thanks to Antje Wiener and Serena Kataoka for their comments and suggestions on an earlier draft of this paper.

Notes

1 In this case, consider particularly the way in which debates regarding genetically modified food are framed. Debates regularly focus on questions of product labelling, etc., and it is only in this 'consumer space' and framed as such that deeper questions regarding cultural norms, ethical and moral considerations are entertained.
2 Of all texts consulted, only the Woodward Jr. *et al.*, *Army Biometric Applications*, devotes more than a paragraph to questions of 'physical privacy', and it only spends two pages.
3 In particular, the decision not to invite – and some argue exclude – Ontario's information and privacy commissioner Ann Cavoukian, who happens to be a world expert on the field but also a critic of the proposed Canadian national identity card, and invite American lawyer Alan Dershowitz who has been an outspoken advocate of biometrics since 11 September 2001, as well as controversially advocating torture as an interrogation technique, suggests the forum participants were chosen with specific intention. On Dershowitz and torture, see Buckley Jr. 2002.

References

Albert, M., Jacobson, D. and Lapid, Y. (eds) (2001) *Identities, Borders, Orders: Rethinking International Relations Theory* (Minneapolis: University of Minnesota Press).

Ali, T. (2002) *The Clash of Fundamentalisms: Crusades, Jihads and Modernity* (New York: Verso).

Andreas, P. and Biersteker, T.J. (eds) (2003) *The Rebordering of North America: Integration and Exclusion in a New Security Context* (New York: Routledge).

Beilharz, P., Robinson, G. and Rundell, J. (eds) (1992) *Between Totalitarianism and Postmodernity* (Cambridge, MA: The MIT Press).

Bennett, C. and Grant, R. (eds) (1999) *Visions of Privacy: Policy Choices for the Digital Age* (Toronto: University of Toronto Press).

'Biometrics to be used to identify illegal immigrants', *Herald Sun*, 11 February 2004. Available at: http://www.heraldsun.news.com.au/ (accessed 12 February 2004).

Booth, K. (1997) 'Security and Self: Reflections of a Fallen Realist', in M.C. Williams and K. Krause (eds) *Critical Security Studies: Concepts and Cases* (Minneapolis: University of Minnesota Press), pp. 83–120.

Borneman, J. (1998) *Subversions of International Order* (New York: SUNY Press).

Bronskill, J. (2004) 'Canada to introduce biometric passports despite privacy concerns', *National Post*, 18 July 2004. Available at: http://www.canada.com/national/nationalpost/news/story.html?id=2e3e0fd2-3d23-45b9-b2c6-45df52bdbf86 (accessed 20 July 2004).

Buckley, Jr., W.F. (2002) 'Tortured thought', *National Review Online*, 29 January 2002. Available at: http://www.nationalreview.com/buckley/buckley012902.shtml (accessed 4 June 2004).

Caldas-Coulthard, C.R. and Coulthard, M. (eds) (1996) *Texts and Practices: Readings in Critical Discourse Analysis* (London: Routledge).

Carr, D. (2002) 'The Futility of Homeland Defense', *The Atlantic Monthly*, January, pp. 53–5.

Chirillo, J. and Blaul, S. (2003) *Implementing Biometric Security* (Indianapolis, IN: Wiley Publishing, Inc.).

Citizenship and Immigration Canada (CIC) (2003) *Biometrics: Implications and Applications for Citizenship and Immigration*, Forum Report, 7–8 October 2003, Ottawa, ON, Canada.

Davis, A. (1997) 'The Body as Password', *Wired Magazine*, 5:7 (July). Available at: http://www.wired.com/wired/archive/5.07/biometrics.html?pg=2&topic=&topic_set= (accessed 4 March 2004).

Davis, J.R. (2000) *Fortunes Warriors: Private Armies and the New World Order* (Vancouver: Douglas & McIntyre).

Donnan, H. and Wilson, T.M. (1999) *Borders: Frontiers of Identity, Nation, and State* (Oxford: Berg Press).

Friedman, T. (1999) *The Lexus and the Olive Tree: Understanding Globalization* (New York: Farrar, Straus, Giroux).

Fukuyama, F. (1992) *The End of History and the Last Man* (New York: Free Press).

George, J. (1994) *Discourses of Global Politics: A Critical (Re)Introduction to International Relations* (Boulder, CO: Lynne Rienner Publishers).

Howarth, D., Norval, A.J. and Stavrakakis, Y. (eds) (2000) *Discourse Theory and Political Analysis: Identities, Hegemonies and Social Change* (Manchester: Manchester University Press).

Klein, B. (1994) *Strategic Studies and World Order* (Cambridge: Cambridge University Press).

Leiss, W. (2004) 'Cultural Politics of Bio-Genetics', seminar at Pacific Centre for Technology and Culture, 12 February 2004, University of Victoria, Victoria, BC, Canada.

Lyon, D. (2001) *Surveillance Society: Monitoring Everyday Life* (Buckingham: Open University Press).

Lyon, D. (2003) *Surveillance After September 11* (London: Polity).

Mann, C. (2002) 'Homeland Insecurity', *The Atlantic Monthly*, September. Available at: http://www.theatlantic.com/doc/prem/200209/mann (accessed 24 October 2002).

Muller, B.J. (2004) '(Dis)Qualified Bodies: securitization, citizenship, and "identity management" ', *Citizenship Studies*, 8:3, pp. 279–94.

Ohmae, K. (1999) *The Borderless World: Power and Strategy in the Interlinked Economy* (New York: Harper Business).

Pieterse, J.N. (1991) 'Fictions of Europe', *Race & Class*, 32:3, pp. 3–10.

Salter, M. (2002) *Barbarians & Civilization in International Relations* (London: Pluto Press).

Silverstein, K. (2000) *Private Warriors* (New York: Verso).

Singer, P.W. (2003) *Corporate Warriors: The Rise of the Privatized Military Industry* (Ithaca: Cornell University Press).

Smith, S. (2004) Singing Our World into Existence: International Relations Theory and September 11. *International Studies Quarterly*, 48, pp. 499–515.

Troyer, L. (2003) 'Counterterrorism: sovereignty, law, subjectivity', *Critical Asian Studies*, 35:2, pp. 259–76.

Walters, W. (2002) 'Mapping Schengenland: denaturalizing the border', *Environment and Planning D: Society and Space*, 20, pp. 561–80.

Wilson, J. (2004) 'Private security firms call for more firepower in combat zone', *The Guardian*, 17 April 2004.

Wilson, T.M. and Donnan, H. (eds) (1998) *Border Identities: Nation and State at International Frontiers* (Cambridge: Cambridge University Press).

Woodward, Jr., J.D. (2001) *Biometrics: Facing Up to Terrorism* (Arroyo Centre, RAND).

Woodward, Jr., J.D., Orlans, N.M. and Higgins, P.T. (2003) *Biometrics: Identity Assurance in the Information Age* (New York: McGraw-Hill).

Woodward, Jr., J.D., Webb, K.W., Newton, E.M., Bradley, M. and Rubenson, D. (2001) *Army Biometric Applications: Identifying and Addressing Sociocultural Concerns* (Arroyo Centre, RAND).

Zureik, E. with contribution from K. Hindle (2004) 'Governance, Security and Technology: the case of biometrics', *Studies in Political Economy*, 73 (Spring/Summer), pp. 113–37.

Chapter 7

Expanding surveillance: connecting biometric information systems to international police cooperation

Nancy Lewis

Canadian news stories grabbing headline attention in recent years included the deportation of Canadian citizen Maher Arar to Syria, and Toronto Police Chief Fantino's suggestions that all arrested persons have their DNA tested. Fantino also proposed that fingerprints collected from persons suspected of criminal behaviour be kept on file, even after charges have been dropped! At first glance these news stories have little in common, save the involvement of law-enforcement agencies. But the connection between these stories is the focus of this chapter: exploring the changing environment of policing in this culture of surveillance (Staples 1997) or surveillance society (Lyon 2001).

First, I should provide the loose threads of the news stories just mentioned. Mr Maher Arar is a Canadian citizen born in Syria, who worked in Ottawa, Canada as a telecommunications engineer. Returning from a family vacation in Tunisia in September 2002, he was detained by US officials while on a scheduled stopover in New York. US officials alleged Mr Arar has links to Al Qaeda. He was deported to Syria, even though he carried a Canadian passport. In an interview with Allison Smith of the Canadian Broadcasting Corporation, Tom Ridge, Director of Homeland Security in the United States, said:

> First of all, I think we need to dispel the notion that this was an arbitrary decision on the part of our government. There was sufficient information within the international intelligence community about

this individual that we felt warranted his deportation back to one of – he had dual citizenship – two countries. The decision was made, based on that information available through the global international intelligence community to effect that outcome.[1]

As a result of his deportation to Syria, Mr Arar spent one year in a Syrian jail where he was tortured.

The issue being debated in Canada relates to the information Canadian police and security agencies shared with American officials. It appears that information collected in Canada by Canadian law-enforcement and security agencies about Mr Arar – who was never charged or convicted of a criminal incident – was entered into a database referred to as SCIS (security criminal intelligence system). This information was subsequently shared with the FBI.

The second news report regarding Toronto Police Chief Fantino's lobbying for the retention of fingerprint information and the further collection of DNA information from suspects charged with lesser criminal offences is a marked change from current practices in Canada. Currently, retaining biometric information such as fingerprints and photographs following criminal charges under the Identification of Criminals Act (1985) is only lawful after conviction for an indictable offence or under the Security of Information Act. Chief Fantino's request flies in the face of current Canadian law, which requires information identifying a person to be stored only after they have been convicted.

Although the collection and storage of biometric information appears unrelated to the case of Mr Arar, it is not. Both are connected through an analysis of the changing nature of social control in this post-industrial or post-modern society, and the corresponding changes in policing evoked. As Western industrialized countries have entered a new period of social, political and economic development, it is marked by the imposition of new methods of formalized social control. Formalized social control within state borders is the mandate of national law-enforcement agencies.

The major premise of this chapter is that law enforcement does not happen in a vacuum, but instead is responsive to the changing social, cultural, economic and political environment. As a result of these changes, the law-enforcement community has incorporated new surveillance technologies and capacities to facilitate its formal mandate of social control. The changing nature of social control has included developing and applying technologies to enhance surveillance, and has increased demands for improved cooperation within the law-enforcement community in Western industrialized democracies. Consequently, social control in a surveillance society rests on the expanded capabilities of police to collect, save, analyse and share information about citizens across international borders and between other national agencies, whether or not these agencies were traditionally connected to law enforcement. Increasingly, the collection of information relates to information about the body, such as DNA, facial recognition and fingerprints, all examples of biometric information. Consequently, changes in the social, political and economic environment of Western industrialized countries have precipitated changes in the way policing is accomplished.

This chapter examines observable changes in the delivery of law-enforcement services as new surveillance technologies and partnerships are incorporated to respond to changing national and international environments. It is exploratory, raising issues of interest that require further analysis. It does not pretend to cover the entire breadth of changes in law enforcement, but instead to offer a sampling of some of the more obvious patterns occurring in Western Europe and North America.

Part 1: Four themes building on existing literature

I begin by drawing on previous literature examining surveillance societies that analysed important concepts useful to the current discussion of expanded surveillance technologies applied in policing. For instance, the growth in surveillance societies rests on creating the body as an objective source of information. Surveillance capacities that focus on the body institute micro-techniques of disciplinary power that self-regulate behaviour to be docile and conformist. However, new surveillance societies maintain the same old, tired social hierarchies that privilege some and deny social benefit to others. Facilitating social hierarchies is a process of social sorting made efficient by the linking of once-discrete information systems into networks of information that can generate and analyse information for purposes not even remotely close to the original purpose of information collection. These four themes are: the body as a site of struggle, micro-techniques of disciplinary power, social sorting and classification into social hierarchies, and leaky containers and assemblages. Applying these themes to the expanded use of surveillance technologies and the sharing of information by the law-enforcement community provides insight into the accomplishment of social control given the tremendous social, political and economic changes.

The body as a site of struggle

Staples observes that the individual's body has become a site of struggle in which the body has become a source of information about the individual.

The body is being used to test truth claims, and to measure possible deviations from the norm. According to Staples (1997: 4) the body is 'to be watched, assessed and manipulated'. For Staples (1997), the more frequent collection of information from the body, to serve an increasing number of public/private functions, demonstrates the diffusion of power and technology to decentralized, daily, local knowledge-gathering activities.

Police Chief Fantino's quest to keep fingerprint information and DNA samples of people not yet convicted of a criminal offence is an example of disciplinary power extending our gaze to an increasing number of citizens and, again, using the body to reveal secrets. Nelkin and Andrews (1999) refer to the gradual expansion of genetic testing for DNA identification as 'surveillance creep'. Increasing numbers of people have their DNA on file, and its collection is no longer limited to those individuals found criminally responsible for the most serious criminal offences. In the United States, military personnel submit a DNA sample, which can be released to a law-enforcement officer investigating a possible criminal matter involving the service member. People who give their DNA in a dragnet have their genetic markers stored in a DNA data bank available for law-enforcement inquiry. Prisoners in many states convicted of property crimes must give up their DNA too.

Marx (1988) predicted increased efficiency and reduced cost of the technology will lead to increased use of surveillance technologies. This is exactly the case with the collection of DNA. DNA collection has gained popularity as the technology required for collection has become less complex, less physically invasive and less costly, and requires less knowledge and skill to use.

Micro-techniques of disciplinary power

Micro-techniques of disciplinary power evoke images of the panopticon. The architectural design of Bentham's prison, the panopticon subjected the inmate to continuous observation by the 'keeper'. The power of the panopticon design is that the inmates never know whether they are being observed, but must assume they are and adjust their behaviour to conform. In this way, inmates watch themselves, by internalizing the gaze of the keeper. It is the randomness of screening that creates the self-disciplining docile body. Micro-techniques of disciplinary power are exercised 'continuously, automatically and anonymously' (Staples 1997: 25).

The principle of the panopticon has been incorporated in many contemporary forms of surveillance, such as random drug tests. Disciplinary power is achieved as individuals conform their behaviour so that their body does not reveal their secrets. Because the screening ceremonies have become enmeshed in our daily routines, the need to give up our bodily fluids is infrequently questioned, continuing the disciplinary regime that is automatic and anonymous.

However, the 'gaze' has moved far beyond those found guilty of criminal offences. Prisoners or those legally defined as deviants are no longer the only group asked to offer up their bodily fluids. Discipline has diffused throughout society so that now countless groups and individuals fall into generalized surveillance regimes. Many minimum wage, service sector jobs require a urine sample for the applicant as a condition of employment. Many high school athletes have to provide a urine sample, and teachers in New York state must submit their fingerprints before employment.

The 'keeper' is no longer necessarily a public employee whose purpose is to protect society. Instead, current surveillance technologies are used by a range of different public and private agencies to 'gaze' at an increasing number of societal members, to create docile consumers, students, employees, aid recipients and citizens. Consequently, disciplinary power transforms and improves the body to become obedient. Disciplinary power effectively achieves social control by creating the body as docile, rendering the 'individual manageable, submissive, teachable ... and pliable' (Staples 1997: 27).

Social sorting

The above examples suggest that disciplinary power has diffused throughout the community, with teachers, students and the working class equally subjected to its disciplinary gaze. But that is not the case as Staples (1997, 2000) and Lyon (2001, 2003) warn. Increased use of surveillance technologies raises important concerns about equality in its application of social control. Staples (1997: 6) makes the important point that historically and cross-culturally, social control experienced by individuals and groups has varied depending on such characteristics as race, ethnicity, class and gender. Hier's (2003: 409) examination of poor, single women receiving social assistance confirms that the application of new surveillance technologies contributes to the 'reinforcement of already existing social fractures'. Abstracted from Staples, and specifically evaluated in Hier, we see that the new systems of surveillance developed from, and remain connected to, 'early modern' systems of surveillance that were designed to 'coordinate and control populations' (Hier 2003: 403). The social need to control populations is a product of social and cultural forces.

Similarly, Lyon (2003) explains the problems with increased surveillance relating to social processes of human decision making. Surveillance technologies are designed and implemented to discriminate between social groups, to collect, categorize and evaluate. Lyon (2003) refers to this process as social sorting. Lyon's (2001: 4) concept of social sorting describes the differential outcomes that result from categorizing groups of people, 'surveillance capacities are used to sort and sift populations, to categorize and to classify, to enhance the life chances of some and to retard those of others'.

As a social process, the entire system of surveillance – from the need to watch, select, collect and code information, to evaluating the information and the power imbued in the information output – reproduces social categories. Social categories of risk, and social hierarchies measured against a model of the privileged, white, middle-aged, middle-class male allow judgements to be made about individuals and groups that include or exclude them from social, political or economic benefits.

Leaky containers and assemblages

Related to his very important observation connecting surveillance to social sorting and inequality, Lyon (2001) more fully develops Staples' (1997) examination of the diffusion of surveillance practices and flows of information. Staples correctly dismisses the 'Big Brother' phenomenon in that there is no centralized, hierarchical power watching and recording our every action. However, Staples (1997) does not continue in his analysis of the diffusion of power to arrive at the decentralized, local knowledge -gathering activities. Lyon's (2001) analysis of 'leaky containers' picks up the disconnected pieces of apparently discrete pools of information and argues the trend in surveillance societies is to move information more freely between once discrete information databases held by institutions. Information collected for one purpose can be used for entirely different purposes.

Similarly, Haggerty and Ericson (2000) use the concept of assemblages to recognize loose connections between these previously discrete information- and data-gathering systems of surveillance. Their idea of the emergent surveillant assemblage theorizes the need of surveillance to bring these once discrete component parts into wider, integrated systems. For Haggerty and Ericson (2000), it is not the body in its totality that is the focus of surveillance technologies; rather, the body is dissected into various data flows, assemblages. Consequently, parts of the body, digitized in leaky containers, will be reassembled in a wider networked system.

Like Staples (1997) and Lyon (2001), Haggerty and Ericson (2000) emphasize the decentralized nature of surveillance. There is no centralized power directing, controlling or storing information. Instead, information systems are loosely connected and unstable. Surveillant assemblages connect once discrete systems, such as state agencies, with other public or private information bases. For instance, Hier's (2003) work that examined welfare services in Ontario demonstrated the 'effectiveness' of the surveillant assemblage as aid recipients' financial information was verified through the use of income tax returns (from a federal database), student loans and other welfare benefits (from various provincial databases).

Social control does not require a centralized panopticon. Instead, social control creating self-regulating docile bodies can happen through a more localized networking of information systems (social sorting). Assemblages, connecting leaky containers, can have an effect similar to that of Bentham's totally closed environment of the panopticon prison.

Part 2: Policing and social change

The discussion in Part 2 of the article records observable changes in the techniques and delivery of policing services as a result of changes driven by surveillance societies. Law enforcement and the regulation of norms do not happen in a vacuum or within the sole discretion of the policing community. Instead, policing occurs within an environment influenced by political, economic and social pressures, and these are increasingly global.

Political pressures include the terrorist attacks in the United States on 11 September 2001. Repeatedly, Canada's immigration and law-enforcement policies have been identified as potential threats to American security. For instance, as US Ambassador Paul Celucci prepared to leave his diplomatic post in Canada, he warned Canadians '"it is inevitable terrorists will attempt to use Canada as a base to strike the United States" and urged Canadians not to be complacent about the threat global terrorism poses to the continent ... [He further argued] "It is inevitable that terrorists would look to Canada as a potential launching pad to get into the US"' (Dawson and Fife 2005).

Economic pressures affecting policing include the liberalization of trade. Increasing liberalization of markets has created new opportunities for crime. Crime and criminals are no longer restricted to one geographic area. Instead, they transcend national borders, finding opportunity for crime around the globe. The global movement of illegal immigrants is a good example of the ability of criminals to forge alliances to commit crimes in response to market pressures. For instance, a market exists in various industrialized countries for cheap, disposable labour (Bales 2004). Other countries have a surplus of labour and the resulting wretched conditions for people with no ability to make an income. Supply meets demand, and through a series of movements, illegal immigrants are transported around the globe.

The adoption of surveillance technologies and the sharing of information with outside agencies, some of which are only remotely involved in law enforcement, necessitate a cultural and operational change in policing. Police culture has generally reinforced an insular police agency, responding with suspicion to outside agencies' requests for cooperation and information sharing. In a speech delivered at the Department of National Defence conference on Network Enabled Operations, Royal Canadian Mounted Police (RCMP) Commissioner Zaccardelli (2004) noted the changing demands of policing have to overcome the traditional police culture:

> Police culture – like military culture – overtly and deliberately creates a sense of higher calling. A bond between the men and women who work the front line that is unique and powerful. The trouble is, those same romantic – although admittedly effective – notions don't blend easily with this new idea that we are in fact inter-dependent, inter-connected and need to share power, resources and even operations with other organizations.

Reiner (2000: 91) describes a core cultural characteristic of police culture as police suspicion, which operationally leads to stereotyping. The police cultural value of suspicion is closely linked to police racism. Through the development of a classification system that allows police officers to contrast the normal with the exceptional, police officers hold very rigid stereotypical views of the 'normal' functioning of society. According to Reiner (2000: 91), 'the particular categories informing [police suspiciousness and stereotyping] tend to be ones that reflect the structure of power in society'. Consistent with surveillance practices such as social sorting, the police cultural characteristic of suspicion works to allow police in surveillance societies to categorize and classify populations and individuals by their perceived level of risk and suspicion.

The growing culture of surveillance (Staples 1997) or surveillance societies (Lyon 2001) is a trend watched closely by the police. Police budget spending on information technology and information management (ITIM) has grown tremendously. The RCMP currently spends 12 per cent of its total budget ($3 billion) on ITIM. Police are lobbying for changes in law and policy that allow them to collect, store and share information.

Toronto Police Chief Fantino's purpose in speaking to the media about his request to retain individuals' biometric information is designed to educate the voters about the police need for this information, while also placing his request on the political agenda in Ottawa.

Examining external police behaviour allows us to make assumptions and predictions about future directions in the role of police in securing social control. What direction will social control by police take as they adopt and apply new surveillance technologies to respond to the growing internal and external pressures to reduce risk and enhance security in their domestic jurisdictions? A review of trends pursued by Western industrialized democracies does not provide a clear picture, with some trends indicating a centralized, 'Big Brother', panopticon style of social control, such as those pursued by European Union nation states, while other trends indicate police surveillance will take on a more decentralized configuration, such as theorized by Haggerty and Erikson (2000) and Lyon (2001). The assemblages linking leaky containers will focus on networking national public and private data banks across various sectors beyond solely law-enforcement information, characteristic of the current North American approach. The remainder of the discussion will focus analysis on the central issue of importance, predicting the future direction of law enforcement in its powerful role of administering social control. Closely associated with this is the second concern, to what extent law-enforcement agencies will intervene in bodily integrity in their quest to collect biometric information.

Centralized surveillance (panopticon)

The underlying assumption of the centralized surveillance approach is that the risks to domestic security come from beyond the nation state's border and, as a result, cannot be addressed by traditional methods of controlling societal members. Such an approach recognizes the global movement of bodies and goods that is beyond the capacity of any one nation state to control. In fact, in a global economy the international movement of goods and bodies is a positive thing. Risks to domestic security identified by those who favour a centralized approach to surveillance to achieve social control include international terrorism and organized crime. The centralized approach to enhanced surveillance has focused on different dimensions in Europe than it has in North America. In Europe a more centralized approach has dominated, given the formation of a common social, economic and political identity within the European Union.

The Treaty on European Political and Monetary Union (the Treaty of Maastricht) came into force on 1 November 1993. The Treaty ushered in a new set of challenges for policing and security among the European member states. According to the Treaty, 'every citizen is free to move and reside freely within the territory of the member states' (Convey and Kupiszewski 1995: 939). However, the challenge is to control the movement of the approximately eight million non-EU citizens moving between member states (Convey and Kupiszewski 1995: 943). Two centralized surveillance systems were instituted by European Union members in an attempt to control immigration from third countries and curtail the spread of crime beyond individual states. The first centralized system of control is Europol, a system of police information exchange available to European Union member states. It came into force on 1 October 1998 and became operational on 1 July 1999 (*European Report* 2004: 408). Activities of interest to Europol include 'drugs-trafficking, human-trafficking, child pornography, money-laundering, Euro-counterfeiting, cyber crime, environmental crime, terrorism and racism' (*European Report* 2004: 408–9).

Schengen Information System is the second centralized surveillance system used by the European Union to control mobile bodies into and through its jurisdiction. In 1985, the leaders of the nine European Community countries signing the Schengen Accord seeking a unified Europe sought not just 'free trade', but also the unimpeded movement between member states for the approximately 250 million residents (Evans 1994: 38). As a result, the Schengen Information System (SIS) was created to facilitate police and customs cooperation in a border-free Europe. SIS is defined 'as a databank for the purposes of tracing criminals, suspects, aliens reported for non-admission, and others' (den Boer, quoted in Warren 1992: 28). In 2002 it was reported that 10 million people were listed in the SIS. Most entries were related to forged or stolen passports or identity cards. As well, 1.3 million convicted and suspected criminals are flagged on its alert system (*European Report* 2002: 481).

The second-generation Schengen Information System is under development. On 26 October 2004, a deal was signed with a multi-national technology consortium to deliver the future Visa Information System (VIS) and the next generation of SIS. It is anticipated that the second-generation SIS system will be in operation by March 2007, and the VIS by the end of 2006. It is notable that the new generation of SIS will be able to bank biometric information, making the job of identifying individuals easier. Dr Frank Paul, Head of Unit, Large Scale IT Systems, European Commission, Director General Justice and Home Affairs recommends that biometric identifiers collected and stored should include a digitized facial image and the mandatory printing of two fingers.[2] Adopting standardized biometric identifiers will verify that the visa documents belong to the person holding them. This represents an interesting trend in the development of new generations of centralized surveillance technologies. Although there is a great deal of interest in these new information systems from the perspective of immigration and migration control, these new systems will not solve the law-enforcement challenges facing the European Union. These challenges stem from the removal of borders between the member states, as well as the challenges faced by all nations from an increasing globalized market structure. The European countries have not been as successful in integrating and sharing law-enforcement information as they been have in sharing immigration-related information. Currently, there is an interest among EU member states to develop a structure to work more cooperatively with other EU police agencies. However, a number of obstacles were identified by police information technology professionals representative of the various European police agencies that prevent information sharing and cooperation.[3] Issues include:

- ownership and control of information
- shared language (the EU recognizes 20 official languages)
- lack of a structure to bring police information technology groups together to discuss the issues
- lack of political commitment and lack of cooperation at various levels
- lack of interest by industry vendors
- lack of a standard system
- lack of resources
- culture of policing (unless the end user/police officer is involved there is no buy-in and the end user needs to work with other partners to prioritize their needs)
- difference in laws between countries

Solutions recommended by conference participants provide a way forward for cooperation and information sharing between police agencies within the EU, but also indicate the infancy of structured cooperative relationships in law enforcement:[4]

- develop a directory of national and international data services and running applications
- develop a web-based community to share information
- produce an organizational contact list (formalized social networks for contact)

- develop a central help desk
- select a sponsor group such as Europol or the Police Cooperative Working Group to hold formal meetings to develop the next steps

North American assemblages

Similar pressures for police cooperation beyond national borders are being felt in North America. The law-enforcement community in North America is driven to information and intelligence sharing by the shared assumption that, 'Scholars, military analysts and policy experts agree: it isn't a matter of IF another large scale terrorist assault will occur in North America or Europe … it is only a question of WHEN' (Zaccardelli 2004). Following the terrorist attacks of 11 September 2001, pressures for integration and cooperation between Canadian and American law enforcement intensified. As RCMP Commissioner Giuliano Zaccardelli stated in a speech on 1 December 2004, 'In a global security environment, our concern is no longer only the protection of borders … The lines of distinction between domestic and international obligations have begun to blur.' Further, outgoing US Ambassador Paul Celucci warned that 'Security trumps trade' (Dawson and Fife 2005). Canada has had to wake up to the fact that 'we sleep next to an elephant! Our culture, our security, our economy, even our identity, are unavoidably affected by America's influence' (Zaccardelli 2004).

Consequently, Canada and the United States are cooperating on a number of projects that increase information flow between law enforcement and the intelligence community. Commissioner Zaccardelli has mused that it is 'only a matter of time until the global law enforcement community utilizes integrated DNA banks, border security systems, even shared criminal records' (Zaccardelli 2004). Currently, however, cooperation between the American and Canadian law-enforcement communities is less characteristic of the European Union centralized approach and more reflective of localized networks partnered to respond to a particular need.

As the following examples of working partnerships demonstrate, there is a range of assemblages sharing information between Canadian and American law enforcement. In addition, there are also assemblages linking information between once discrete national agencies. Examples of North American police cooperation include Integrated Border Enforcement Teams and protocols to share fingerprint information between American and Canadian police agencies.

Although Canada/US Integrated Border Enforcement Teams (IBET) were originally developed in 1996 to address cross-border crimes along the American and Canadian west coast, IBETs have increased in frequency and importance. Currently there are fifteen geographical regions with IBETs operating. The IBET model is designed to create partnerships among American and Canadian police agencies at the local, state, provincial and federal levels to respond to crimes that profit from cross-border relations, such as smuggling of illegal drugs, weapons, liquor, tobacco, migrants and vehicles. IBETs facilitate the sharing of information between Canadian and US police and law enforcement. Increased and sustained funding of IBETs is one of the measures implemented by Canada to respond to the terrorist attacks of 11 September 2001. The RCMP received $135 million dollars dedicated to IBETs to continue partnerships with American law enforcement through 2005–6.[5]

A second example of increased structured information sharing between Canadian and US law enforcement is the cooperation between the FBI and the RCMP to exchange information related to 'persons of interest'. This is done through the exchange of biometric information from fingerprint identification. This exchange of information protocol is currently limited to specified people within each agency. That is, the officer on the street in Chicago, for example, cannot query the Canadian Police Information System directly, but must follow an established protocol that links his or her request through specific individuals within the FBI and RCMP.

In addition to programmes and projects to increase police cooperation beyond national borders, there is increasing interest and activity in the linking of leaky containers nationally, within both Canada and the United States. The Canadian programme of Integrated National Security Enforcement Teams (INSET)[6] is an example of assemblages such as those Haggerty and Ericson (2000) and Lyon (2001) describe. The formalization or creation of a structure to share information and analysis of intelligence among such leaky containers as the RCMP, Canada Border Services Agency (CBSA), Citizenship and Immigration Canada (CIC), Canadian Security Intelligence Service (CSIS) and provincial and municipal police services is an example of the pooling of information. In addition, the RCMP, under the guidance of the National Security Policy, is forging stronger alliances with the Department of National Defence.

The formation of the US Customs and Border Protection agency, centralizing the operations of US Customs, US Immigration, Animal and Plant Health Inspection Service and the US Border Patrol under the authority of the Department of Homeland Security occurred as the result of the terrorist attacks of 9/11. The single, unified border agency is an example of the formalization and securing of once discrete pools of information. As a centralized agency, the US Customs and Border Protection agency has access to vast amounts of surveillance technology and information from Advance Passenger Information System (APIS), to the Office of Intelligence and the National Targeting Center. The US Customs and Border Protection agency is an example of linking information between once discrete agencies. However, in this case more than just information was linked to create greater efficiency and effectiveness in achieving the agency's mandate. The example of the US Customs and Border Protection agency questions the notion of linking leaky containers and assemblages that are by their nature localized and decentralized. Perhaps centralization of public agencies with shared mandates, not just formalized agreements for information sharing between decentralized or localized agencies, is the future direction of law enforcement.

Conclusions

This chapter applied concepts from the surveillance literature and found that policing in both the North American context and Western Europe is responding to the changing political, economic and social environment of the post-modern society by developing protocols and programmes to link police information beyond the level of the individual agency, including to police agencies beyond national borders. There are trends operating in law enforcement predicted by the surveillance literature. For instance, the surveillance literature places great importance on examining the body as a site of struggle. This chapter agrees that current law-enforcement practice and future trends indicate that the body is under siege. In fact, increasing collection and uses of biometric information are being planned for future generations of information systems. Surveillance creep is the reality, as surveillance technology becomes less complex and less expensive, and continues to disperse into the community. The fact that there is no agreement among various national agencies regarding a standard biometric indicator does not appear to be a stumbling block. Some in the law-enforcement field predict we will have a multi-biometric environment and develop ITIM to work in this environment.

It remains to be seen whether or not the increase in the use of biometrics shared between once discrete agencies will have the effect of creating self-regulating docile bodies. For that to occur, people would have to know the extent of the networked information about them, flowing between agencies and across international borders. There is room here for further research to examine micro-techniques of discipline across different populations, such as criminal offenders who have their DNA stored, or consumers who have their credit and financial information profiled and widely available to other commercial enterprises. Will this shape their future decision making or behaviour?

More research is needed to determine how the core cultural characteristic of police suspicion is used to sort and categorize individuals and groups. Even more important is the question of whether or not police agencies across international borders using the same information will define characteristics of suspicious persons similarly. After all, definitions and societal responses to deviance change over time, and between different societies.

The chapter revealed many instances in which law-enforcement agencies in North America and Western Europe have instituted protocols and programmes to collect and share information from once discrete information pools. However, the current review indicates that there is not one preferred networking or partnership arrangement. Instead, some arrangements fit Lyon's (2001) model of social sorting characterized by loosely networked protocols, while others reveal a more centralized partnership such as the European experience or the creation of the US Customs and Border Protection agency. Configurations of leaky containers or centralized surveillance systems will depend on a number of factors, including the legislative and political environment in the countries of information origin and destination.

The clear conclusion from a discussion of these law-enforcement information-sharing programmes and protocols is that the changing social, political and economic environment has resulted in changes to traditional police operations. Traditional police culture characterized by the statement 'The way things get done around here' has been noticeably impacted by the changing requirements of social control and the availability of surveillance technologies. Will there be a globalized DNA data bank in the future, one centralized police force for the European Union, or a totally integrated police system in North America? We are not there yet, and given the challenges identified by leaders in police information technology in Europe, we are a long way off from such panoptic visions. However, given the lightning speed of information technology development, such possibilities may be available before the political and social environments have planned for it.

Notes

1   Source: Interview with Allison Smith, CBC, 3 October 2003. Available at: http://www.cbc.ca/news/background/arar
2   Presentation by Dr Frank Paul, AGIS Programme, 'Police Information Technology Co-Operation in an enlarged European Union', Wednesday 19 May 2004.
3   Workshop on AGIS Programme, 'Police Information Technology Co-Operation in an enlarged European Union', Friday 21 May 2004.

4   Workshop on AGIS Programme, 'Police Information Technology Co-Operation in an enlarged European Union', Friday 21 May 2004.
5   Source: http://www.rcmp-grc.gc.ca/security/ibets_e.htm
6   Source: http://www.rcmp-grc.ca/security/insets_e.htm

References

Bales, K. (2004) *Disposable People: New Slavery in the Global Economy* (Los Angeles: University of California Press).

Convey, A. and Kupiszewski, M. (1995) 'Keeping up with Schengen: migration and policy in the European Union', *International Migration Review*, 29:4, pp. 939–64.

Dawson, A. and Fife, R. (2005) 'Don't Lose Fear of Terrorists, U.S. Envoy Cellucci Warns', *The Ottawa Citizen*, Monday 7 February 2005, p. A5.

European Report (2002) 'Justice and Home Affairs: Council Moves to Add Al-Qaeda Members to Schengen Information System', 26 June 2002, p. 481.

European Report (2004) 'Justice and Home Affairs: Data Exchanges with Europol Up by 39% in 2003', 7 July 2004, p. 408.

Evans, D. (1994) 'Bordering on the Ridiculous (development of Schengen Information System)', *Computer Weekly*, 24 March 1994, pp. 38–42.

Haggerty, K. and Ericson, R. (2000) 'The Surveillant Assemblage', *British Journal of Sociology*, 51:4, pp. 605–22.

Hier, S.P. (2003) 'Probing the Surveillant Assemblage: on the dialectics of surveillance practices as processes or social control', *Surveillance and Society*, 1:3, pp. 399–411.

Lyon, D. (2003) *Surveillance as Social Sorting: Privacy, Risk and Digital Discrimination* (New York: Routledge).

Lyon, D. (2001) *Surveillance Society: Monitoring Everyday Life* (Buckingham: Open University Press).

Marx, G. (1988) 'Do Monitoring Technologies Threaten Employee Privacy Rights?' *Editorial Research Reports*, 2:12, p. 489.

Nelkin, D. and Andrews, L. (1999) 'DNA Identification and Surveillance Creep', *Sociology of Health and Illness*, 21:5, pp. 689–706.

Reiner, R. (2000) *The Politics of the Police* (Oxford: Oxford University Press).

Staples, W.G. (2000) *Everyday Surveillance: Vigilance and Visibility in Postmodern Life* (Lanham: Rowman and Littlefield Publishers).

Staples, W.G. (1997) *The Culture of Surveillance: Discipline and Social Control in the United States* (New York: St Martin's Press).

Warren, P. (1992) 'Continental Cop-out', *Computer Weekly*, 8 October 1992, pp. 26–8.

Zaccardelli, G. (2004) *Speech-Cooperation and Coordination in the New Security Environment*, Department of National Defence Network Enabled Operations: Ottawa). Available at: http://www.rcmp-grc.gc.ca/speeches/sp_new_security_e.htm

Chapter 8

What happens when you book an airline ticket? The collection and processing of passenger data post-9/11

Colin J. Bennett

In 1999 I wrote a paper with a similar title (Bennett 1999) based on a series of case studies for the European Commission on the collection, processing and dissemination of personal data by multi-national businesses, including the international airline industry (Raab *et al.* 1998). The paper traced the flows of data from the time of booking an airline ticket, through the check-in process, to the flight and the landing.[1] The case study examined the flows of data through an increasingly complex series of scenarios concerning the identity and tastes of the traveller, his 'frequent flyer status' and the nature of the ticketed route. The study allowed me to draw some tentative generalizations about the practices of typical international air carriers with regard to the processing of personal information, the characteristics of the larger surveillance network and the prospects for international regulation.

At the time of writing, little attention was paid to personal data protection issues by the airline industry. It was then difficult to find interested or expert officials within the major airlines who could provide accurate descriptions of the personal information processing practices of the industry. Few companies had appointed Chief Privacy Officers and few had explicit codes of practice. It was also difficult to find knowledgeable people from the community of outside activists and regulators who had paid much attention to the issue. There has, however, been a dramatic increase in the attention paid to the personal data processing activities of the airline industry since 11 September 2001. Passenger Name Record (PNR) data has been aggressively sought by US and international law-enforcement agencies as the basis of pilot projects for passenger profiling systems. This has caused a major transatlantic row between the Europeans and the US over the legality (under the EU's 1995 Data Protection Directive) of transferring such data to the US for processing, given the presumed 'inadequacy' of American privacy protection standards. In addition, the construction of Advanced Passenger Information (API) databases and the introduction of trusted traveller systems, often accompanied by biometric identifiers, have brought the question of the processing of travel data sharply into profile.

This paper attempts to update the earlier 1999 version in light of developments since 9/11.[2] Again, this paper eschews abstraction in favour of a very detailed empirical description of 'what happens when you do indeed book an airline ticket'. It describes two scenarios, both based on recent personal experience. The first outlines the relatively simple trip that I took to attend the conference at which the first draft of this article was presented: a flight via one airline (Air Canada) within one country (Canada, from Victoria, British Columbia to Toronto, Ontario, with onward flights to Kingston and Ottawa, Ontario). It outlines the personal information practices of the booking process, the check-in process, and the frequent flyer programme. At each stage, I have tried to discover what information about me is collected by whom, for how long it is retained, and who might have access to it. A second scenario takes the onward leg of my journey to New York rather than to Ottawa, and investigates how current and future changes in the rules of Canadian and US border control agencies have affected the flows of personal data about me.

Although the paper concludes with some reflections of a more theoretical nature, it is explicitly based on some firm assumptions about how we should be studying the 'everyday' nature and implications of personal surveillance systems (Lyon 2001). I am critical of some of the literature on the surveillance (or privacy) implications of information and communications systems and networks. The analysis of social or individual risk is often based on exaggerated claims about the potential for the linkage and communication of personal data, on extrapolations about surveillance potential from highly abnormal cases, and on hypotheses about what roles new technologies might perform in the abstract, with very little grounded analysis of its role in real, dysfunctional organizations within which fallible but mainly well-intentioned individuals make choices and decisions. 'Our physical bodies are being shadowed by an increasingly comprehensive data body', asserts Felix

Stalder in his critique of privacy in the very first issues of *Surveillance and Society* (Stalder 2002). Perhaps, but is it possible to observe this body of data? Can one find one's 'digital persona' (Clarke 1994)? The common assumptions in the literature are that one's 'data shadow' is becoming more latent, comprehensive, integrated, finely tuned, and thus more pernicious. Through this very narrow, and hardly generalizable, case study based on the 'politics of personal experience' I wish to raise some searching questions about these and other assumptions within the surveillance literature.

Victoria–Toronto–Kingston–Toronto–Ottawa–Toronto–Victoria

The reservation

Airline flights can be reserved in one of four ways: first, directly from the airline's own reservation system (by phone or at its website); second, through a travel agent who will have access to international computerized reservation systems or global distribution systems (GDS);[3] third, if reward points are being used, through the toll-free number or website associated with the airline's frequent flyer programme; and fourth, over the Internet, through services such as www.travelocity.com, www.expedia.com or www.travelport.com.

On 24 June 2004, I followed the instructions of the conference organizers and reserved return flights from Victoria to Kingston with onward connections to Ottawa through a local travel agency based in Kingston, Ontario. All Canadian travel agencies are now covered by either federal or provincial privacy legislation, and should be developing their own privacy policies and appointing privacy protection officers. It seems, however, that only the larger agencies, such as Thomas Cook, have taken these initiatives.[4] The Association of Canadian Travel Agencies (ACTA) also provides guidance concerning obligations under the new legislation, although the professional standards promulgated by ACTA have yet to incorporate privacy protection.[5] Thus, no agency should be revealing information in my customer profile to anybody else (without my consent) unless it is for the express purpose of reserving travel arrangements for me,[6] or is otherwise required by law.

Like many Canadian travel agents, this one used the Galileo reservation system to book my flight and collected my name, address, e-mail, credit card number and Aeroplan frequent flyer number. Travel agencies pay an annual fee to Galileo for access to this system, and for the presumed convenience, speed and possible cost savings to their clients. Galileo International, Inc. is one of the leading global distribution systems (GDS).

Their services connect approximately 44,000 travel agency locations to 470 airlines, 24 car rental companies, 56,000 hotel properties, 430 tour operators and all major cruise lines throughout the world. Located in Greenwood Village, near Denver, Colorado, Galileo's Data Center handles, on average, over 175 million requests for information per day. At peak times the company processes more than 2,915 messages per second.[7] GDSs like Galileo are the central repository for vast amounts of information related to an individual's travel. They are the central hubs which link all providers of travel services. They play a similar role to that played by the credit bureaus in relation to the financial industry (Hasbrouck 2004).

Thus, when a prospective traveller discloses air travel plans to a travel agent, the agent enters the data into the Galileo system, either via an encrypted Internet portal protected by SSL technology or by a direct communication link. The Galileo system then electronically contacts the airline(s) in question to ascertain whether the requested flight is available. If it is, the travel agent completes the reservation in the Galileo system. Galileo then transmits the reservation data to the travel suppliers involved in the booking – solely Air Canada in this case. If the airline is hosted on a different GDS, information about the flight(s) on that airline is sent to the airline's host system. The standards for information sharing between airlines are governed by the Airline Interline Message Procedures Manual (AIRIMP).

I was then e-mailed an electronic ticket, issued by Air Canada, which includes a ticket number, the name and place of the booking agent, the entire itinerary and the price for each leg (plus taxes). The electronic ticket includes the statement: 'Carriage and other services provided by the carrier are subject to conditions of carriage which are hereby incorporated by reference. These conditions may be obtained from the issuing carrier.'[8] It also states that 'this receipt may be required at check-in and must be presented to customs and immigration if requested.' My itinerary and e-ticket could also be viewed online by typing in the reservation locator number and my last name at www.viewtrip.com, a website operated by Galileo.[9]

At this point in the process, the travel agent's role is typically complete. Certain billing and scheduling issues may be raised after the completion of travel. For example, an airline might contest the quoted price of a fare because certain booking conditions were not met. As the travel information is no longer online (see below), the agency would have to retrieve a hard copy from Galileo. With these exceptions, the only records of travel that might be kept by an individual agency relate to the accounting information. The data-retention practices of travel agencies differ widely, however.

The record – the PNR

When my flight was booked, a Passenger Name Record (PNR) was created on Galileo's reservation system.[10] It is probable that my PNR simply included the five mandatory fields of data: the Passenger's Name, Itinerary or Routing Information, Recipient (reservation booking personnel), Phone Contact and Ticket Number. There are two supplementary categories contingent upon the construction of the PNR: a Special Service Request field and an Other Service Request field, into which information might be entered depending on the special needs and preferences of the traveller (seat assignment, meals, wheelchair needs and so on). Some of the materials contained within these fields are available to other carriers through an inter-operability mechanism, while others are exclusive to the carrier itself. A General Remarks Category is available to the operator as well. Some carriers will also 'overlay' their checkpoint information (seat numbers, baggage, frequent flyer) onto the PNR through their own systems at check-in. Some carriers (typically chartered carriers) do not enter formal PNR information, particularly where the carrier has an agreement with a 'Tour Operator', but are provided with a basic 'manifest' of passenger information by the operator with whom they have a contract.

A PNR may be amended by different agencies through different channels at different times. For complex travel arrangements, therefore, there may be several PNRs created and stored on different GDSs. An example of the possible complexities is given by Hasbrouck (2004):

> If, for example, you make a reservation on United Airlines (which outsources the hosting of its reservations database to the Galileo CRS/GDS) through the Internet travel agency Travelocity.com (which is a division of Sabre, and uses the Sabre CRS/GDS), Travelocity.com creates a PNR in Sabre. Sabre sends a message derived from portions of the Sabre PNR data to Galileo, using the AIRIMP (or another bilaterally-agreed format). Galileo in turn uses the data in the AIRIMP message to create a PNR in United's Galileo 'partition'.

Once a PNR is created, an audit trail logs each entry in the PNR history with the date, time, place, user ID and other information of the travel agent, airline staff person, automated system or any other person (such as a company secretary) who requested the entry or change. Each entry in each PNR, even for a solo traveller, may thus contain personally identifiable information on several people.

In my case, the profile is not that interesting. But it could also include the credit card information, alternative addresses, phone numbers and emergency contacts. It may contain notes about tastes and preferences, as well as personal notes intended for the use of the travel agency.[11] PNRs can therefore reveal an enormous amount about our travel preferences, and therefore our tastes and behaviours. They show:

> where you went, when, with whom, for how long, and at whose expense. Behind the closed doors of your hotel room, with a particular other person, they show whether you asked for one bed or two. ... Through meeting codes used for convention and other discounts, PNRs reveal affiliations – even with organizations whose membership lists are closely-held secrets not required to be divulged to the government. Through special service codes, they reveal details of travelers' physical and medical conditions. Through special meal requests, they contain indications of travelers' religious practices – a category of information specially protected by many countries. (Hasbrouck 2004)[12]

Airlines also, of course, transport special categories of persons – deportees, unaccompanied minors, refugees, and so on.

The PNR created for my travel was collected in Canada, and is therefore subject to Canadian privacy legislation. A recently constructed privacy policy for Galileo Canada stipulates in greater detail how this information is collected, stored and disclosed. Galileo Canada discloses personal information to the extent necessary or related to successfully completing the reservation. Thus,

> personal information is disclosed to the travel agency and travel suppliers selected by the traveler and others involved in the transaction, such as the traveler's credit card company, insurance company, and otherwise as necessary on important public interest grounds or as required by law, court order, or as requested by a governmental or law enforcement authority or in the good faith belief that *disclosure is otherwise necessary or advisable.*

Certain ticketing information in the Galileo system is optionally available to the airlines. Personal information may also be disclosed in any other manner upon the consent of the traveller involved or to anyone who Galileo Canada reasonably believes is seeking the information as the agent of the traveller. They also reserve the right to disclose personal information in connection with the sale or transfer of all or substantially all of the assets of Galileo Canada or Galileo International, Inc. to a third party.[13] The PNR data remains online for up to 72 hours after the completion of travel. After that it is archived for three years in the Galileo Data Center, after which it is destroyed.

The Galileo Canada privacy policy applies only to personal information collected in Canada. No general privacy protection policy appears on the parent site of Galileo.[14] As a global distribution system, however, this policy is not significantly different from that applied throughout the entire global operations and which has been driven principally by European rules.[15] A series of regulations on Computerized Reservation Systems (dating from 1989, 1993 and 1999) have governed the services between GDSs and suppliers, to ensure fair competition. These regulations also include bans on the transfer of personal data to third parties.[16] The 1995 EU Data Protection Directive reinforces these conditions. Thus, to all intents and purposes, the rules for personal data processing expressly defined under Canadian law would apply to Galileo's global operations.

It is commonly assumed that the PNR is a standard, while in fact they can vary in size and format. In the 1970s, the International Air Transport Association (IATA) tried to establish certain standards and inter-operability mechanisms. More recently, the International Civil Aviation Organization (ICAO) has been considering the development of an international standard to implement uniform practices.[17] The issue has really been brought to the fore by the request by the US Department of Homeland Security (DHS) for the PNR data and Advance Passenger Information (API) data from all international flights arriving in the US. This prompted questions from the European Union about what PNR data might actually be included. The DHS then came up with a list of 39 separate data elements, subsequently reduced to 34.[18]

In June 2004, the US Department of Homeland Security head Tom Ridge signed an agreement with the EU that would allow US Customs and Border Protection (CBP) to collect airline PNR data from flights between the US and EU. Once implemented, the agreement will be in effect for three and a half years, with re-negotiations to start within one year of its expiry date. Under the accord, data will be retained by CBP for three and a half years unless associated with an enforcement action. In addition, only the 34 PNR data elements will be accessed by CBP to the extent collected in the air carriers' reservation and departure control systems and CBP will filter and delete 'sensitive data' (on medical conditions, meal preferences, religious affiliations, etc.) as agreed by CBP and the European Commission. At writing, the entire agreement is under review by the European courts.

The departure: the departure control system

Typically, 24 hours before departure, relevant fields from the PNR are transferred to the airline's Departure Control System (DCS), and the check-in agents will 'edit' the flight list to make sure there is the appropriate weight distribution, to establish fuel requirements, to order meals, and to ascertain that those with special needs have been properly accommodated. When I check in for my flight at Victoria International, Air Canada check-in staff would enter my last name (or the locator code) on the DCS, but they would not necessarily have access to the complete PNR. They would add my seat allocation (if necessary) as well as the information on any checked baggage. Around five to ten minutes before departure, a complete list of passengers by seat number is printed (Passenger Information List) and given to the in-charge flight attendant. The records for each flight are purged from the DCS within 24 hours after the flight has landed, and then archived in Air Canada's headquarters in Montreal.[19] If there are special requests from third parties after the PNR has been archived, they would have to be made in writing and considered at Air Canada headquarters.

Air Canada's databases are password-protected for its own staff and check-in agents, with different levels of access depending on status in the organization. Employees, agents and contractors' staff needing access all have to complete an application form which also serves to remind them about the need for confidentiality. To access the system, users have to input their ID and a self-selected password (which has to be changed at regular intervals). The history of any changes to a PNR is recorded. There is an audit trail of all access to the DCS. If a passenger is taking an ongoing flight with a domestic carrier, the onward flight appears as an Air Canada coded flight on the passenger's ticket. The details transferred would only be the relevant stage booking, the immediately prior connecting flight and any special needs. 'Second' carriers do not have direct access to the complete journey details, booking contacts or PNR history. Air Canada employees in Canada will have been made aware through training of the general policy about the disclosure of reservations information. In general, employees are told not to disclose information about a passenger, including via the telephone, unless the information is given to: a colleague/another airline or agent for the purpose of reservation booking or ticket issue; the passenger himself and you have taken the necessary steps to ensure that this person is the passenger; some other person, and the passenger has clearly consented to this and there is a record of this in the PNR; an appropriate person or organization in an emergency to prevent injury or damage to someone's health. Employees are also advised orally that requests from the police or law-enforcement bodies must be referred to the investigations unit, and those relating to legal proceedings to the legal department.

Airline personnel work, however, in a number of different settings that might guide the ways in which these rules are interpreted. A greater variety of more urgent requests arise within the airport context from local law-enforcement authorities (who have jurisdiction over most airports), from the federal Royal Canadian Mounted Police (RCMP), or from customs and immigration officials. Working within a closer environment, personal contacts obviously develop between individuals from different authorities. Air Canada staff are also, of course, frequently asked to check whether Mr or Mrs X is on a particular flight. They should not give out such information; anecdotal evidence suggests, however, that they often do.[20]

Responsibility for the process or pre-board screening is now the responsibility of the Canadian Air Transport Safety Agency (CATSA), the main institutional response of the Government of Canada to the events of 11 September 2001. On 1 April 2002, CATSA assumed financial responsibility for pre-board screening by reimbursing airlines for the cost of the service. At Victoria International, the pre-board passenger screening is contracted to a company called Aeroguard, the main organization responsible for pre-board screening in Canadian airports.[21] On entering the screening area, I was welcomed by the sign: 'Security measures are being taken to observe and inspect passengers. No passengers are obliged to subject to a search of their persons and goods if they do not choose to board an aircraft.' There would, however, be very few circumstances under which Aeroguard personnel would seek passenger identification. Any attempt to take surreptitiously a prohibited object onboard would almost certainly be a matter for intervention by an official from Commissionaires Canada, the company contracted to provide general security services at the airport, and/or by the RCMP.

The Victoria Airport Authority (VAA) is obviously responsible for ensuring that security measures are strictly enforced, but they do not now supervise the passenger or baggage screening process. There would be very few circumstances, therefore, where the VAA would need to know any identifiable passenger information. The one exception would be the video-surveillance system. When I boarded my flight at Victoria, my image would probably be captured on three sets of digital cameras (at pre-boarding, the curb and the ramp). Those tapes would be retained by the VAA for a week before being destroyed.[22]

Collecting 'points'

I have been a member of Air Canada's Aeroplan for about 15 years, and am now a 'Prestige' member. My Aeroplan number appears on the PNR and on my boarding card. Aeroplan is a division of Air Canada, though it has a separate privacy policy and Chief Privacy Officer. I have a profile with Aeroplan which will have been collected over the years from me personally when I enrolled, from partners (hotels, credit card companies, car rental companies and other airlines) from whom I have earned miles, and from other companies who are not Aeroplan partners to whom I might have consented to the disclosure of my information. None of these partners, however, should be disclosing any details about the various transactions, beyond the aggregate miles accumulation. Aeroplan's Direct Marketing System Club Profile Database is located in Point-Claire, Quebec.

Controversy erupted in July of 2001 when, in an attempt to conform to the provisions of the Personal Information Protection and Electronic Documents Act (PIPEDA), Aeroplan released a brochure entitled 'All About Your Privacy', outlining the conditions under which Aeroplan collected, retained and disclosed the personal information of its members. The brochure was made available to approximately 60,000 of the nearly 6 million members of the Aeroplan programme. It identified the many situations in which Air Canada would disclose the personal information of Aeroplan members, including sending membership lists to Aeroplan partners, who send 'information of interest' to Aeroplan's members. Membership information was also disclosed to companies outside of the Aeroplan programme for similar purposes.

Former Canadian Privacy Commissioner George Radwanski launched an investigation into the policies and practices of Aeroplan, to ensure that they were conforming with the provisions of PIPEDA. On 20 March 2002, Radwanski released his findings after a nine-month investigation and found that Aeroplan had 'not met its obligations under Principles 4.2.4, 4.3, 4.3.1, and 4.5 of Schedule 1 of the Act', concerning consent for the disclosure of personal information. He recommended that Air Canada should

> inform all Aeroplan members as to the collection, use, and disclosure of their personal information; explain to all Aeroplan members the purposes for the collection, use, and disclosure of their personal information. This is not done adequately in the current version of the 'All about your privacy' brochure; seek positive (i.e., opt-in) consent from all Aeroplan members regarding all information-sharing situations outlined in the brochure; establish appropriate procedures for obtaining positive consent; and execute appropriate agreements with all the direct-mailing houses it employs as agents

to ensure that the personal information of Aeroplan members is protected in accordance with the Act.[23]

The Privacy Commissioner also found that, prior to the distribution of the brochure in July of 2001, received by fewer than 1 per cent of Aeroplan customers, Air Canada had made no attempt to obtain consent for the retention and disclosure of personal information. Radwanski also determined that the 'opt out' portion of the brochure constituted a 'negative option', wherein members were unwittingly providing consent unless they negated the possibility by virtue of a check mark. The Commissioner condemned the practice by ruling that 'negative or opt-out consent is not sufficient for any of the five situations described in the brochure'.

Aeroplan has subsequently amended its Privacy Policy to include a recognition of the 'importance of privacy for the Aeroplan Program', which includes a reference to the newly appointed Aeroplan Privacy Officer. The amended policy also addresses Aeroplan's commitment to privacy protection, which includes acceptance of responsibility for the personal information collected; a statement of justification for the collection of personal information; the limitations upon the collection, use, retention and disclosure of personal information; a statement concerning the importance of consent and accuracy; and a statement ensuring security, transparency, and a mechanism for addressing complaints.[24] It still, however, relies on the opt-out procedures for securing consent. On the website, and on brochures periodically sent to subscribers, customers are allowed to check a number of boxes if they do not want their personal information shared with other airlines, hotels, car rental companies, travel partners, financial partners, retail and entertainment services and telecommunication partners.[25]

Adding a border

Toronto–New York

At each leg of my journey from which I take departing flights with Air Canada (Victoria, Toronto, Kingston and Ottawa) my basic PNR is accessed and updated by Air Canada personnel. At each departing point, it is removed from the system within 72 hours of the completion of that leg of my travel. With this relatively simple trip within Canada, data on my flight arrangements obviously have appeared on the systems at these airports. But it is also held in Greenwood Village, Colorado and in Point-Claire, Quebec. Let us now analyse an onward flight to New York rather than to Ottawa, again with Air Canada. Let us 'add a border' to the scenario and trace my data shadow as I enter the United States and then return to Canada. Let us also say that I am attending a conference in New York, for which my hosts are paying my travel expenses and a modest honorarium.[26]

The North American Free Trade Agreement (NAFTA) allows certain 'Professionals' in 63 approved categories to enter the United States to carry out professional activities pursuant to a contract or an offer of employment, under the TN Classification. The visitor is advised that 'in addition to your proof of Canadian citizenship a letter from your prospective employer, or a signed contract may assist in your inspection by United States Immigration and Naturalization Service (USINS) officials.'[27] The letter or contract should include: job title and detailed summary of your duties; starting date and anticipated length of stay; arrangement for payment; proof that you have the necessary degree to work in the profession for which you are to be engaged; and professional-level qualifications (certified copies of your diploma/ alternative credentials). The TN Visa also serves as a work permit and can be presented to the US Social Security Administration to receive a Social Security Number. The TN classification is generally issued for one year (with a $50 fee) and is renewable as long as you can demonstrate that your employment is temporary. If I were not performing any paid work, I would not require a visa and could travel between the US and Canada with one of the following documents: a Canadian passport; a Canadian government-issued birth certificate with government-issued photo ID; a Canadian Certificate of Naturalization, Canadian Certificate of Citizenship (laminated card) or Canadian driver's licence only when travelling from the US to Canada on the return portion of a roundtrip ticket.[28]

I would go through US Customs and Immigration Service (USCIS) at Toronto's Pearson International Airport. At that point, I would submit this documentation and fill in a USCIS Form I-94 (Arrival-Departure Record) with the VISA classification, the date I arrived in the United States and the 'Admitted Until' date, the date when my authorized period of stay expires. The USCIS inspector might ask me questions about the purpose of my trip, how long I would be in the United States, and my residence while in New York. The I-94 would be surrendered when I leave the United States.

There are, in fact, four separate inspections on entry to the United States: Public Health, Immigration, Customs and Agriculture. Most people would talk to one Immigration official, and one Customs official. For Customs purposes, I am also required to fill in a Customs Declaration

Form (Form 6059B) which requires: name; birth date; number of family members travelling; US address; passport number; country of residence; countries visited on the trip prior to US arrival; airline number; primary purpose of trip; whether I am bringing in fruits, plants, food, insects, meats, animals, animal/wildlife products, disease agents, cell cultures, snails, soil from a farm, ranch, or pasture; whether I have been in close proximity to livestock; whether I am carrying more than $10,000 in currency or monetary instruments; whether I have commercial merchandise; and the total value of all articles that will remain in the US. The small print on the back of the form states ironically that the authority for collection is the 1995 Paperwork Reduction Act, that my response is mandatory and that the 'average burden associated with this collection of information is 4 minutes per respondent'.

All the information submitted through this application process on Forms I-94 and 6059B is theoretically protected by the US Privacy Act of 1974. USCIS could, however, reveal that information to an extensive list of federal, state or local agencies for law enforcement, public safety and other 'routine uses'. At this point in my travel, therefore, the list of US government agencies to which this information might potentially be revealed is extensive. Section 215 of the USA PATRIOT Act also authorizes the FBI to request an order 'requiring the production of any tangible things (including books, records, papers, documents, and other items)' relevant to an investigation of international terrorism or clandestine intelligence activities, without the traditional 'probable cause' test. This immigration data may, therefore, be disclosed, disseminated, matched or profiled within government with few restrictions. With the exception of the new USA PATRIOT Act requirements, this was also the case before September 11.

To whom in the United States, however, might the API or PNR data be revealed? Several schemes require discussion in this regard. The first is the US/Canada Smart Border Initiative signed between the two countries in December 2001. This constitutes a large package of security measures, including agreements on inter-operable biometric standards, permanent resident cards, refugee asylum claims processing, and the NEXUS programme to expedite air, land and sea crossings for pre-approved low-risk travellers. Canada and the United States have also agreed to share API and PNR data on 'high-risk' travellers destined to either country. The automated Canada-US API/PNR data-sharing program was due to be in place in Spring 2003. The two countries have also agreed on the co-location of customs and immigration officers in Joint Passenger Analysis Units to more intensively cooperate in identifying potentially high-risk travellers.[29]

Beyond these bilateral initiatives, the US has proposed three more general schemes for the collection and analysis of airline passenger data. The first, and most controversial, was the Computer Assisted Passenger Profiling System (CAPPS), the second generation of an earlier measure. The CAPPS II version was designed to receive PNR data from a new integrated database, cleanse and format the data, perform a risk assessment and then assign a risk 'score' to individual passengers entering the United States. The second-generation system was to rely on experimental data-mining algorithms to find patterns in the government and commercial databases available on individuals. In January 2003, the Transportation Security Administration (TSA) published a federal register notice announcing the creation of a new system of record called the Aviation Security Screening Records (ASSR) database. The notice described a system that would allow the government access to unlimited amounts and kinds of data from other proprietary and public sources: Passenger Name Records (PNRs) and associated data; reservation and manifest information of passenger carriers and, in the case of individuals who are deemed to pose a possible risk to transportation security, record categories may include risk-assessment reports, financial and transactional data, public source information, proprietary data, and information from law-enforcement and intelligence sources.[30] As a result of an enormous volume of criticism from Congress, civil liberties groups and other interests, Tom Ridge, the Secretary of Homeland Security, declared CAPPS II dead in July 2004, a statement that raised a series of further questions about what would happen to the millions of records already collected.

Secondly, and as a result of recommendations of the United States National Commission on Terrorist Attacks upon the United States (2004), a successor to the CAPPS system emerged in August 2004. Secure Flight is intended to be confined simply to terrorist-related activities. Under this proposal, airlines will still have to submit passenger data to the agency, which will use an expanded, unified watch list run by the Terrorist Screening Center to flag potential threats. Homeland Security officials hope law-enforcement and intelligence groups will add more data to the watch list if they are assured the information will not be provided to private companies. That matching process is currently being tested with millions of passenger records, which the Transportation Security Administration ordered airlines to turn over in November 2004. The TSA further wants to test whether the information passengers provide to airlines can be verified using massive commercial databases run by companies such as LexisNexis and Acxiom. The government has claimed that this system is very different from its CAPPS predecessor because privacy considerations have been built in from the outset. Civil liberties groups remain sceptical. They point to the fact that the watch lists currently in use have already been shown to be inaccurate, as exemplified by the high-profile example of Senator Ted Kennedy repeatedly misidentified as a suspected terrorist. It remains unclear how individuals who are improperly flagged will be protected.

A third, and related, proposal is the US-VISIT programme. The programme is a response to the Enhanced Border Security Act of 2002, wherein Congress directed the DHS to initiate controls on entry and exit points into the United States. Proposals were received in January 2004 and a contract was awarded to Accenture LLP on 28 May 2004. According to DHS:

US-VISIT is part of a continuum of security measures that begins overseas, when a person applies for a visa to travel to the United States, and continues on through entry and exit at US air and seaports and, eventually, at land border crossings. The US-VISIT program enhances the security of US citizens and visitors by verifying the identity of visitors with visas. At the same time, it facilitates legitimate travel and trade by leveraging technology and the evolving use of biometrics to expedite processing at our borders. US-VISIT is helping us demonstrate that we remain a welcoming nation and that we can keep America's doors open and our nation secure.[31]

At the end of 2004, US-VISIT entry procedures were in place at 115 airports (including the major Canadian airports) and 14 seaports. It is scheduled to be expanded to the 50 busiest land ports of entry and to all 165 land ports of entry by 31 December 2005. US-VISIT begins at the US consular offices issuing visas, where visitors' digital fingerscans and photographs are collected and checked against a database of known criminals and suspected terrorists. When the visitor arrives at the port of entry, the same biometrics are used to verify that the person at the port is the same person who received the visa. This programme does not apply to citizens of 27 countries that participate in the Visa Waiver Program, although such citizens will need to submit machine-readable passports (or a valid US Visa) as of October 2004. US-VISIT has also been subjected to considerable scrutiny from a privacy perspective. Information gathered from US-VISIT may be shared with the usual list of federal agencies plus 'appropriate federal, state, local or foreign government agencies when needed by these organizations to carry out their law enforcement responsibilities.'[32] Canadian citizens are not yet subject to these rules, even though Canada is not a party to the Visa Waiver Program. Thus, at the moment, given my Canadian citizenship, there would be nothing different about my entry into the United States under the circumstances outlined above, from what would have occurred pre-9/11. Returning to Canada, however, would be a different story.

New York–Toronto

On my return to Canada, I would, as traditionally, be required to fill in immigration landing cards, and would be required to provide the following information: name, permanent address, date and place of birth, nationality, passport number, flight number, purpose of visit and the value of all goods being brought back to Canada. On arrival, I would surrender this card to Canada Customs which, some weeks later, will be processed and entered into the Canada Customs information system. Airline personnel will not have access to the information provided on these cards, although it may be shared and matched with data from other federal agencies.[33]

The collection and retention of the personal information of airline passengers entering Canada is regulated by the *Customs Act* of 1985. Canadian law also now requires that all commercial carriers and charter carriers provide the newly created Canadian Border Services Agency (CBSA) with information about all passengers and crew destined for Canada. The legislative amendments necessary to implement this initiative were included in Bill C-11, the Immigration and Refugee Protection Act, which received Royal Assent on 1 November 2001, Section 269 of which outlines the obligations of the carriers:[34]

> On the request of an officer, a commercial transporter must provide on departure of their commercial vehicle from the last point of embarkation before arriving in Canada the following information in writing on each person carried:
>
> (a) their surname, first name and initial or initials of any middle names;
> (b) their date of birth;
> (c) the country that issued them a passport or travel document or, if they do not have a passport or travel document, their citizenship or nationality;
> (d) their gender;
> (e) their passport number or, if they do not have a passport, the number on the travel document that identifies them; and
> (f) their reservation record locator or file number.

Passenger reservation information
(2) At any time after a commercial transporter undertakes to carry a passenger to Canada, the commercial transporter must provide an officer access to its reservation system or, on the request of an officer, provide in writing all reservation information held by the commercial transporter on passengers to be carried to Canada.

These regulations require that commercial carriers, charter operators, travel agents and owners/operators of a reservation system who undertake to carry persons to Canada must, at the time of departure, provide the Minister of Citizenship and Immigration with access to specific information on all passengers and crewmembers en route to Canada. The API data is collected at check-in time, and is transmitted by the carrier or reservation system prior to the arrival of the conveyance. At present these regulations only apply to air travel. It is argued that obtaining passenger information in advance of the arrival of a commercial conveyance will provide immigration officials with additional time to assess the specific risk of individual passengers and focus their attention on the passengers who pose the highest risk before they arrive at the border.

In order to receive the API/PNR data from the databases of the concerned third parties, Canada Customs and Revenue Agency (CCRA) contracted with the Société Internationale de Transportation Aéronautique (SITA) to provide the technology to bring API/PNR to Canada. CCRA developed a new tool entitled PAXIS, which is the user-end application needed to access API/PNR data, and began collecting this information in October 2002.[35] That information is now stored in the new Advance Passenger Information/Passenger Name Record (API/PNR) database. In March 2003, the more precise PNR data from airlines' departure control systems came online, and more and more airlines are increasingly becoming compliant. To effectively carry out this initiative, Canada Customs has established combined CIC/CCRA passenger assessment units (PAUs) at the three main Canadian airports (Vancouver, Toronto and Montreal). The primary role of the PAUs is to identify those travellers who, based on the information obtained from API/PNR, should be referred for an immigration 'examination'.

The construction of this database was the subject of a very high-profile conflict between the Canadian government and the former Privacy Commissioner, George Radwanski, the result of which were certain constraints on how this information might be used. Advance Passenger Information (API) – which consists only of passport information such as name and date of birth and does not include any specific travel information – will continue to be stored for six years and can be widely shared under Section 107 of the Customs Act. The much more detailed Passenger Name Record (PNR) will immediately be purged by the CCRA of all meal and health information.

PNR data will still be held for six years, but use and access will vary by length of retention. For the first 72 hours, it will be used by customs and immigration officers to assess risk. From 72 hours to two years, the information will be depersonalized and used, without names attached, only by intelligence officers and analysts. The information can be re-identified with the traveller's name only when necessary for customs purposes. During this two-year period, information will only be shared with other agencies or departments for non-customs purposes if a warrant has been obtained, including for tax-evasion purposes. From two years to six years, the information can only be used to fulfill the CCRA's mandate regarding the security of Canada, rather than all customs purposes. It will be used on a depersonalized basis unless the Commissioner of the CCRA personally approves re-personalizing it based on reason to suspect that the name or other identifying elements are necessary to deal with a high-risk person. During this final period, information can only be shared with agencies that have a national security mandate, where there are reasonable grounds to believe that the information relates to a real or apprehended threat. Commissioner Radwanski hailed this compromise as a great victory for the privacy rights of Canadians.[36] Others were more sceptical.[37]

Conclusions

The literature on privacy, surveillance and all the attendant issues surrounding the processing of personal information is replete with images and metaphors about how each individual has a 'data shadow' (Stalder 2002) or perhaps a 'digital persona' (Clarke 1994). The new networked society (Castells 1996) produces a proliferation of remotely captured and stored personal data that may or may not correspond with an individual's actual personality or behaviour. These fragments of personal data supposedly exist in a non-transparent, mystical and complex world over which the individual has little knowledge and no control. In the theoretical literature of post-modernity, this condition supports wider arguments about the dissolution of the 'subject' and of traditional borders between individual and society, public and private, self and other, and so on (e.g. Poster 1990).

Whether in its more sophisticated and theoretical version, or its more rhetorical or polemical variant, this theme is rarely supported by detailed empirical investigation into the nature of databases and the flows of information between them. We are left with a range of often insightful conclusions about the nature of the surveillance society, none of which have been, or indeed can be, subjected to rigorous empirical scrutiny. That empiricism is necessary if analysts and advocates are to understand the fundamentally contingent or 'Janus-faced' nature of contemporary surveillance practices (Lyon 2001), and also to comprehend how their worst effects might be remedied.

Certainly the endeavour of tracing my data shadow with respect to the flights described in this paper resonates with some important themes in the contemporary literature. The collection of personal information is largely characterized by a process of automatic 'data capture' (Agre 1994), rather than visual monitoring. Unawares, I left behind a 'data trail' (Cavoukian and Tapscott 1997). Most of these transactions have taken place at a distance, reinforcing Lyon's point about 'disappearing bodies' (2001: 16–27). To the extent that 'my' data, even concerning a simple flight within Canada, have ended up in the United States, supports larger points about globalization and especially about the 'de-localized' border (Lyon 2003: 110); I did not have to cross a geographical or national border for 'my' data to do so.

If one confines the analysis for the moment to the travel *within* Canada, certain conclusions can be reached about my abilities as a data subject to access my information and to control its circulation. The following organizations have had access to the basic information about my flight plans: the local travel agency, Galileo, Air Canada and Aeroplan. The Victoria and Toronto Airport Authorities would also have access to my images captured at various stages in both airports. Each of these institutions is regulated by federal privacy protection legislation and should therefore be abiding by the standard fair information practices.[38] With the exception of the travel agent, each institution has developed a tailored code of practice for the benefit of consumers and employees. From my brief interviews with representatives from these organizations, I became convinced that the protection of the personal information of travellers was something that each took very seriously. There are of course important differences between rules and practices, and I have already noted how informal networks develop in an airport environment which can facilitate the unwarranted sharing of personal information.

Thus, for anyone with a little time and energy, it is possible to discover who has what information, when about a particular flight itinerary. These institutions rarely receive requests for personal information, but they are all obligated to provide it – even Galileo Canada, which claims that it is not. The prevailing assumption in much of the literature that surveillance is removed, invisible, non-transparent, mystical, complex and so on, is therefore overdrawn. It is difficult to trace one's 'digital persona', but it is not impossible. While it is common in the surveillance literature to critique the concept and policies of privacy protection, it is also true that those very policies oblige organizations to be far more forthcoming about what data they collect and store. Transparency of 'systems of records' is one of the unrecognized values of information privacy and data protection policy. Privacy is not *the* antidote to surveillance (Stalder 2002), but it is the only conceptual and legal framework available to achieve some organizational accountability and transparency.

Have I been the subject of surveillance or, more precisely, 'dataveillance' (Clarke 1989)? Again, the literature would suggest that any capture of personal information (however benign) constitutes a surveillance process. Surveillance, Lyon contends, is 'any collection and processing of personal data, whether identifiable or not, for the purposes of influencing or managing those whose data have been garnered.' It is simply the outcome of the 'complex ways in which we structure our political and economic relationships' (2001: 2). Marx (1988) has also argued that there is a 'new surveillance' – routine, everyday, invisible and pre-emptive. Linked to this broad definition is the power of classification and sorting. It is a powerful means of creating and reinforcing social identities and divisions (Gandy 1993; Lyon 2003).

Without dissenting from these judgements, two insights suggest themselves as a result of the case studies above. First, my personal data (so far as I know) has not been processed for any purpose beyond that of ensuring that I am a valid passenger on the days and flights reserved. It has not been analysed, subjected to any investigation, manipulated or used to make any judgement about me. No doubt, a certain amount of data mining of de-identified information occurs within the industry to analyse general travel patterns and demands. No doubt, had I not opted out under the Aeroplan privacy policy, my data might have ended up with a variety of Aeroplan's partners, and I might have received related, and unrelated, promotional materials.

It seems, however, that there is a fundamental difference between the routine capture, collection and storage of this kind of personal information, and any subsequent analysis of that information from which decisions (benign or otherwise) might be made about me. The new process for API/PNR analysis serves to highlight the distinction. As a passenger, when I return to Canada, that information is automatically transferred ahead of my arrival to the CCRA's Passenger Assessment Unit at the Canadian airport, and it is systematically analysed. Anybody within a 'high-risk' category is then subject to further investigation. The crucial process, therefore, is not the capture and transmission of the information, but the prior procedures, and the assumptions that underpin them, about who is or is not a high-risk traveller. Surveillance might be 'any collection and processing of personal data, whether identifiable or not.' If we are to use such a broad definition, however, we need to find another concept to describe the active intervention of human agents who then monitor that data to make decisions about individuals. 'Surveillance' conflates a number of distinct processes. To describe what has happened to me as surveillance perhaps serves to trivialize the real surveillance to which some individuals, perhaps with 'risky' surnames and meal preferences, can be subjected during air travel.

Surveillance is, therefore, highly contingent. If social scientists are to get beyond totalizing metaphors and broad abstractions, it is absolutely necessary to understand these contingencies. Social and individual risk is governed by a complicated set of organizational, cultural, technological, political and legal factors. The crucial questions are therefore distributional ones: Why do some people get more 'surveillance' than others (Bennett and Raab 1997, 2003)? But to address those questions, it is crucial to conduct the kind of finely tuned empirical studies such as the one attempted above.

These case studies have revealed something about the information flows when a fairly typical traveller books an airline ticket. In this context, the nature and extent of the surveillance, and thus of individual risk, is highly dependent on methods of booking, on local practices, on legal rules, on networks and interfaces, and on the behaviours and preferences of the individual. Students of surveillance have a responsibility to study these processes in far greater detail. We must try to trace the information flows, and thus interrogate Castells' major hypothesis about the 'space of flows' within the network society, in which 'dominant functions are organised in networks pertaining to a space of flows that links them up around the world, while fragmenting subordinate functions, and people in the multiple space of places, made of locales increasingly segregated from one another' (Castells 1996: 476). 'What happens when you book an airline ticket' is a complex question, but it is not unfathomable. My tentative answers certainly reveal a dominant network, represented by Galileo and other global distribution systems, as well as a number of segregated locales, at which localized data capture, but hardly pernicious surveillance, has occurred.

Notes

1 Available at: http://web.uvic.ca/polisci/bennett/index.htm#online

2 My thanks to Dean Murdock for the diligent and careful research assistance upon which this paper is based.

3 The travel industry is served by four main 'reservation system' service providers – 'Global Distribution Systems'. Two companies have emerged as giants of the industry. Sabre, the larger of the two companies and pioneer of the service, and Galileo offer computerized reservation systems to airlines, travel agencies, rental companies and hotel chains. The others are Worldspan and Amadeus.

4 http://www.thomascook.ca/About/PrivacySecurityOnline.aspx
My customer profile includes the following: name, designation, contact information, preferred language, nationality, date of birth, membership numbers (for frequent flyer points), credit card numbers, passport number, e-mail address, my flying preferences (seat, meals, etc.) and my beneficiary (for insurance purposes).

5 Source: http://www.acta.ca

6 Typical pressures arise when a travel agent is asked whether a third party is on a particular flight; when client profiles are transferred from one agency to another; and when client data have to be communicated in cases of emergency.

7 Source: http://www.galileo.com

8 Nothing in the Air Canada conditions of carriage statements (that appear on the reverse of paper tickets) mentions the collection and disclosure of personal information. Air Canada's privacy policy is available at: http://www.aircanada.com/en/about/legal/privacy/policy.html

9 See the critique of the security of these web portals by Edward Hasbrouck, 'Who's Watching you While you Travel?' Available at: http://www.hasbrouck.org/articles/watching.html

10 There are no indications on the Galileo system that a passenger can access his or her PNR from Galileo. Indeed, the Galileo Canada website expressly indicates that 'as a processor of data, Galileo Canada does not conduct business directly with individual travelers. Upon request, individual travelers may have access to their own data held by the Galileo system by contacting the travel agent involved in the booking' (Source: http://www.galileocanada.ca/privacy/2/). I asked the travel agency for my PNR and was told that it was not their practice to disclose this information as they were only accessing the remote network. Although I did not press the issue, the travel agency would legally be responsible for providing access.

11 Hasbrouck (2004) suggests the following: 'prefers king bed', 'prefers room on low floor in hotels', 'always requests halal meal', 'won't fly on the Jewish sabbath', 'uses wheelchair, can't control bowels and bladder', 'prefers not to fly Delta Airlines'. Travel agents might add information like 'difficult customer – always changing his mind'.

12 Air Canada provides the following meal choices: Asian vegetarian, bland/ulcer, child, diabetic, fruit platter, gluten-free, Hindu non-vegetarian, kosher, low calorie, low cholesterol, low salt, Muslim vegetarian, non-lactose, oriental, regular, vegetarian (lacto-ovo), and vegetarian. It provides the

following Special Needs options: assistance climbing steps, assistance when on plane, blind, hearing impaired, wheelchair in terminal.

13 Galileo Canada Privacy Policy available at http://www.galileocanada.ca (my emphasis).

14 There is just a policy that applies to the collection of information through the website itself.

15 Telephone conversation with Thomas de May, Chief Privacy Officer, Galileo, 5 August 2004.

16 See: European Parliament, Directorate General for Research, *Working Paper on The Rights of Airline Passengers* (1999). Available at: http://www.europarl. eu.int/workingpapers/tran/105/default_en.htm

17 FAL/12-WP/74, 153/04, 'Airline Reservation System and Passenger Name Record Access by States'. ICAO Facilitation Division – Twelfth Session, Cairo, Egypt, 22 March to 2 April 2004. Available at: http://www.icao.int/ icao/en/atb/fal/fal12/documentation/fal12wp074_en.pdf

18 PNR Data Elements Required from Air Carriers and Global Distribution Systems (GDS) Federal Register / Vol. 69, No. 131/Friday, July 9, 2004. 1) The PNR record locator code. 2) Date of reservation. 3) Date(s) of intended travel. 4) Name. 5) Other names on PNR. 6) Address. 7) All forms of payment information. 8) Billing address. 9) Contact telephone numbers. 10) All travel itinerary for specific PNR. 11) Frequent flyer information. 12) Travel agency. 13) Travel agent. 14) Code share PNR information. 15) Travel status of passenger. 16) Split/Divided PNR information. 17) E-mail address. 18) Ticketing field information. 19) General remarks. 20) Ticket number. 21) Seat number. 22) Date of ticket issuance. 23) No show history. 24) Bag tag numbers. 25) Go show information. 26) OSI information. 27) SSI/SSR information. 28) Received from information. 29) All historical changes to the PNR. 30) Number of travelers on PNR. 31) Seat information. 32) One-way tickets. 33) Any collected APIS information. 34) ATFQ fields.

19 Telephone interview with Gail Paul, Air Canada manager, Victoria International Airport.

20 I am indebted on this point to a paper written by a former student, who had worked as a customs agent at Vancouver International Airport. Khushwant Dhillon, 'Profiling by Canada Customs at Vancouver International Airport'. (Admn 548, April 2002).

21 Source: http://www.aeroguard.ca/index.html

22 Interview with Bruce MacRae, Victoria International Airport Authority, 3 August 2004.

23 News Release on 20 March 2002, from the Office of the Privacy Commissioner of Canada. Available at: http://www.privcom.gc.ca/media/nr-c/02_05_b_ 020320_e.asp

24 Aeroplan 'Privacy Policy'. Source: https://www.aeroplan.com/en/about/ privacy.jsp The new policy reads:

   1. We will only collect the personal information necessary to administer the Aeroplan Loyalty Program and to offer our members rewards, benefits, products, goods and services under the Program.

2. We do not collect, use or disclose personal information about a member without the consent of the member, except where required by law.
3. From time to time we may transfer personal information to our agents for processing in order to determine which members may be most interested in rewards, benefits, products, goods and services offered by Aeroplan or its Partners. We use contractual and other means to protect your information while it is being processed by our agents.
4. To increase opportunities for members to accumulate miles under the Program, to facilitate the redemption of miles under the Program, or to obtain special benefits for members, Aeroplan® may temporarily share personal information with a Partner. Use by the Partner for any purpose other than the Aeroplan Loyalty Program is strictly prohibited.
5. We will provide our members with a detailed explanation, when they enroll and periodically thereafter, of how they can have their name deleted from the lists we share with our Partners. Our members may contact us at any time at the address below to have their names deleted from the lists.
6. We maintain the security and confidentiality of the information furnished by our members according to the strictest standards. Compliance with these standards is constantly verified and revised as needed.
7. In the administration of the Aeroplan Loyalty Program, if we communicate information to our Partners, agents, or representatives, we assume the responsibility arising from these communications and take actions to ensure that the commitments and rules set forth in this Policy are observed by our Partners, agents, or representatives.
8. We require every organization that provides us with administrative or information processing support services to comply with this Policy and with the privacy protection rules it contains.
9. Our members are entitled to examine the information we hold regarding them, subject to the restrictions provided by law, and may request rectification of inaccurate or incomplete information. If applicable, we will disclose this information to the person concerned or rectify it promptly.

25 Source: https://www.aeroplan.com/en/about/removal.pdf Aeroplan 'Opt-Out request form'. I have 'opted-out'.
26 Many of the relevant rules have been derived from the website: http://www.foreignborn.com
27 Source: http://www.dfait-maeci.gc.ca/nafta-alena/temp_entry-en.asp
28 Canadian permanent residents and landed immigrants now require government-issued photo ID (The Maple Leaf card) when travelling to the United States.
29 Department of Foreign Affairs and International Trade, Smart Border Action Plan Status Report. Available at: http://www.dfait-maeci.gc.ca/can-am/menu-en.asp?act=v&mid=1&cat=1&did=2465
30 Federal Register: 15 January, 2003 (Volume 68, Number 10)][Notices] [Page

2101-2103] at: http://a257.g.akamaitech.net/7/257/2422/14mar20010800/edocket.access.gpo.gov/2003/03-827.htm

31 Source: http://www.dhs.gov/dhspublic/interapp/content_multi_image/content_multi_image_0006.xml

32 Source: http://www.dhs.gov/interweb/assetlibrary/USVISITPrivacyPolicy.pdf

33 In 1999, the Federal Privacy Commissioner challenged the constitutionality under the search and seizure provisions of the Canadian Charter of Rights and Freedoms of a data matching arrangement between Canada Customs and Human Resources Development Canada (HRDC) for the comparison of these customs data with unemployment insurance records. At issue is HRDC's practice of collecting data from the Customs declarations of every returning traveller to identify employment insurance claimants (supposedly available for work) who were out of the country while receiving benefits.

34 The Public Safety Act also regulates access to API/PNR data. See: http://www.tc.gc.ca/mediaroom/releases/nat/2002/02_gc004e.htm

35 Customs Act, Section 107 (1) reads: 'The Minister may, under prescribed circumstances and conditions, require any prescribed person or prescribed class of persons to provide, or provide access to, prescribed information about any person on board a conveyance in advance of the arrival of the conveyance in Canada or within a reasonable time after that arrival.'

36 Source: http://www.privcom.gc.ca/media/nr-c/2003/02_05_b_030408_e.asp

37 See, for example, the analysis of the Canadian Civil Liberties Association at: http://www.ccla.org/privacy/api-pnr.shtml

38 Ironically, the only institution that bears no legal responsibility for data protection is Queen's University; Ontario universities still are not regulated under Ontario's Freedom of Information and Protection of Privacy Act.

References

Agre, P. (1994) 'Surveillance and Capture: two models of privacy', *The Information Society*, 10, pp. 101–27.

Bennett, C. (1999) 'What Happens When you Buy an Airline Ticket? Surveillance, globalization and the regulation of international communications networks', paper presented to annual meeting of Canadian Political Science Association, Sherbrooke, Quebec, at: http://web.uvic.ca/~polisci/bennett/index.htm#online

Bennett, C. and Raab, C. (1997) 'The Distribution of Privacy Risks: who needs protection?', *The Information Society*, 14, pp. 263–74.

Bennett, C. and Raab, C. (2003) *The Governance of Privacy: Policy Instruments in Global Perspective* (Aldershot, UK: Ashgate Press).

Castells, M. (1996) *The Rise of the Network Society Vol. 1* (Oxford: Blackwells Press).

Cavoukian, A. and Tapscott, D. (1997) *Who Knows? Safeguarding your Privacy in a Networked World* (New York: McGraw-Hill).

Clarke, R. (1989) 'Information Technology and Dataveillance', *Communications of the ACM*, 31, pp. 498–512.

Clarke, R. (1994) 'The Digital Persona and its Application to Data Surveillance', *The Information Society*, 10 (2); also at: http://www.anu.edu.au/people/Roger. Clarke/DV/DigPersona.html

European Union (1995) *Directive 95/46/EC of the European Parliament and of the Council on the Protection of Individuals with regard to the Processing of Personal Data and on the Free Movement of Such Data* (Brussels: OJ No. L281, 24 October 1995).

Gandy, O. (1993) *The Panoptic Sort* (Boulder: Westview Press).

Hasbrouck, E. (2004) 'Travel Privacy', in *Privacy and Human Rights Yearbook 2004* (Washington, DC: Electronic Privacy Information Center).

Lyon, D. (2001) *Surveillance Society: Monitoring Everyday Life* (Buckingham: Open University Press).

Lyon, D. (ed.) (2003) *Surveillance as Social Sorting: Privacy Risk and Digital Discrimination* (London: Routledge).

Marx, G. (1988) *Undercover: Police Surveillance in America* (Berkeley: University of California Press).

Poster, M. (1990) *The Mode of Information* (New York: Polity Press).

Raab, C., Bennett, C., Gellman, R. and Waters, N. (1998) *Application of a Methodology Designed to Assess the Adequacy of the Level of Protection of Individuals with Regard to Processing Personal Data: Test of the Method on Several Categories of Transfer* (Luxembourg: Office for Official Publications of the European Commission, at: http://europa.eu.int/comm/internal_market/en/media/dataprot/studies/adequat.htm).

Stalder, F. (2002) 'Privacy is not the Antidote to Surveillance', *Surveillance and Society*, 1:1, at: http://www.surveillance-and-society.org/journalv1i1.htm

United States National Commission on Terrorist Attacks upon the United States (2004) *The 9/11 Commission Report* (New York: Norton).

Chapter 9

Potential threats and potential criminals: data collection in the national security entry-exit registration system[1]

Jonathan Finn

On 5 June 2002 United States Attorney General John Ashcroft announced the National Security Entry-Exit Registration System (NSEERS). The initiative captures and archives biographic data and images of the faces and fingerprints of select foreign nationals visiting or residing in the United States on temporary visas. Because all of the 19 individuals involved in the 11 September 2001 hijackings entered the United States on valid temporary visas, NSEERS was promoted as a program to prevent future terrorist attacks and enhance border security through rigorous documenting and monitoring of visitors to the United States.

The registration system is based in a 1996 Congressional mandate, entitled the Illegal Immigration and Immigrant Responsibility Act, that the United States develop a comprehensive entry-exit registration system to record nearly all of the country's 35,000,000 annual visitors. On 5 January 2004 the United States Visitor and Immigrant Status Indicator Technology program (US-VISIT) was implemented to fulfill this mandate and to succeed NSEERS. Both programs collect detailed biographic information along with fingerprint scans and full-face, frontal photographs (hereafter referred to as photographs) from persons entering the United States. In over a year of operation, NSEERS had compiled data on 177,260 individuals (USDHS 2003). By comparison, in just three months of operation, US-VISIT had processed 3,002,872 individuals (USDHS 2004).

The tremendous difference in the data collected within these registration systems points to a primary feature of NSEERS and forms the basis of this paper. Both programs are based in the 1996 Congressional mandate for an entry-exit registration system. Both utilize similar technology and collect similar data. However, where US-VISIT records nearly all foreign nationals entering the United States, registration in NSEERS was selectively applied almost exclusively to Arab and Muslim men. This overtly discriminatory practice was justified under the rubric of a 'war on terrorism' and as a necessary response to a national security threat described as invisible and omnipresent.

This paper examines the collection of personal identification data in the National Security Entry-Exit Registration System. The development and implementation of NSEERS is examined to foreground discussion of data collection and its impact on persons subject to registration. I argue that the construction and implementation of NSEERS was not a necessary response to the events of 11 September 2001 but that it was reactionary and retaliatory. Data collection in NSEERS functioned less to enhance border security, than to code, categorize and display certain bodies as potentially threatening and as warranting continued surveillance. This in turn had immediate and far-reaching effects on the identities, rights and freedoms of individuals subject to registration.

Background and implementation

The original proposal for the National Security Entry-Exit Registration System was published in the 13 June 2002 Federal Register (67 FR 40581).[2] The proposal was drafted by Larry D. Thompson, then acting Attorney General, and called for written responses and commentary to be received by 15 July. The document, 'Registration and Monitoring of Certain Non-immigrants,' amended Parts 214 (Non-immigrant Classes) and 264 (Registration and Fingerprinting of Aliens in the United States) of the Code of Federal Regulations, the codification of rules published in the Federal Register.

Although NSEERS announced new and far-reaching powers to the presiding government agencies and officials, the program was based in earlier efforts to formally document visitors to the country. The authority to register individuals in the United States dates to a 1952 section of the Immigration and Nationality Act (Kobach 2003). The formal application of this provision reached a peak during the 1990s, during which the authority to register non-immigrants was sporadically exercised. In 1991 a final rule published in the Federal Register called for the registration and fingerprinting of non-immigrants from Iraq and Kuwait entering the United States (56 FR 1566). This was in response to Iraq's then recent invasion of Kuwait, and the United States' subsequent involvement in that conflict. Two years later, the Attorney General published a notice in the Federal Register calling for the fingerprinting and registration of non-immigrants from Iraq and Sudan (58 FR 68157). On 5 September 1996 a Federal Register notice called for the fingerprinting and registration of non-immigrants from Iran and Libya (61 FR 46829). Finally, on 21 July 1998 Attorney General Janet Reno published a document to consolidate and amend all previous registration requirements. Attorney General Reno's notice called for the registration, fingerprinting and photographing of non-immigrant aliens from Iran, Libya, Iraq and Sudan (63 FR 39109).

Although Attorney General Reno's 1998 notice established the basis for a registration system, the registration requirements were routinely waived for the vast majority of non-immigrants entering the country. Prior to the implementation of NSEERS, the majority of persons entering the United States were only required to complete an I-94 form, detailing their plans while in the United States and providing contact information. Thus, one goal of NSEERS was to enforce the 'general registration' requirements (the collection of biographic information, fingerprints and photographs) outlined under Attorney General Reno's 1998 notice. However, in addition to the enforcement of 'general registration', NSEERS also announced distinctly new capabilities for law-enforcement and border security programs and personnel. New 'special registration' requirements were developed for a new class of non-immigrants, loosely defined as 'certain non-immigrant aliens', that were believed to require closer scrutiny.

The 2002 proposal included a vague justification for the 'special registration' of these individuals, which simply stated: 'the United States frequently acquires information that indicates that a specific alien's or class of aliens' activities within the United States should be more closely monitored' (67 FR 40582). In addition to the general registration requirements, those subject to 'special registration' would have to provide more detailed biographic information and would be required to report to INS offices upon arrival to the United States, again 30 days after arrival and annually for re-registration. Further, those subjected to special registration had to report any change of address, school or employment within ten days of the change and had to report to an INS office at their time of departure from the United States.

In conjunction with the new special registration requirements, the NSEERS proposal also enabled the Attorney General to call on 'certain non-immigrant aliens' residing in the United States to report to INS for registration. This is a particularly problematic feature of NSEERS and one that clearly distinguishes it from other registration programs. Where past registration procedures documented only persons entering the country, NSEERS allowed for the collection of identification data retroactively from persons already residing in the country. Thus, the collection of personal identification data in the National Security Entry-Exit Registration System functioned in two ways: at ports of entry (POE registration) and through 'call-in' registration. In the former, individuals entering the country through any of the 317 air, land or sea ports of entry are registered directly on-site. In the latter, individuals residing in the United States can be called to register at a specified office or location through a notice published in the Federal Register.

Significant penalties resulted for failing to comply with any of the registration requirements. As outlined in the proposed rule, 'because failure to complete registration is an unlawful activity, the alien shall thereafter be presumed to be inadmissible to the United States' (67 FR 40584). In addition, failure to register or making a false statement during registration carries a maximum $1000 fine or six months in prison; failure to provide change of address or other information carries a maximum $200 fine or imprisonment for 30 days; and failure to comply with any of the registration procedures renders the alien 'removable' from the country and 'inadmissible' in the future.

The NSEERS proposal was published as final rule in the 12 August 2002 Federal Register (67 FR 52584). Fourteen comments on the proposal were received within the month-long period allowed for by the Attorney General. Concerns ranged from the legal basis for such a program and the potential for discrimination and violation of due process rights to the tremendous power afforded to the Attorney General. Despite these concerns, the 12 August publication notes 'this final rule adopts the proposed rule without substantial change' (67 FR 52584). In fact, the single set of changes made to the document was clearer indication that the registration system would be paperless, that the data would be collected electronically. In an overtly symbolic move, the new registration system would take effect at select ports of entry a year to the day after the terrorist attacks, on 11 September 2002. The system was operable at all ports of entry on 1 October 2002.

The general registration requirements of Attorney General Reno's 1998 publication to document individuals entering the country from Iran, Iraq, Libya and Sudan were met through the initial implementation of NSEERS. However, shortly after publication of the final rule in August of 2002, Attorney General Ashcroft greatly expanded the list of nations whose residents would be subject to special registration. This is most clearly exemplified in the four published notices for call-in registration. All four calls focused on men, 16 years of age or older, who were admitted to the United States on or before 30 September 2002, the date port of entry registration began. The first call, on 6 November 2002, required citizens and nationals of Iran, Iraq, Libya, Sudan and Syria to report for registration (67 FR 67766). The second call, on 22 November 2002, was directed at citizens and nationals of Afghanistan, Algeria, Bahrain, Eritrea, Lebanon, Morocco, North Korea, Oman, Qatar, Somalia, Tunisia, United Arab Emirates and Yemen (67 FR 70526). The third call, on 16 December 2002, targeted citizens and nationals of Pakistan and Saudi Arabia.[3] The fourth and final call for registration was published on 16 January 2003 and added nationals and citizens of Bangladesh, Egypt, Indonesia, Jordan and Kuwait to the list.

By the end of the call-in registration period, 25 countries had been

Table 9.1 The four 'call-in' registration periods in NSEERS

Date of Call	Countries Listed
6 November 2002	Iran
	Iraq
	Libya
	Sudan
	Syria
22 November 2002	Afghanistan
	Algeria
	Bahrain
	Eritrea
	Lebanon
	Morocco
	North Korea
	Oman
	Qatar
	Somalia
	Tunisia
	United Arab Emirates
	Yemen
16 December 2002	Pakistan
	Saudi Arabia
16 January 2003	Bangladesh
	Egypt
	Indonesia
	Jordan
	Kuwait

identified as warranting special registration and close monitoring. The presentation of these call-in periods in Table 1 emphasizes the extent to which the registration system focused extensively on Arab and Muslim men, foreign nationals of North Korea being the primary exception. Together with POE registration, these call-in registrations produced significant amounts of personal identification data. By 30 September 2003 NSEERS had processed 177,260 individuals. Of these 93,741 individuals were registered at ports of entry and 83,519 were registered through the call-in notices (USDHS 2003).

Both the proposal and eventual application of NSEERS drew significant protest from professional and lay audiences. Comments on the 13 June proposal identified concerns and fears that were later taken up in protests throughout the country by concerned residents and by civil and human rights groups, including the American Civil Liberties Union, Amnesty International and the American-Arab Anti-Discrimination Committee (Buchanan 2003; Garvey, Groves and Weinstein 2002; McGann 2003; Redd 2003). The central area of concern was the selective application of NSEERS and the seemingly unlimited authority of the Attorney General to call on bodies for registration.

The amendment to Part 264 (Registration and Fingerprinting of Aliens in the United States) of the Code of Federal Regulations detailed the three ways in which individuals could be subject to special registration:

1. Non-immigrant aliens who are nationals or citizens of a country designated by the Attorney General, in consultation with the Secretary of State, by a notice in the Federal Register.

2. Non-immigrant aliens who [sic] a consular officer or an inspecting officer has reason to believe are nationals or citizens of a country designated by the Attorney General ...

3. Non-immigrant aliens who meet pre-existing criteria, or who [sic] a consular officer or the inspecting officer has reason to believe meet pre-existing criteria, determined by the Attorney General or the Secretary of State to indicate that such an aliens' presence in the United States warrants monitoring in the national security interests. (67 FR 52592)

As outlined above, the task of deciding which individuals or groups should be subject to special registration was the responsibility of the offices of the Attorney General and Secretary of State. Vague terminology such as 'certain non-immigrant aliens', 'pre-existing criteria' and 'intelligence-based criteria' provided the legal basis for the selective application of NSEERS registration. Not only can the Attorney General require members of entire nations to register simply by citing the country in the Federal Register, but consular officers and inspecting officers throughout the world can impose similar requirements on individuals and groups based on their 'belief' that the persons in question warrant registration.

In response to concerns surrounding the seemingly arbitrary criteria for data collection, the final rule of NSEERS included the following statement, which is equally vague if not dismissive: 'The criteria by which an alien may be required to make a special registration cannot be made public without defeating the national security and law-enforcement effectiveness of the criteria' (67 FR 52588). The selective and discriminatory application of NSEERS at the discretion of the Attorney General was shielded by a rhetoric of national security. In her analysis of NSEERS, Kathryn Lohmeyer (2003), J.D. Candidate at the Whittier Law School, argues that by exploiting this rhetoric, Attorney General Ashcroft was able to supercede the constitutional rights of registrants to due process and equal protection. She further argues that NSEERS employed the 'plenary power' doctrine, a provision of the US Constitution that gives Congress complete control over immigration policy and allows for differential treatment of citizens and non-citizens. This effectively precluded any judicial or federal review of the program. Lohmeyer rightly concludes that the selective application of special registration was not just discriminatory but that it was antithetical to international laws governing the fair and equal treatment of individuals.

The Homeland Security Act of 2002 officially abolished many of the federal agencies involved in NSEERS, amalgamating them with numerous other agencies under the Department of Homeland Security. Similarly, the efforts of Attorney General John Ashcroft to oversee NSEERS were transferred to Secretary of Homeland Security, Tom Ridge. This transformation of power and the conglomeration of previously disparate federal departments and offices under the unified Department of Homeland Security was paralleled by the announcement of a new registration system, the United States Visitor and Immigrant Status Indicator Technology program (US-VISIT).

US-VISIT accomplishes the same goals as NSEERS but is considerably larger in scope, ultimately collecting fingerprints, photographs or other biometric data from all aliens entering and leaving the country. The program was officially launched on 5 January 2004 and it is scheduled to be in full operation at all ports of entry by 31 December 2005. At full implementation, the program will compile data on each of the 35,000,000 individuals who visit the United States annually. The scope of US-

VISIT – politically, economically and culturally – and the compilation of an increasingly inclusive identification database demand serious and continued critical attention. Nonetheless, it is sufficient here to note that US-VISIT developed as a complete entry-exit registration system to succeed NSEERS and fulfill the 1996 Congressional mandate.[4]

The efficacy of NSEERS to enhance border security and prevent future terrorist attacks is difficult, if not impossible, to discern. The Department of Justice, Immigration and Naturalization Service, and now the Department of Homeland Security, cite statistics of detentions, arrests and deportations through NSEERS as proof of the program's success. Of the 177,260 persons registered through 30 September 2003, 2,870 were detained and 143 identified as criminals (USDHS 2003). The majority of offences were violations of various immigration laws, such as overstaying a visa or presenting fraudulent documents. To suggest that detaining or charging a person with a criminal act for these offences aided in the prevention of a terrorist attack is speculative at best. What then is the purpose of special registration?

In his extensive work on fingerprint identification, Simon Cole (1998, 2001) shows that the technique's adoption into United States law-enforcement practices during the early twentieth century worked in concert with broadening criminal laws to bring more bodies under police surveillance. In a similar manner, the tremendous discretionary power of the Attorney General under NSEERS increased the number of individuals monitored by law-enforcement and immigration departments. Yet, despite the heightened capabilities of digital technologies to collect and archive masses of data (recall that US-VISIT processed over three million individuals in three months), the Attorney General focused on the registration of Arab and Muslim men. This selective application of an entry-exit system suggests another function or purpose of NSEERS. The program was less a necessary or rational response to the events of 11 September 2001 than it was reactionary and retaliatory. Criteria for data collection were derived from 19 individual bodies and expanded to encompass millions of bodies and entire geographic areas. That is, because the 19 individuals involved in the hijackings were adult males from specific Arab and Muslim countries, then all adult males from all Arab and Muslim nations were categorically suspicious and therefore warranted increased scrutiny and monitoring.

The development of US-VISIT with its more comprehensive and democratic collection of data is, in theory, a more realistic attempt to address border security concerns. This is not to suggest that US-VISIT is benign, but to highlight the extent to which NSEERS specifically targeted certain bodies. Under the guise of national security, NSEERS was sped into application despite varied concerns and criticism. The program was proposed on 30 June 2002, adopted as rule on 12 August and in operation by 11 September. NSEERS yielded blanket authority to the Attorney General, which was subsequently exercised on certain bodies. True to David Lyon's description of surveillance in the wake of September 11: 'hastily formulated legislation came first', the technology and application followed (2003a: 20).

While the efficacy of NSEERS to protect national security is uncertain, its impact on the identities, rights and freedoms of those subject to registration is clear. In what follows I want to address some of the primary impacts of data collection in the registration system. For purposes of clarity, the discussion is divided into two broad, but inter-related categories: direct impact and public impact. The former focuses on the immediate and future consequences of special registration on persons subject to that process. The latter examines the impact of processes of data collection as they took place within the public arena.

Direct impact of data collection

The tremendous capabilities of digital technologies to collect, store, process and exchange data lay at the foundation of contemporary law-enforcement and surveillance practices. The seemingly anonymous and ubiquitous gaze of CCTV cameras serves as the premier example of a disembodied surveillance apparatus that transcends traditional spatial and temporal constraints. NSEERS relies on these enhanced capabilities for the rapid collection, exchange and use of biographic data, fingerprints and photographs of 'certain non-immigrant aliens'. Importantly, data collection in NSEERS also functions at a much more rudimentary level: that of the body. The collection of identification data directly from individual bodies, and the future uses of that data, present both immediate and far-reaching consequences for bodily identity, with the rights and limitations it affords.

Special registration places severe limitations on the mobility of individuals subject to the process. Under the initial rule, individuals subject to special registration were forced to report in person to an INS office at arrival, 30 days after arrival, and again on an annual basis. On 2 December 2003 a notice in the Federal Register suspended both the 30-day and annual re-registration requirements (68 FR 67578). The notice also marked the official transition in power from the Department of Justice and Immigration and Naturalization Services to the new Department of Homeland Security (DHS) and the parallel transfer in authority over the registration system from Attorney General John Ashcroft to Secretary of Homeland Security Tom Ridge. In the notice, Secretary Ridge suggests that the suspension of re-registration requirements will ultimately benefit those subject to registration by placing fewer restrictions on them and by reducing an estimated 103,000 hours of work (45 minutes per interview and 30 minutes preparation by each alien multiplied by the 82,532 aliens that would be subject to re-registration over a six-month period). However, in practice the new procedures accomplish the same goals and, I argue, place stronger limitations on the mobility of those subject to special registration. The new procedure is outlined in the notice:

> At the time of admission, DHS will advise all non-immigrant aliens subject to special registration that they *may* be required to appear for additional registration interviews upon notice. DHS will separately notify those aliens selected to appear before DHS. (emphasis added)

The procedure for notification is then outlined:

> Notification under these regulations may be given to the alien in a manner reasonably calculated to reach the alien, which shall include, but is not limited to, notice by publication in the Federal Register, a letter sent via standard US postal mail to the last address provided by the alien to DHS using regular mail, an e-mail to the address provided to DHS during a previous NSEERS registration interview, or in-person delivery. (68 FR 67580)

Under the new procedure, aliens have ten days to contact DHS from the date of publication or of post. Failure to contact DHS in a timely manner constitutes a violation of the registration requirements and is grounds for deportation and future inadmissibility. The new procedure may free the individual from the requirements of re-registration but simply replaces them with others. The new requirements assume that the individual will remain tied to a specific address and places undue burden on the individual to monitor the Federal Register as they *may* be called on for further information. An individual's capabilities to be mobile, which may well be a condition of employment or required for health or reasons of emergency, are greatly hindered by this process.

In addition to restricting the mobility of individuals, NSEERS also places registrants under increased surveillance. Law-enforcement and immigration databases house the 'data-images' (Laudon 1986) or 'data-doubles' (Lyon 2003b) of individuals subject to NSEERS registration. An individual's ability to work and live as a member of society are greatly influenced through the deployment of such data (Lyon 1988, 1994). Once collected, personal identification data can be accessed, interpreted and re-interpreted based on mutable conceptions of what constitutes criminality, deviance or threat. The individual's identity as a threat to national security, a criminal, deviant or normal body can change depending on the deployment of data.

To exemplify, the 'data-image' of a Pakistani man working in the United States during the year 2000 might attest to his purchasing habits, travel and employment history, his temporary and permanent addresses, and other biographic information. During the year 2000 this man exists as a non-resident alien; as an individual working in the United States on a valid temporary visa. The third notice of call-in registration, on 16 December 2002, requires this man to report to a local INS office for special registration. This process adds more detailed information as well as fingerprint scans and a photograph to his 'data-image'. Most importantly, the man's identity as a valid non-resident alien working in the United States on a temporary visa is reconfigured into someone who constitutes a potential threat to national security and warrants closer scrutiny and continued monitoring. Nothing about this living body has changed, yet his rights and freedoms and his ability to work and function in the United States are now contested and restricted.

The impact on individual identity through NSEERS registration is also affected by the cooperation of NSEERS with other law-enforcement databases. Fingerprint scans taken during the registration process are checked against databases of known criminals and terrorists as well as a large archive of latent prints collected from 'known' terrorist locations throughout the Middle East by United States military. Utilization of this latent archive is cause for particular concern, as what constitutes a known terrorist location is unclear but seems to be equated with race. Fingerprint and other data collected through NSEERS is also linked to the archives of the National Crime Information Center (NCIC), an immense law-enforcement information archive containing 17 cross-referenceable databases and uniting 80,000 criminal justice agencies throughout the United States, the US Virgin Islands, Puerto Rico and Canada (FBI 1999). Suppose the Pakistani man from the previous example is questioned in relation to a local, minor offence in which he was simply present. Prior to his registration in NSEERS, a search through NCIC databases may not be cause for concern if the retrieved data simply attests to employment history and other biographic information. However, after registration a search would identify the man as an NSEERS registrant. The man's cooperation with the call-in notice places him within a category of suspicion, which follows him and can have numerous and varied impacts on his identity.

Public impact of data collection

On 24 March 2003, five days after the United States launched its primary military campaign against Iraq, I was travelling in the United States and was at a stop-over in the Atlanta airport. The numerous televisions in the terminal were tuned to CNN, which ran a continuous stream of war coverage that was eagerly monitored by crowds surrounding the televisions. Amid this activity a message was repeatedly broadcast over the PA system announcing that the Homeland Security threat level was currently at orange and that passengers should report any suspicious activity to law-enforcement.

The activity and announcement in the Atlanta airport point to the very public nature of the 'war on terrorism'. Within this war the public is co-opted in surveillance practices and in the maintenance of national security. The Department of Homeland Security's colour-coded 'Citizen Guidance on the Homeland Security Advisory System' asks that citizens be alert for and report suspicious activity to authorities. Similarly, the message in Atlanta asked that we, the patrons of the airport, report any suspicious activities to law-enforcement.

The move to co-opt the public in the protection of national security and in the war on terrorism is based around a rhetoric that describes an enemy that is invisible and omnipresent. Consider the following remarks prepared for Attorney General Ashcroft's public announcement of NSEERS:

> On September 11, the American definition of national security was changed forever. A band of men entered our country under false pretenses in order to plan and execute a murderous act of war ...
> In this new war, our enemy's platoons infiltrate our borders, quietly blending in with visiting tourists, students, and workers. They move unnoticed through our cities, neighborhoods, and public spaces. They wear no uniforms. Their camouflage is not forest green, but rather it is the color of common street clothing. Their tactics rely on evading recognition at the border and escaping detection within the United States. Their terrorist mission is to defeat America, destroy our values and kill innocent people. (USDOJ 2002)

The passage above describes an enemy that is seemingly undetectable.

He wears the same clothes as we do and walks unnoticed among us. How then are we to locate or make this enemy visible in order to protect national security? To return to the Atlanta airport example, what might count as suspicious and warrant reporting?

Throughout the tremendous media activity leading up to the war with Iraq the suspicious and potentially dangerous body had been coded in a specifically visual way. Race, represented by skin colour, became a central means of identification. Although the enemy, as outlined by Attorney General Ashcroft, may wear the same clothes that we do and he may occupy the same roles that we do (as a tourist, student or worker), he is nonetheless visually distinguishable from 'us'. Why else would we be asked to keep watch? Newspapers, magazines, television and Internet sources continually displayed the brown-skinned faces of (almost exclusively male) Arab and Muslim persons as the focus of the war on terrorism. Racial profiling was employed at ports of entry to literally separate persons according to perceived levels of potential threat.

The collection of identification data in NSEERS reflected a parallel emphasis on race and nationality as categories of suspicion. At POE registration 'certain non-immigrant aliens' are routed through separate lines and are subject to increased scrutiny and detention. Similarly, Attorney General Ashcroft called on individuals working, studying and travelling in the United States from Arab and Muslim countries to present themselves for registration at local INS offices. Fearing humiliation, incarceration and potential deportation, large numbers of people waited until the last possible day to register. The snaking lines of Arab and Muslim men outside registration offices were clear examples of the race-based categorical suspicion of NSEERS. These images were captured by the press and represented in newspapers across the country and internationally. For example, a story in the 11 January 2003 edition of the *New York Times* includes an image displaying 'men from mostly Arab or Muslim countries' outside an INS office in Detroit in response to the second call-in registration period ('Facing a Registration Deadline' 2003). A more alarming scene is documented in the 11 January 2003 edition of the *Globe and Mail* (Houpt 2003). An image beside the headline 'Thousands with US visas race to meet INS deadline' depicts 'foreign-born men' lined up outside a New York City INS office, literally barricaded from the surrounding environment by a fence. The fence as barricade also appears in a 22 March 2003 story in the *New York Times* (Cardwell 2003), with the title 'Pakistani and Saudi Men Find Long Lines for Registration'.

A brief search of American newspapers yields scenes similar to those described above as well as others documenting the registration process.

An image in the *San Francisco Chronicle* (Hubbell 2003) shows immigrants leaving a local INS office following registration. Images in the *Los Angeles Times* (Mcdonnell and Mena 2003) and the *Pittsburgh Post-Gazette* (Thomas 2003) show registrants being counselled by lawyers and volunteers. An image in the *Orlando Sentinel* (Brewington 2003) displays an individual being fingerprinted at a Detroit INS office. An image in Baltimore's *The Sun* (Shane 2003) depicts a Pakistani family at the Pakistani Embassy listening to a discussion of the registration rules. And a story in the *Buffalo News* (Bonfatti 2003) contains an image of a Pakistani family waiting in a crowded refugee centre trying to cross into Canada before the registration deadline.

The images depicted and referenced above are part of the tremendous sums of images, moving and still, which have documented, and been deployed in, the war on terrorism. Importantly, these images are not simply static documents. As part of a larger visual culture they are dynamic sites where meaning, knowledge and identity are negotiated. They function as interactive screens or spaces through which social experience and knowledge are exercised, imposed and learned. The continued dissemination and consumption of visual materials through a multiplicity of media channels aids in the transmission of social codes and in the formation of identities of self and other (Manning 1999).

Understood as dynamic rather than static objects, the deployment and circulation of images documenting 'special registration' contribute to the construction and reinforcement of race-based categorical suspicion. An aggregate category – Arab and Muslim men – was created and coded as a potential threat to national security. This process had two main consequences. First, it contributed to the development of a rhetoric that justified the discriminatory treatment of individual Arab and Muslim men. Second, the continued presentation and re-presentation of Arab and Muslim men subject to the registration process gave a visual 'face' to this potential threat, enabling the public to participate in the war on terrorism (as in the reporting of suspicious activity and persons). The continued production and consumption of visual materials – live, recorded, still and moving – contributed to the formation of false binaries of self and other, normal and deviant, and American and potential threat.

Conclusion: the public display of power

Initiatives such as NSEERS and US-VISIT are indicative of a society and culture of surveillance.[5] Within such a space, registration and monitoring programs benefit from the tremendous capabilities of digital technology in the collection, storage and use of personal identification data. However, these programs do not simply increase the administrative and communications capabilities of the state but also, as David Lyon (1994: 50–1) argues, constitute a reversal of the presumption of innocence. Within the contemporary culture of surveillance the individual body is increasingly treated as a site of potential threat.

The application of any surveillance technology or program necessarily reflects the interests, desires and mission of its employers. In the abstract, a program such as US-VISIT may enhance the security of the United States border through the documentation and monitoring of each of the country's visitors. In its potentially democratic treatment of bodies, US-VISIT shares many parallels with existing registration systems in Switzerland, the United Kingdom, Germany, Spain, France and the Netherlands (USDOJ 2002).[6] It could be argued that having one's personal information collected in this and other formats is a necessary precondition for life in a surveillance society. However, the selective application of registration requirements in NSEERS is overtly discriminatory and betrays any such rationale. The efficacy of NSEERS to enhance border security is highly debatable. What are clear are the numerous consequences and challenges the program poses to the identities and capabilities of individuals, groups and nations.

The implementation and application of the National Security Entry-Exit Registration System was a reactionary and retaliatory response to the events of 11 September 2001. The program was sped into application without sufficient review, and gave unyielding authority to the Attorney General to collect aggregates of personal identification data not just from persons entering the country, but retroactively from persons residing in the United States. Far from the mundane collection of data through daily transactions, activities and through the ubiquitous gaze of CCTV that is the hallmark of a contemporary culture of surveillance, the net effect of data collection in NSEERS was to code, categorize and display 'certain' bodies as potentially threatening and potentially criminal.

The collection of data in NSEERS marks a curious aberration from the subtle and diffuse 'micro-physics of power' (Foucault 1979) characteristic of the modern state. In contrast to the anonymous, all-seeing gaze of the contemporary surveillance apparatus, the selective application of registration requirements in NSEERS represents an overt and public display of state power. This power is targeted at specific persons and is exercised directly on the body. Individuals registered at ports of entry are processed through separate lines and are fingerprinted and photographed while non-registrants pass by. Those subject to call-in registration stand behind fences in lines snaking out of INS offices. What we see throughout these events and in the media representations of them are Arab and Muslim men put on display, coded and identified as potential threats to national security. The production and consumption of these scenes by non-registrants reinforces this identity, simultaneously validating the viewer's own role as a participant in the war on terrorism and as a defender of national security. The overtly discriminatory collection of data in the National Security Entry-Exit Registration System promulgates a false dichotomy of 'us' and 'them', of 'American' and 'potential threat' that has had and will continue to have lasting impacts on the identities and abilities of individuals, groups and nations.

Notes

1 The author gratefully acknowledges that financial support for this research was received from an Initiatory Research Grant through Wilfrid Laurier University.
2 The federal register is 'the official daily publication for rules, proposed rules and notices of Federal agencies and organizations, as well as executive orders and other presidential documents'. The citation format [67 FR 40581] refers to [Volume 67, Federal Register, p. 40581]. This format is used throughout government documents and is used in this paper as well. The Federal Register from 1994 to the present can be accessed and searched through the United States Government Printing Office's website. Available at: <http://www.gpoaccess.gov/fr/index.html>
3 Armenia was mistakenly included in this call, but was removed from the list two days after the initial publication [67 FR 77642].
4 Although US-VISIT is the successor to NSEERS it did not completely replace the program. Individuals can still be subject to special registration under NSEERS at the discretion of the Secretary of Homeland Security.
5 On the development of a society or culture of surveillance, see Lyon (1994), Marx (1985, 1988) and Staples (1997).
6 The announcement of NSEERS included a comparison of the program with the registration systems of the countries cited.

References

Bonfatti, J.F. (2003) 'Between Two Worlds; Pakistanis pack a refugee center in Buffalo', *Buffalo News*, 7 March, p. A1.
Brewington, K. (2003) 'Immigrants Sign Up in INS Antiterror Push', *Orlando Sentinel*, 11 January, p. A1.
Buchanan, W. (2003) 'Hundreds Protest INS Registration: Men from 13 countries sign in', *San Francisco Chronicle*, 11 January.
Cardwell, D. (2003) 'Pakistani and Saudi Men Find Long Lines for Registration',

New York Times, 22 March, p. D2.

Cole, S. (1998) 'Manufacturing Identity: A History of Criminal Identification Techniques From Photography Through Fingerprinting', PhD diss, Cornell University.

Cole, S. (2001) *Suspect Identities: A History of Criminal Identification and Fingerprinting* (Cambridge: Harvard University Press).

'Facing a Registration Deadline' (2003) *New York Times*, 11 January, p. A9.

Federal Bureau of Investigation (FBI) (1999) 'Inauguration of the Integrated Automated Fingerprint Identification System (IAFIS)', 10 August Press Release. Available at: <http://www.fbi.gov/pressrel/pressrel99/iafis.htm> (accessed November 2002).

Foucault, M. (1979) *Discipline and Punish: The Birth of the Prison*, Alan Sheridan (trans) (New York: Vintage Books).

Garvey, M., Groves, M. and Weinstein, H. (2002) 'Hundreds Are Detained After Visits to INS; Thousands protest arrests of Mideast boys and men who complied with order to register', *Los Angeles Times*, 19 December, p. A1.

Houpt, S. (2003) 'Thousands with US visas race to meet INS deadline', *Globe and Mail*, 11 January, p. A13.

Hubbell, J.M. (2003) 'Immigrants register before final deadline', *San Francisco Chronicle*, 26 April, p. A17.

Kobach, K. (2003) 'National Security Entry-Exit Registration System', 17 January Foreign Press Center Briefing. Available at: <http://fpc.state.gov/16739pf.htm> (accessed 6 July 2004).

Laudon, K. (1986) *The Dossier Society: Value Choices in the Design of National Information Systems* (New York: Columbia University Press).

Lohmeyer, K. (2003) 'The Pitfalls of Plenary Power: a call for meaningful review of NSEERS "Special Registration"', *Whittier Law Review*, 25:1, pp. 139–79.

Lyon, D. (1988) *The Information Society: Issues and Illusions* (Cambridge: Polity).

Lyon, D. (1994) *The Electronic Eye: The Rise of Surveillance Society* (Minneapolis: University of Minnesota Press).

Lyon, D. (2003a) *Surveillance after September 11* (Cambridge: Polity).

Lyon, D. (2003b) 'Surveillance as Social Sorting: Computer Codes and Mobile Bodies', in D. Lyon (ed.) *Surveillance as Social Sorting: Privacy, Risk and Digital Discrimination* (New York: Routledge), pp. 13–30.

Manning, P.K. (1999) 'Reflections: The Visual as a Mode of Social Control', in J. Ferrell and N. Websdale (eds) *Making Trouble: Cultural Constructions of Crime, Deviance and Control*, Social Problems and Social Issues Series, J. Best (ed) (New York: Aldine De Gruyter), pp. 255–75.

Marx, G. (1985) 'The Surveillance Society: the threat of 1984-style techniques', *The Futurist*, June, pp. 21–6.

Marx, G. (1988) *Undercover: Police Surveillance in America* (Berkeley: University of California Press).

Mcdonnell, P. and Mena, J. (2003) 'Round 2 of INS Sign-ups Goes Well', *Los Angeles Times*, 11 January, p. B1.

McGann, C. (2003) 'Protestors Accuse INS of "Very Un-American" Registration; Hundreds Rally in Seattle; Many Fear Tracking Will be Used to "Target and

Profile"', *Seattle Post-Intelligencer*, 14 January, p. B1.

Redd, C.K. (2003) 'Protestors Rally Against INS Rules Effort Decried as Racial Profiling', *Boston Globe*, 21 February, p. B3.

Shane, S. (2003) 'Registration rules puzzle, anger Pakistanis in US', *The Sun* (Baltimore), 5 January, p. 3A.

Staples, W.G. (1997) *The Culture of Surveillance: Discipline and Social Control in the United States*, Contemporary Social Issues, George Ritzer (ed) (New York: St Martin's Press).

Thomas, L. (2003) 'Register or Risk Deportation', *Pittsburgh Post-Gazette*, 16 March, p. C1.

United States Department of Homeland Security (USDHS) (2003) 'Fact Sheet: Changes to National Security Entry/Exit Registration System', 1 December Press Release. Available at: <http://www.dhs.gov/dhspublic/display?content=3020> (accessed 22 June 2004).

United States Department of Homeland Security (USDHS) (2004) 'US-VISIT Statistics'. Available at: <http://www.dhs.gov/dhspublic/interapp/editorial/editorial_0437.xml> (accessed 9 July 2004).

United States Department of Justice (USDOJ) (2002) 'Attorney General Prepared Remarks on the National Security Entry-Exit Registration System'. Available at: <http://www.usdoj.gov/ag/speeches/2002/060502agpreparedremarks.htm> (accessed 14 July 2004).

Chapter 10

Imperial embrace?: identification and constraints on mobility in a hegemonic empire

John Torpey

I have previously argued that the ability to 'embrace' its members effectively – to identify them individually and to draw a boundary around them collectively – is a key attribute of modern nation states, a fact that massively promoted the *'revolution identificatoire'* that has characterized the development of modern state bureaucracy. Meanwhile, Emmanuelle Saada has noted that 'the colonial setting played the role of a laboratory for the "identifying State"' (Saada 2003: 17). There is indeed good reason to think that this is the case; in German Southwest Africa, for example, the German government developed in the course of its domination of colonial populations a number of the techniques later applied against the Jews. Against the backdrop of recent developments, however, one wonders whether the nation state wasn't, in turn, the 'laboratory' for empire itself – a new kind of empire (if that is the correct term) embodied by the post-Cold War United States.

This chapter explores the question of whether or not the United States is an 'empire' – which is of course in significant part a matter of definition – and how the practices of identification and restrictions on movement associated with the 'identifying State' relate to the question of empire. I argue that, in contrast to the modern European overseas empires, and much to the chagrin of some of its contemporary cheerleaders, the United States is not and lacks even the desire to be an empire in any very useful sense. Hannah Arendt (1973: 125–34) detested European imperialism for refusing to extend the laws of the metropole to the subjugated territories, as the Romans had done, and thus ruling over their domains tyrannically; in contrast, the United States seems to want to extend its laws to the territories it invades, but not actually to rule over them (directly, at least). Hence, for example, George Bush has said of the intervention in Iraq, 'I sent American troops to Iraq to defend our security, not to stay as an occupying power. I sent American troops to Iraq to make its people free, not to make them American.'[1] For the time being, to be sure, any major decisions about policy are made in Washington, not Baghdad, but the objective – on both sides of the political aisle – is to get out of Iraq, not deeper into it. This is true in general of American dominance, which is more 'soft' than 'hard'.

To the extent that it could be described as an empire at all, then, I suggest that we might call it a 'hegemonic empire', in which those dominated by the United States often welcome the possibility of sharing in what they take to be 'the American dream'. The usual imperial arrangement whereby various groups are subordinated to a dominant lineage and ethnic or religious group does not fit the case of American 'empire' very well, as the United States population itself is so diverse and multi-faceted, the product of constant infusions from outside. Despite US military dominance of the world, its population has come to feel itself (and to some extent it really is) threatened in a novel manner by enemies who are not embodied in states but in loose networks of like-minded warriors externally (Al Qaeda) and in large numbers of predominantly non-white miscreants internally. In this context, the efforts to identify at a distance those wishing to come to the territory of the centre, and the incarceration of both domestic social castoffs and potential non-state attackers from outside, are part of a far-flung policing-cum-war machinery that is intended to protect the inhabitants of a country that experiences itself as threatened by those not enthusiastic about, or a part of, a middle-class, consumption-oriented populace. Attempts to embrace and constrain these elements are driven by a new kind of 'fear factor', one that has emerged from the post-Cold War deterioration of traditional class and ethical solidarities.

Getting a grip on a hegemonic empire

In the aftermath of 9/11, only the second externally initiated attack on the United States since the War of 1812, the country has moved vigorously to enhance its capacity to track persons all over the world. The US-VISIT program – under the auspices of the Department of Homeland Security – 'seeks to supplant the nation's physical borders with what officials call virtual borders' and 'to track visitors long before they set foot' in the United States (Lichtblau and Markoff 2004). This project goes far beyond the important administrative innovation of 'remote control', a development that Aristide Zolberg (forthcoming) has shown was a major advance in nation states' efforts to forestall unwanted immigration, beginning in the early twentieth century. At the same time, the United States has also moved to ensure its access to cannon fodder should it need more military recruits – a major concern during the 2004 election campaign with its accusations of the Bush administration's deployment of a 'backdoor draft' and a matter of continuing concern to the US military. Thus the December 2001 'smart border' declaration signed with Canada 'will prevent conscientious objectors (and cowards) from finding sanctuary across the northern border' (Sutherland 2004). It has also given Border Patrol officers the power to exclude potential entrants at the Canadian and Mexican borders (Swarns 2004b). In carrying out this intensified effort to keep terrorists out of American territory, the Border Patrol has created checkpoints as much as 100 miles from the actual border that it calls 'Functional Equivalents of the Border', moving the effective boundaries of the country far inland (Blumenthal 2004).

Since 9/11, the United States government has also moved to require 27 industrialized countries whose citizens do not currently require visas to enter the United States to provide them with tamper-proof machine-readable passports. The program has hit major obstacles, however, leading to requests for delays in implementation beyond the initial 26 October 2004 deadline ('Passport Deadline in Doubt' 2004; Swarns 2004d). Before stepping down as the first Secretary of the Department of Homeland Security, Tom Ridge recommended that the US government also begin to issue passports with a full set of the bearer's fingerprints, on the assumption that 'the change would induce foreign governments to do the same on the passports they issue' (Wald 2005). In an effort 'to ensure that travelers do not vanish into the shadows after their arrival in the country', the government is also expanding its efforts to track the departures of those required to have a visa to enter the United States, taking fingerprints and digital photographs of them at eleven US airports ('Program Tracking Foreign Visitors' 2004; Swarns 2004a). In addition, the government is experimenting with programs to allow 'frequent fliers' to undergo streamlined security checks at airports in exchange for giving the authorities more information about themselves than does the average traveller. 'Among the areas in which the government wants to gain experience [with these programs] is the issuing of "biometric" identification cards, incorporating data on fingerprints or iris scans, to thousands of people, and using them routinely in short transactions' (Wald 2004a; 'Program Enlists About 10,000 Frequent Fliers' 2004). Among these various options, the National Institute of Standards and Technology, the government agency responsible for determining such matters, has found that fingerprint systems 'performed better as a group than facial recognition systems', although it continues to test such systems ('Fingerprint Systems Superior' 2004).

Meanwhile, largely poor would-be entrants must run a 'gauntlet of death' at the United States' southern border, taking serious risks in pursuit of the opportunity to earn considerably higher wages than those available to them at home. Yet there are thought to be some 10 million illegal migrants inside the territory of the United States, perhaps half of whom entered the country legally (and who shift into illegality simply by overstaying their visas). They play an important role in the country's economy, particularly in places like California that receive a large number of Mexican immigrants ('Crosses on Border' 2004). From the point of view of citizenship, these persons may be US citizens-in-waiting who will eventually be granted or acquire American citizenship, but in all events their US-born children will do so automatically by dint of the United States' *jus soli* ('law of the soil') procedure for attributing citizenship. One generation on, members of these groups will be full-fledged members of the nation state. While they exist in legal limbo, however, one might regard them as 'outsiders within'; they are the citizenship equivalent of ghosts – there, but not really there from the point of view of full, political membership.

In part as a result of the presence of so many 'undocumented' residents (a misnomer, really, as they may have all kinds of documents – just not authentic papers attesting American citizenship), talk of introducing a national identity card has grown louder; such documents would help identify 'insiders within' – that is, those legitimately inside the national territory and hence fully authorized to be and remain in the country and to enjoy access to the political system ('A National ID' 2004). Of course, such identity cards are only as good as the documents used to acquire them, and cannot identify those who may wish to do a people harm – unless they have already fallen under the suspicion of the authorities in the first place. This shortcoming explains the call for federal standards for the issuance of driver's licences and birth certificates now controlled at the state level, 'a problem highlighted by the ease with which the September 11 hijackers were able to obtain such documents' (Swarns 2004a). As part of the legislation overhauling the United States' intelligence activities, the Department of Homeland Security will henceforth issue regulations on the documentation required before a state may grant a driver's licence (Wald 2004d). Some critics see this as a step on the road to a national ID card or, indeed, 'a system of internal passports' (Wald 2004d).

These considerations address the efforts of the world's leading power to regulate entry into and presence and mobility within the country's territory. Yet in recent years the United States has also come to administer an 'extralegal penal empire' (Sontag 2004) in various parts of the world, in which 'detainees' may be subjected to treatment without the benefit of the protections accorded to prisoners under various Geneva Conventions. This confinement operation involves the now-infamous Abu Ghraib prison in Iraq, Afghanistan's Bagram Air Base, Guantánamo Bay, and 'secret prisons now holding the thousands who have been arrested and confined by American and allied forces since the attacks of September 11' (Danner 2004). According to a report by the International Committee of the Red Cross, 'between 70 per cent and 90 per cent of the persons deprived of their liberty in Iraq had been arrested by mistake' (Danner 2004). Strikingly, those detained may also disappear into the carceral system without their families having any idea of their whereabouts or how to find them. Some of those who disappeared had done so because Secretary of Defense Donald Rumsfeld had ordered that they be secluded from the prying eyes of monitoring groups (Schmitt and Shanker 2004). This is hardly surprising, given the discovery of a memo from 4 January 2004 and written by the top legal adviser to the then-senior American commander in Iraq, Lt. General Ricardo Sanchez, unabashedly laying out what the memo's title called a 'New Plan to Restrict Red Cross Access to Abu Ghraib' (Shanker and Elliott 2004).

At the same time, some of those held in the penal archipelago have been detained 'as much for what officials do not know about them as for what they do' (Golden and Van Natta 2004); sometimes, the lack of information begins with the very identity of the person in question, as some of the prisoners have refused to give their names. The information value of many of the prisoners held at Guantánamo Bay has been regarded by knowledgeable experts – including analysts of the CIA – to have been much over-estimated. Indeed, as of June 2004 – nearly two years after they were first incarcerated – 'investigators have been able to deliver cases for military prosecution against only 15 of the suspects" (Golden and Van Natta 2004). Then, in November 2004, a federal judge found that President Bush had over-stepped his constitutional authority and improperly ignored the Geneva Conventions by establishing at Guantánamo Bay military commissions designed to try detainees as war criminals (Lewis 2004).

The abuse at Abu Ghraib may yet be deemed a war crime, despite efforts by Bush administration lawyers to interpret the statutes on torture narrowly with the objective of circumventing the relevant international and American law (Hoge 2004). A March 2003 memo prepared for the administration

contains a curious section in which the lawyers argued that any torture committed at Guantánamo would not be a violation of the anti-torture statute because the base was under American legal jurisdiction and the statute concerns only torture committed overseas. That view is in direct conflict with the position the administration has taken in the Supreme Court, where it argued that prisoners at Guantánamo Bay are not entitled to constitutional protections because the base is outside American jurisdiction. (Lewis and Schmitt 2004)

This would seem to be the legal equivalent of 'having it both ways', and the Supreme Court would have none of it. On 28 June 2004 all of the justices save Clarence Thomas ruled that 'enemy combatants' both in the United States and in Guantánamo Bay must be given the opportunity to challenge their detention before a judge or other 'neutral decisionmaker'. The Court also ruled that federal judges had jurisdiction to consider petitions for writs of habeas corpus from any of the hundreds of non-citizens held at Guantánamo Bay who believe they are being detained illegally. Contrary to the administration's claim that Guantánamo Bay was outside the US and hence outside those judges' jurisdiction, the military base in Cuba is in fact 'territory over which the United States exercises exclusive jurisdiction and control', according to the Court (Greenhouse 2004b). The Bush administration has appealed these rulings, but in January 2005 a federal judge held that the detainees at Guantánamo Bay 'were clearly entitled to have federal courts examine whether they have been lawfully detained' (Lewis 2005).

In all events, the available evidence indicates that the abuse of Iraqi prisoners is not 'the isolated acts of a rogue night shift', but systemic and pervasive – despite a directive by President Bush ordering that all people detained by the United States as part of the war on terrorism be treated properly 'even if the United States considered them not to be protected by the Geneva Conventions'. The documents relating to Abu Ghraib that were released by the administration were predictably selective, and criticized as self-servingly so by, among others, Senator Patrick Leahy and the editorial writers of the *New York Times* (Stevenson 2004; 'Abu Ghraib, Stonewalled' 2004).

Against this background, one might characterize those persons held in US custody abroad as 'outsiders without' – violators of what the United States military or government regard as the security concerns of the US, and without protection either by US law or by international laws related to the treatment of prisoners in wartime. Surely the transgressions that took place in Abu Ghraib were a function of the extra-legal character of the American military occupation in Iraq (Fisher 2004; see also Danner 2004 and Tyler 2004). These misdeeds are also a result of the fact that the United States military 'is being swiftly privatized before our eyes', and 'in an astonishing lapse on the part of American legislators, the actions of the tens of thousands of [military] contractors in Iraq are not governed by any comprehensive body of criminal law' (Keefe 2004). The situation of those detained in overseas US prisons thus bears some resemblance to what Hannah Arendt once said about the stateless populations of Europe: 'their plight is not that they are not equal before the law, but that no law exists for them' (Arendt 1973).

The kinds of abuses that have been uncovered in the overseas penal empire, meanwhile, are thought to be not uncommon in prisons in the United States themselves, 'where a number of guards at Abu Ghraib worked in their civilian lives' (Zernike and Rohde 2004). Indeed, the preoccupation with terrorism has led to at least one case of a poor innocent disappearing into the federal prisons for months on suspicion of terrorism. A visa over-stayer from Nepal who was arrested for photographing – apparently unbeknown to him – a building containing an FBI office in New York City 'was swallowed up in the government's new maximum security system of secret detention and secret hearings, and his only friend was the same FBI agent who had helped decide to put him there'. The prison in Brooklyn where the man was detained has been cited by the Department of Justice's inspector general for 'a pattern of physical and mental mistreatment of post-9/11 detainees', including 'slamming detainees into walls, mocking them during unnecessary strip-searches, and secretly taping their conversations with lawyers'. According to the man's Legal Aid lawyer, as a result of the secret system operated by the Bush administration Justice Department, 'there is no way to know' whether non-citizens continue to be treated in a manner similar to that of the unfortunate Nepalese man (Bernstein 2004; see also Dow 2004).

Not surprisingly, perhaps, the development of the overseas penal empire follows the emergence over the past two decades of a massive 'prison-industrial complex' in the United States itself, which has involved an enormous growth of penal institutions and prison populations (Butterfield 2004b). This remarkable expansion of the 'correctional population' has occurred despite declines in the rates of crimes of property and violence from 1993 to 2002 to 30-year lows (Wald 2004b; Butterfield 2004a). In addition to the growth in the numbers of those imprisoned, the average length of sentences grew from 23 months in 1995 to 30 months in 2001 (Butterfield 2004c). Some insist that the treatment of foreign prisoners in such notorious locales as Iraq's Abu Ghraib is only the overseas analogue of the treatment accorded prisoners in the United States itself (Herbert 2004).

In contrast to the illegal immigrant population ('outsiders within'), these US citizens are 'insiders without' – that is, inside the territory but outside the society and often without access to its political system. The population held in the US prison system is disproportionately non-white, especially black (African-American); indeed, one in ten black men aged 25 to 29 were in prison in 2003 (Butterfield 2004c). The system contains so many poorly educated blacks that incarceration has come to be viewed as 'a new stage in the life course of young, low-skill black men' (Pettit and Western 2004). To a considerable extent, the rise in incarceration rates has been a result of the more vigorous prosecution of drug-related offences and longer and mandatory sentencing of those convicted. Often, the segregation from the larger society also entails exclusion from its political system due to the fact that many states disenfranchise convicted felons, even after they leave prison (Staples 2004; Behrens, Uggen and Manza 2003).

In the eyes of David Garland, a leading specialist on these matters, the massive expansion of carceral institutions and populations in recent years reflects a shift from the 'old regime' of 'penal welfarism', in which the dominant expectation was of reform and rehabilitation, to a regime of 'punitive segregation' that aims only 'to punish and exclude' (Garland 2002: 140). The emphasis on anticipatory action to forestall crime in Garland's interpretation of the new regime of crime control eerily resonates with the Bush administration's arguments about the need for preventive strikes against what it deems threatening countries. The shift in punishment regimes is tied to changes in the political economy and, in the United States itself, to changes in the status of blacks in American society as a result of the 'civil rights revolution'. Punitive segregation has been accompanied by a massive movement of whites out of the cities and into suburbs, increasingly including gated communities that offer privatized security arrangements for those who can afford such quarters. It seems more than coincidental that the boom in such housing took off soon after the adoption of landmark laws that sought to guarantee the legal equality of blacks in American society (Blakely and Snyder 1997).

One might argue that the inhabitants of the 'penal empire', both domestic and foreign, are forced migrants of a sort – expelled by government power for shorter or longer periods into zones from which they cannot return – but from which they will eventually return, like most forced migrants, aggrieved and embittered (if they return at all). Once their freedom of mobility is restored to them, they are likely to have difficulty re-integrating into the society from which they came and resentment about what has happened to them. As one Arab commentator put it with regard to the prisoners held in Cuba, 'Guantánamo is a huge problem for Americans. … Even those who were not hard-core extremists have now been indoctrinated by the true believers. Like [in] any other prison, they have been taught to hate. If they let these people go, these people will make trouble' (Golden and Van Natta 2004). Indeed, upon release, several

Afghan detainees returned to the battlefield as commanders or fighters for the Taliban. Similarly, observers of the Spanish prisons have found the radical Islamists regard the jails as prime recruiting grounds as well (McLean 2004).

To be sure, at least some of those caught up in the penal empire are guilty of crimes of one sort or another, or may bear animus towards the United States and its way of life and wish to do Americans harm. But the crimes for which so many have been incarcerated domestically are clearly of an ephemeral nature, not the sort of thing that will remain on the books whenever the current wave of repression passes. Similarly, if the 'war on terrorism' was being conducted more clearly under the auspices of international law, many of those held overseas would be freed; in many cases, however, the current US government simply does not wish to conform to the dictates of that law. Whether domestic or foreign, those detained may spend the remainder of their lives under various kinds of surveillance and restricted mobility, on the basis of the identities now stored in the many databases linked together for security and other purposes (Pear 2004). Whether citizens of the United States or not, individuals are increasingly subject to one or another form of 'embrace' by the American state. Contrary to traditional conservative strictures against the growth of government power, the United States in recent years has moved energetically to mobilize the state with the aim of protecting the population and territory, and this has meant a significant effort to enhance its grip on persons within and without (Swarns 2004c; Brooks 2004). Meanwhile, private parties seek residential and other arrangements that segregate them from groups regarded as dangerous, recalcitrant and deviant.

And yet despite this major drive towards an enhanced embrace of both domestic and external populations, the US Supreme Court has recently been forced to address the very basic question of whether individuals can be required to identify themselves to the authorities or not. A Nevada man who was pulled over by the police refused (11 times!) to give his name to the arresting officer. This refusal violated a Nevada law requiring people in suspicious circumstances to tell police their names; 20 US states and a number of cities and towns had such laws on their books at the time of this incident. The man, Larry D. Hiibel, refused to identify himself on the ground that doing so would violate his rights under the Fourth Amendment (unreasonable search and seizure) and the Fifth Amendment (avoiding self-incrimination). Ultimately, the Supreme Court upheld the man's conviction, arguing that the divulgence of the man's name was reasonably required under existing statutes and did not entail a violation of the constitutional rights he invoked. But the Court was sharply divided; the vote was 5–4 to sustain the lower courts' ruling. In dissenting opinions, several justices (the more liberal ones) argued that the requirement to identify oneself did overstep the authority of the law. Despite losing the particular cause at issue, Marc Rotenberg, the executive director of the Electronic Privacy Information Center (EPIC), one of the leading groups working to defend privacy rights, noted that the Court's majority had raised constitutional doubts about whether a demand for identification documents, as opposed to merely the person's name, would be acceptable. Rotenberg stressed his concern about the relationship between a possible national ID card and the potential for tapping into the vast amounts of information stored in inter-linked databases.

This case suggests that, despite what some would argue is a drift towards (or indeed the *fait accompli* of) 'empire' (in the sense of a political system of unilateral arbitrariness, legal unaccountability and tyrannical rule over other populations), the United States still has many of the legal safeguards that characterize liberal democracies as opposed to authoritarian states. The law can't do much with people whose identities are unknown – other than incarcerate them, which is not a very good or defensible solution when the offence is minor. But there is clearly a significant division of opinion over whether or not individuals may be compelled to reveal to officials who they are, and the indications are that the issue will have to be revisited later (Greenhouse 2004a, 2004b). In the heart of the 'empire', it may turn out that persons may legitimately refuse to tell the authorities who (and hence to some degree 'what') they are.

The question of empire

Against this background, we may return to the question posed at the outset: Is the United States behaving in these various efforts like an empire? There are perhaps four basic answers to this question:

1) Yes, the United States is an empire, and that's a good thing (or would be if put properly into practice). Those who answer in this fashion tend to be neo-conservatives and certain human-rights liberals. The former endorse its intervention in Iraq; the latter want it to intervene in Darfur. Thus Samantha Power has recently written of the United States as an 'empire of human rights' – if only it lived up to its commitments in this regard (Power 2003).[2]

2) Yes, the United States is an empire, and that's a bad thing. This is the response of the traditional anti-imperialist left, perhaps best represented by Noam Chomsky. Those in this camp see the United States as enormously powerful and with a habitual tendency to invade and oppress other countries, especially the smaller and weaker.

3) No, the United States is not an empire, nor should it be. It should avoid foreign entanglements, as the Founding Fathers once recommended, and look after its own concerns. Pat Buchanan is a leading representative of this view.

4) No, the United States is not an empire, and that's bad. That is, the United States has the power to intervene in parts of the world that need fixing, but it is too isolationist and too unwilling to engage with the rest of the world to assume the obligations of empire. This is the view of the British (and now Harvard) historian Niall Ferguson, which he has laid out in a number of his writings. Ferguson wishes the United States and its citizens were less parochial and more willing to assume the mantle of the British empire.

Yet these views often seem to over-state the power of the United States and to misrepresent its nature. One measure of the 'empire' is its worldwide military presence and capacity. These are undoubtedly great and, indeed, unmatched by any other country. With regard to the overall level of US military power, Paul Kennedy has recently stated, on the basis of *Time* magazine's recent estimate, that the United States has 368,000 people in its 'national service' stationed in 120 countries (Kennedy 2004). Still, as was noted earlier, the United States is moving dramatically towards the privatization of its military forces. This is partially a matter of trying to 'outsource' certain activities in order to reap supposed gains of efficiency and cost. It is also an effort to appear to be 'downsizing' the military at a time when Americans have little stomach for large-scale military losses and when there is little doubt that a draft would provoke major upheaval. With developments such as these taking place in the world's leading power, we may be witnessing the end of the Westphalian period that Max Weber had used to define the modern state as that entity with a monopoly on the legitimate use of violence (Keefe 2004; Ignatieff 2000).

At the same time that the United States has such unchallengeable resources for projecting force and intimidating potential opponents around the world, the Bush administration is clearly moving towards a rearrangement of American military forces based on a rethinking of their uses. For example, the Pentagon plans to replace two Army divisions (typically including three brigades and 20,000 men) with a single brigade in Germany, and a 'wing' of F-16 fighters currently based there will be moved to Turkey. These plans comprise 'the most significant rearrangement of the American military around the world since the beginning of the Cold War, according to American and allied officials' (Gordon 2004). Similarly, plans are afoot to withdraw 12,500 American troops from South Korea. According to Defense Secretary Donald Rumsfeld, 'It is not numbers of things. ... It is capability to impose lethal power, where needed, when

167

needed, with the greatest flexibility and with the greatest agility' (Brooke and Shanker 2004).

What is striking, however, from the point of view of considering the nature of American power is that significant elements in both regions regret this departure of American power. Despite the recent *contretemps* between the United States and 'old Europe', anti-Americanism probably remains far stronger in South Korea. Yet in each of the above-mentioned zones from which American troops are to be withdrawn, influential voices would prefer them to stay. These facts suggest that the United States is not the hated 'empire' that many claim it is; the element of what Joseph Nye called 'soft power' in contemporary American dominance cannot be gainsaid. To some extent, the use of the term 'empire' to describe the United States is simply a way of tarring it with a brush that is no longer defensible. In the post-colonial age of the nation state, empires are not acceptable or legitimate forms of political organization. They smack of heteronomy – 'subjection to an external law or power', according to the *Oxford English Dictionary* – and lack of democratic participation.

Those who wish to deride the United States by using the term 'empire' to characterize it may have an inflated view of its capacities. There are signs of weakness in the American 'empire' that suggest that the country is not as powerful as is often claimed – whether by supporters or detractors. Hence Emmanuel Todd has argued that American power has over-reached in the sense that it is becoming increasingly dependent upon foreigners for its current consumption and, as a result of growing deficits in trade and current accounts, dangerously vulnerable to changes in policy and behaviour by other countries – especially Japan and China, which hold a large per centage of American debt. Similarly, mobilizing his 'IEMP' (ideological, economic, military and political) model of power to analyse contemporary developments, Michael Mann argues that the United States has become increasingly weak economically because of the size of its trade deficits and the extent of foreign ownership of American financial assets. Both of these commentators see the US as a giant with clay feet, militarily unchallengeable but economically rather shaky (Todd 2003; Mann 2003). There is, of course, debate among economic analysts over the long-term significance of these developments (Uchitelle 2004). The point remains that, however predominant in military terms at present, American supremacy is likely to be neither eternal nor long unimpeachable.

Conclusion

Contemporary American dominance, if not 'empire', involves to a considerable extent efforts to strengthen the state with the aim of extending its embrace to those whose movements it wishes to constrain, whether these are undesirables from without or from within. The latter – 'insiders without' – are persons subject to a more stringent degree of constraint and control than had been sought for persons similarly situated in the previous regime of crime control. In addition to the efforts to strengthen state control over such persons, recent developments in crime control have pushed in the direction of greater private efforts to prevent crime and segregate stigmatized populations. The increased spread of preventive strategies with regard to domestic crime resonates with new military and security doctrines that promulgate anticipatory interventions against rogue elements deemed to represent an external threat; these may be held as 'outsiders without', beyond the reach of either US law or international law. The movements of 'outsiders within' are made more complicated and subject to greater surveillance, but mainly with the aim of locating and apprehending terrorists. Many 'outsiders within' – the 'illegal aliens', predominantly from Latin America – remain a population vital to the wellbeing of the American economy, and hence a group that is 'wanted but not welcome' (Zolberg 1987). Perhaps most emblematic of the current constellation, however, are the 'outsiders without' – those detained by American entities overseas and frequently deprived of the rights that would normally accrue to 'enemy combatants' under international law, or to beneficiaries of American law under the constitution.

Despite opposition from the Supreme Court (Dworkin 2004), the Bush administration has been inclined to ignore such documents as the Geneva Conventions and such organizations as the Red Cross. Its disregard for these bulwarks of the international order has inflamed world opinion and given rise to an increasing proclivity to regard the United States as an empire – or even a 'rogue nation' (Prestowitz 2003). Perhaps Raymond Aron's notion of the US as the political equivalent of a platypus – as an 'imperial republic', that is – remains apt (Aron 2003). If the United States is an empire, it is one that is currently demonstrating a tremendous interest in controlling the movements of persons within and across its borders – not a characteristic typically associated with empires.

Notes

1 Speech on 24 May 2004.
2 William Shawcross appears to straddle the divide between these two groups; see Shawcross (2004) and Asmus (2004).

References

'A National ID' (2004) *New York Times* national edition, 31 May, p. A20.

'Abu Ghraib, Stonewalled'(2004) *New York Times* national edition, 30 June, p. 22.

Arendt, H. (1973) *The Origins of Totalitarianism* (New York: Harcourt Brace).

Aron, R. (2003) 'The Imperial Republic', in T. Judt (ed.) *The Dawn of Universal History: Selected Essays from a Witness to the Twentieth Century* (New York: Basic Books).

Asmus, R. (2004) 'Using American Power: Definite and Opposite Views', *New York Times* national edition, 3 March, p. B7.

Behrens, A., Uggen, C. and Manza, J. (2003) 'Ballot Manipulation and the 'Menace of Negro Domination': racial threat and felon disenfranchisement in the United States, 1850–2000', *American Journal of Sociology*, 109:3, pp. 559–605.

Bernstein, N. (2004) 'In FBI, Innocent Detainee Found Unlikely Ally', *New York Times* national edition, 30 June, p. A1, C14.

Blakely, E. and Snyder, M.G. (1997) *Fortress America: Gated Communities in the United States* (Washington, DC and Cambridge, MA: Brookings Institution/Lincoln Institute of Land Policy).

Blumenthal, R. (2004) 'New Strains and New Rules for Agents Along Mexican Border', *New York Times* national edition, 13 August, p. A13.

Brooke, J. and Shanker, T. (2004) 'US Plans to Cut Third of Troops in South Korea', *New York Times* national edition, 8 June, pp. A1, A12.

Brooks, D. (2004) 'How to Reinvent the GOP', *New York Times Magazine*, 29 August.

Butterfield, F. (2004a) 'Violent Crime Dropped by 3 Per cent in 2003', *New York Times* national edition, 25 May, p. A18.

Butterfield, F. (2004b) 'US "Correctional Population" Hits New High', *New York Times* national edition, 26 July, p. A10.

Butterfield, F. (2004c) 'Despite Drop in Crime, An Increase in Inmates', *New York Times* national edition, 8 November, p. A14.

'Crosses on the Border' (2004) *New York Times* national edition, 1 June, p. A18.

Danner, M. (2004) 'Torture and Truth', *New York Review of Books*, 10 June, p. 47.

Dow, M. (2004) *American Gulag: Inside U.S. Immigration Prisons* (Berkeley: University of California Press).

Dworkin, R. (2004) 'What the Court Really Said', *New York Review of Books*, 12 August, pp. 26–9.

'Fingerprint Systems Superior in ID Tests' (2004) *New York Times* national edition, 5 July, p. C5.

Fisher, I. (2004) 'Searing Uncertainty for Iraqis Missing Loved Ones', *New York Times* national edition, 1 June, pp. A1, A8.

Garland, D. (2002) *The Culture of Control: Crime and Social Order in Contemporary Society* (Chicago: University of Chicago Press).

Golden, T. and Van Natta, Jr., D. (2004) 'Exaggeration Seen on Value of Guantánamo Detainees', *New York Times* national edition, 21 June, pp. A1, A12.

Gordon, M.R. (2004) 'A Pentagon Plan to Sharply Cut GIs in Germany', *New York Times* national edition, 4 June, pp. A1, A10.

Greenhouse, L. (2004a) 'Supreme Court Hears Case of Man Who Withheld ID', *New York Times* national edition, 23 March, p. A14.

Greenhouse, L. (2004b) 'Justices Affirm Legal Rights of "Enemy Combatants"', *New York Times* national edition, 29 June, pp. A1, A14.

Herbert, B. (2004) 'America's Abu Ghraibs', *New York Times* national edition, 31 May, p. A21.

Hoge, W. (2004) 'UN Rights Chief Says Prison Abuse May be War Crime', *New York Times* national edition, 5 June, p. A5.

Ignatieff, M. (2000) *Virtual War: Kosovo and Beyond* (New York: Metropolitan Books).

Keefe, P.R. (2004) 'Iraq: America's Private Armies', *New York Review of Books*, 12 August, pp. 48–9.

Kennedy, P. (2004) 'Mission Impossible?', *New York Review of Books*, 10 June, p. 18.

Lewis, N.A. (2004) 'US Judge Halts War-Crime Trial at Guantánamo', *New York Times* national edition, 9 November, pp. A1, A14.

Lewis, N.A. (2005) 'Judge Extends Legal Rights For Guantánamo Detainees', *New York Times* national edition, 1 February, pp. A12.

Lewis, N.A. and Schmitt, E. (2004) 'Lawyers Decided Bans on Torture Didn't Bind Bush', *New York Times* national edition, 8 June, pp. A1, A10.

Lichtblau, E. and Markoff, J. (2004) 'US Nearing Deal on Way to Track Foreign Visitors', *New York Times* national edition, 24 May, pp. A1, A18.

Mann, M. (2003) *Incoherent Empire* (New York: Verso).

McLean, R. (2004) 'Spanish Prisons Provide Pool of Recruits for Radical Islam', *New York Times* national edition, 31 October, p. 8.

'Passport Deadline in Doubt' (2004) *New York Times* national edition, 15 June, p. A18.

Pear, R. (2004) 'Survey Finds US Agencies Engaged in "Data Mining"', *New York Times* national edition, 27 May, p. A24.

Pettit, B. and Western, B. (2004) 'Mass Imprisonment and the Life Course: race and class inequality in US incarceration', *American Sociological Review*, 69, pp. 151–69.

Power, S. (2003) 'Das Empire der Menschenrechte', in U. Speck and N. Sznaider (eds) *Empire Amerika: Perspektiven einer neuen Weltordnung* (Munich: DVA), pp. 138–55.

Prestowitz, C. (2003) *Rogue Nation: American Unilateralism and the Failure of Good Intentions* (New York: Basic Books).

'Program Enlists About 10,000 Frequent Fliers' (2004) *New York Times* national edition, 5 September, pp. 1, 14.

'Program Tracking Foreign Visitors to be Expanded' (2004) *New York Times* national edition, 4 August, p. A14.

Saada, E. (2003) 'The History of Lessons: power and rule in imperial formations', *Items & Issues*, 4:4, p. 17.

Schmitt, E. and Shanker, T. (2004) 'Rumsfeld Issued an Order to Hide Detainee in Iraq', *New York Times* national edition, 17 June, pp. A1, A8.

Shanker, T. and Elliott, A. (2004) 'Rumsfeld Admits He Told Jailers to Keep Detainee in Iraq Out of Red Cross View', *New York Times* national edition, 18 June, p. A13.

Shawcross, W. (2004) *Allies: The US, Britain, Europe and the War in Iraq* (New York: Public Affairs).

Sontag, S. (2004) 'Regarding the Torture of Others', *New York Times Magazine*, 23 May, p. 29.

Staples, B. (2004) 'How Denying the Vote to Ex-Offenders Undermines Democracy', *New York Times* national edition, 17 September, editorial page.

Stevenson, R.W. (2004) 'Orders by Bush About Prisoners Set Humane Tone', *New York Times* national edition, 23 June, pp. A1, A10.

Sutherland, R. (2004) 'Draft Dilemma', *The Guardian*, 31 May. Available at: http://www.guardian.co.uk/g2/story/0,3604,1228178,00.html

Swarns, R.L. (2004a) 'Some Steps Put in Place to Aid Border Security', *New York Times* national edition, 26 July, p. A12.

Swarns, R.L. (2004b) 'US to Give Border Patrol Agents the Power to Deport Illegal Aliens', *New York Times* national edition, 11 August, pp. A1, A11.

Swarns, R.L. (2004c) 'Government to Take Over Watch-List Screening', *New York Times* national edition, 17 August, p. A14

Swarns, R.L. (2004d) 'US Acts to Notify Foreigners of Tougher Rules for Visits', *New York Times* national edition, 11 September, p. A16.

Todd, E. (2003) *The Breakdown of the American Order* (New York: Columbia University Press).

Tyler, P. (2004) 'UN Chief Ignites Firestorm by Calling Iraq War "Illegal" ', *New York Times* national edition, 17 September, p. A11.

Uchitelle, L. (2004) 'US and Trade Partners Maintain Unhealthy Long-Term Relationship', *New York Times* national edition, 18 September, pp. B1, B4.

Wald, M.L. (2004a) 'Program Would Ease Security a Bit for Frequent Fliers', *New York Times* national edition, 16 June, p. A15.

Wald, M.L. (2004b) 'Most Crimes of Violence and Property Hover at 30-Year Lows', *New York Times* national edition, 13 September, p. A12

Wald, M.L. (2004c) 'Congress Close to Establishing Rules for Driver's Licenses', *New York Times* national edition, 11 October, p. A21.

Wald, M.L. (2004d) 'US to Specify Documents Needed for Driver's Licenses', *New York Times* national edition, 9 December, p. A27.

Wald, M.L. (2005) 'Ridge Wants Fingerprints in Passports', *New York Times* national edition, 13 January, p. A22.

Zernike, K. and Rohde, D. (2004) 'Forced Nudity of Iraqi Prisoners is Seen as a Pervasive Pattern, not Isolated Incidents', *New York Times* national edition, 8 June, p. A11.

Zolberg, A. (1987) 'Wanted But Not Welcome: alien labor in western development', in W. Alonzo (ed.) *Population in an Interacting World* (Cambridge, MA: Harvard University Press), pp. 36–74.

Zolberg, A. (forthcoming) *A Nation by Design: Immigration Policy in the Fashioning of America* (Cambridge, MA: Harvard University Press).

Chapter 11

Fencing the line: analysis of the recent rise in security measures along disputed and undisputed boundaries

John W. Donaldson

1. Introduction

1.1 Images of a borderless world

The tearing down of the Berlin Wall and emphasis on cross-border cooperation within a globalized world was believed in the 1990s to have harkened in an age when the inclination was to be towards new ideas and practices which sought to distance the notion of the international boundary as a linear barrier (Laitinen 2003: 37). It is true that the conditions of globalization in the modern world – including the flow of information across boundaries, the rise in international trade, the proliferation of corporations with worldwide influence, the ease of international travel and, most significantly, the increase in the number of regional economic unions – have affected the traditional characteristics of a boundary as a distinct line of separation.[1] These factors led to a notion that absolute state sovereignty over fixed parcels of territory was being eroded.[2] This process was succinctly defined as 'de-territorialisation' and was described by Newman as:

> This notion of absolute form of political legitimacy that occurs within a rigidly defined state territory, determined by the course of human-made boundaries, is being called into question. State sovereignty is, so it is argued, being broken down as boundaries

have become more permeable than in the past and no longer fulfil one of their basic functions – to act as physical barriers to transboundary movement. (Pratt and Brown 2000: 20)

Even in the midst of presumed 'de-territorialisation', many nation states and their populations remained passionate about territory.[3] However, the pervading sense of global insecurity in the wake of the 11 September 2001 attacks has led many more states to re-examine their territorial boundaries less as areas of interaction with neighbouring states, and more as areas that need to be monitored and secured.

1.2 Boundaries, defence and territorial conflict

Historically, states viewed their boundaries from a defensive perspective, as the ramparts from which to defend their territory. The securing of a land boundary along its entire length, over hills and mountains, across streams, rivers, etc. was traditionally intended to meet an organized military threat from an opposing state, usually within a dispute over territory (i.e. fear of conquest). Some famous historical examples of extensive, man-made boundary defences include the Great Wall of China, the Roman Hadrian's Wall, the French Maginot Line and, more recently, the Iron Curtain between East and West Germany.[4] Changes in military technology through the twentieth century led to a decline in the boundary as a line of defence, as forces and tactics gained mobility and weapons gained range. These developments were indicative of warfare between large organized military forces, able to quickly seize and hold territory. But states have identified new threats, outside the context of combat between national armies, which have prompted a return to old defensive measures.

That traditional notion of a defensively secured boundary continues in long-running territorial disputes around the world such as in Korea, where standard military forces stretch along a boundary or line facing opposing military forces. It was thought such measures were becoming increasingly anachronistic in a post-Cold War world, which envisioned an end to the macro-territorial conflict between opposing state military forces. Nevertheless, recently two states within prolonged territorial disputes, India and Israel, have begun establishing boundary defence and security measures. The nature of these recent measures reflects the new threats to states, identified as small irregular forces (e.g. terrorists/ insurgents), illegal immigration and smuggling, rather than state-versus-state conflict. But within the potential settlement of these territorial disputes, boundary security measures may have much more effect on the legal and political battles than on actual battlefield tactics.

1.3 Boundary security outside territorial disputes

The events of 11 September 2001 have re-awakened the traditional sense of the international boundary as a line of defence for the state. In the period following the terrorist attacks on the United States, many countries around the world initially tightened security at airports, sea ports and major crossing points along land boundaries, in an effort to thwart the movement of militants and terrorists. Subsequently, popular demand for protection from terrorists has expanded to include a call for governments to address other cross-boundary problems, including weapons and drugs smuggling and illegal immigration. Under the influence of popular opinion clamouring for increased security, and with attention already focused on the major points of entry, many governments have focused substantial security resources along their land boundaries.

The increase in boundary security measures in the post-September 11 environment has occurred along boundaries or through territories which are both in dispute and not in dispute between neighbouring states. Such measures along agreed and undisputed boundaries are certainly nothing new, but the scale and number of the recent increases has occurred at a time when the separation between the territories of two states was hoped to be more cooperative and less definitive; more zonal and less than linear. Under this argument, fixed boundary defences within territorial disputes such as Korea could have been considered simply an exception, a relic of another time where standard forces faced off over large tracts of territory. Concepts of 'de-territorialisation' envisioned less rigid definition of territory with no real need for boundary defences along agreed boundaries between seemingly friendly neighbouring states. However, it now seems apparent that the international community is disapproving of states that have not imposed tight boundary security measures. The popular concept seems to be that states with insecure boundaries might be used as potential harbours for trans-national militants/terrorists.

This study hopes to give an overview of the exact nature of the new boundary security measures introduced within disputed territory and along several undisputed boundaries. From analysis of the case studies, it will be seen what influence the imposition of border security measures might have in terms of dispute settlement and perceptions about bilateral relations.

2 Boundary security measures in disputed areas

2.1 Territorial and boundary disputes

It is important, at the outset, to make the difficult distinction between territorial disputes and boundary disputes. With significant overlap and no clear distinction between the two types, many disputes could easily be defined as relating to both territory and boundaries. Territorial disputes involve the disputed title to sovereignty usually over a large area of territory and its population. In some cases a territorial dispute may not involve land boundaries, as in the case of disputed islands[5] or in cases where the extent of territory is clearly defined. However, a territorial dispute will often have a boundary element, in terms of defining the exact extent of the disputed territory. Boundary disputes on land concern the precise definition of the course of an international boundary between two states. Sovereignty over territory is usually not the central focus of a boundary dispute, but rather the exact definition of territory. Obviously it can be argued that even in a boundary dispute where the territory involved may be very small, that the dispute involves claims to sovereignty, but the issues involved with boundary definition are more specific.

In many cases the boundary element is an extremely important aspect of the territorial dispute and usually manifests in the post-conflict settlement process. Although the scale of territory in dispute is usually much smaller, a boundary dispute can be just as volatile as a territorial dispute. So while territorial and boundary disputes can be distinguished very roughly as separate categories, a boundary dispute can very easily develop from a territorial dispute. As J.G. Merrills (1999: 98) points out '... because establishing title and determining its extent are separate questions, deciding that a particular piece of territory belongs to a certain state may generate further disputes about boundaries.'

3 Recent boundary security measures in Kashmir and the West Bank

The territorial disputes between India and Pakistan over the province of Jammu/Kashmir, and between Israel and Palestine are perhaps the two highest-profile territorial disputes, as they involve disputed title over large areas of territory and population. In neither case does the dispute exclusively concern the actual position of an international boundary, although it will certainly need to be addressed in the settlement of the territorial dispute. Most importantly for this discussion, there have been recent, unilateral efforts to erect border security measures, including fencing and walls, between the opposing sides. These efforts have both been sharply criticized, particularly by the opposing parties, in relation to their influence in the potential settlement of these territorial disputes.

3.1 India and Pakistan (Kashmir/Jammu – The Line of Control)

The dispute between India and Pakistan over the region of Jammu and Kashmir dates back to 1947 when the Maharajah of Kashmir agreed to accede to the newly independent state of India. Pakistan refuted this accession and fighting broke out in 1948. In 1949 a cease fire line was agreed by the two sides in the Karachi Agreement, but fighting broke out again in 1971 and several areas on either side of the cease fire line changed hands. The two sides signed another cease fire agreement in 1972 (the Simla Agreement) which established the Line of Control (LoC), generally following the 1949 cease fire line with several minor deviations.

Current situation

The LoC essentially marks the limit of the respective forces as defined in the 1972 Simla Agreement. No official buffer zone has ever officially been established,[6] but the forces are certainly separated at varying distances along the LoC by something akin to an informal no-man's-land. Scattered gunfire is frequently exchanged, although a current

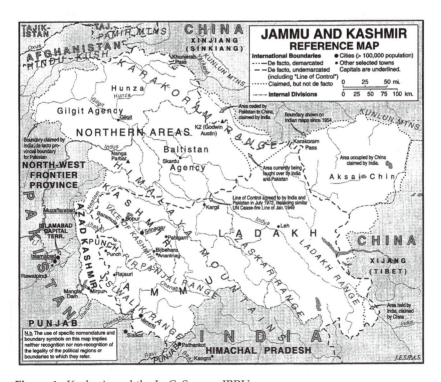

Figure 1. Kashmir and the LoC. Source: IBRU

cease fire established in 2003 appears to be holding. The extent of the military fortifications along the LoC is unknown, but certainly involves a large number of static emplacements originally intended to defend against military forces. The UN Military Observer Group India/Pakistan (UNMOGIP) ostensibly continues to observe the cease fire although it has very little influence over the opposing forces, possessing only 44 military observers.[7] The LoC itself has never been marked on the ground by fencing or other means.[8]

Fence along the LoC

With opposing military forces in a deadlock along the Line of Control, India currently believes its most immediate threat is from Kashmiri militants who cross the LoC from Pakistani-controlled areas and commit terrorist attacks within Indian-held Kashmir. These are not regular Pakistani military forces, although Islamabad has in the past admitted to giving the militants what it termed 'moral support'. In the recent climate of the 'war on terror', Pakistan has made efforts to restrict the activities of the Kashmiri militants within areas under its control. Nevertheless, in 2001 India began construction of a 340 mile-long fence (in some places electrified) along its side of the LoC, including a variety of motion and thermal imaging sensors to detect cross-boundary incursions. Temporary mud walls reportedly were built in some areas to protect those constructing the fence itself from Pakistani shelling and snipers. There is no reason to believe that the boundary fence is a strategic component of India's military defence against a full-scale assault by Pakistan's military forces. Instead, it is clearly meant to monitor and deter the movement of small groups and/or individuals across the LoC.

Pakistan has reacted sharply to India's actions, believing that such fencing is an effort by India to validate the LoC as an official boundary between the two states. This is despite the fact that India's fencing does not directly follow the LoC and is actually well behind the line itself (up to several miles in some places). But in the context of the dispute, Pakistan continues to claim the whole province of Jammu/Kashmir, and therefore any division of the province might be perceived as a loss of territory. India also continues to claim title to the entire Jammu/Kashmir region, but the LoC places a substantial portion of the region under Indian control. Therefore, with the territorial upper hand, it is clear that India is less eager to settle the status of the region *en masse*.[9] Whether or not India had any degree of territorial aspirations in mind when choosing to construct the fencing, it is the sense of permanence implied by the fence that has prompted such a strong retort from Pakistan, which views the fencing by India as a unilateral validation of the LoC as a permanent division, a hardening of the line into an international boundary.

3.2 Israel and Palestine (West Bank)

The situation in the volatile region of Israel and the Occupied Territories of the West Bank and Gaza Strip (Palestine) remains another long-standing and intransigent territorial dispute. After the Second World War and Britain's withdrawal from its mandate in Palestine, the UN divided the mandate area into Jewish and Arab states.[10] Arab populations within Palestine and in neighbouring Arab states objected to the partition and Jewish forces fought Arab forces to maintain an independent Israel. Several armistice agreements were signed in 1949 which established armistice lines separating the areas held by opposing forces. In 1967, Israeli forces, pre-empting an attack by the neighbouring Arab states, crossed the armistice 1949 lines and occupied areas beyond the lines. Therefore, since 1967 the West Bank has been occupied by Israeli forces, with no organized state military force in opposition on the ground in the West Bank or Gaza Strip. With this in mind, the Palestinians in the occupied territories have relied on irregular militants to engage the occupying Israeli military force, resulting in terrorist activities on both sides.

1949 Armistice: The 'green line'

Because there is no formal military force opposing Israel's occupation of the West Bank, it is easy to lose sight of the fact that this was once a territorial dispute with a separation of opposing military forces. On 3 April 1949, the armistice line, or 'green line', was drawn in the West Bank, separating Jordanian and Jewish forces.[11] In most places it eventually constituted a single line[12] but in Jerusalem and several other areas, two cease fire lines formed no-man's-land areas. A UN contingent monitored the cease fire, but it gradually eroded from the armistice line after 1949 and by 1967 there was little appreciable UN presence. The 'green line' has been the topic of much discussion in the myriad settlement plans proposed up to the present day, but it has certainly never held the status of an international boundary. As is the case in Kashmir, Korea and Cyprus, the 'green line' is simply a cease fire line indicating the position of military forces at the conclusion of hostilities.

However, from 1949 until 1967 this line did serve as the *de facto* boundary between Israel and the Arab-controlled territories. Since 1967, with Israeli occupation of the West Bank, the 'green line' generally ceased to function as a *de facto* boundary.[13] However, criticism of this legally questionable occupation has kept memories of the 'green line' at the forefront of negotiations. In addition, Palestine continues to claim that the 1949 'green line' did gain a high degree of legal validity from the wording of Article 1(i) of the 1967 UN Security Council Resolution

242 which called for: 'Withdrawal of Israel armed forces from territories occupied in the recent conflict.' The reference to 'territories' is believed by many to refer to those territories east of the 'green line'.

2003: Israel–Palestine security barrier and wall

In 2003 Israeli forces began construction of a new security wall in an attempt to restrict the movement of irregular militant forces accused of conducting suicide bombings within Israel. The Israeli government officially refers to this as the 'security barrier', while the Palestinian Authority (and many outside observers) have used various other terms, including 'apartheid wall'. In some more populated areas, particularly around East Jerusalem, the security wall consists of a massive 18 to 20 foot-high concrete wall with frequent watch towers.[14] In less-densely populated areas the fortifications include a security fence, less-frequent watch towers and a variety of motion sensors, thermal imaging and sanded-track to identify crossing points. It is even rumoured that remotely controlled automatic machine guns will be installed in some places along the barrier. Monitoring is so advanced that the Israeli military claims it can respond to an intrusion along the barrier within six minutes in some places (particularly around Jerusalem).

As with India's fence along the LoC, Israel's security cordon is not designed to repel full-scale, organized military assault, such as the positions along the 'de-militarised zone' between North and South Korea. One key difference is that Israel has built sections of the barrier well beyond the 1949 armistice line, while India's fencing is entirely within its side of the LoC. Much of the controversial course of the Israeli security barrier does not follow the 1949 'green line'; instead it cuts a looping path well to the east, encircling a number of large Jewish settlements, and projected expansions to settlements. This has left many Palestinian villages and towns cut off from one another and, in many cases, from the fields in which people work, schools in which children study and markets where they shop. Interrupting the normal movement patterns of residents in the areas, there is the potential for the population patterns to shift as Palestinians are left detached by the security barrier.

4 Conclusions on the recent boundary security measures in disputes areas

4.1 Meeting the threat

The security measures put in place by both India and Israel are more focused on surveillance rather than on direct military confrontation.[15]

These measures are reflexive of the perceived threat which prompted them to be put into place and the environment within which they are placed.[16] The threats being addressed are small groups or individual militants and/or arms smugglers, which pose a security risk in terms of terrorist attacks on civilian population or military installations. However, such forces are unlikely to gain and actually hold territory. The fortifications, emplacements and military presence along Korea's DMZ (one might also include the forces of Eritrea and Ethiopia along the UN-monitored temporary security zone and, at one time, the former emplacements through Cyprus) were designed to meet a large-scale opposing military threat. The threat in those situations was that opposing forces had the capability to gain and hold territory, unlike the security threats in Kashmir and Israel which have provoked the recent boundary security measures.

4.2 Boundary dispute from territorial dispute

These two territorial disputes can be shown against the backdrop of the Eritrea–Ethiopia boundary dispute, which exemplifies the development of a boundary dispute from a territorial dispute. After Eritrea's 30-year conflict for separation from Ethiopia, Eritrea gained independence in 1993. But at this settlement of the territorial dispute, the position of the boundary remained unclear. With simmering animosity, a boundary war ensued from 1998 to 2000. At the conclusion of these hostilities a second settlement phase emerged where the boundary was the key issue. An arbitral tribunal, the Eritrea–Ethiopia Boundary Commission (EEBC), was set up to delimit the boundary. Unfortunately, as critics have argued, this second settlement process between 2000 and 2002 was somewhat rushed as the EEBC was given a hurried schedule for arbitration. The decision of the EEBC in 2002 has also been criticized for not addressing the more sensitive issues involved in the boundary dispute in a pragmatic rather than legalistic manner, especially concerning the position and significance of the village of Badme. Consequently, tensions between Eritrea and Ethiopia have again increased, still within the context of a boundary dispute, which continues to sour relations and deter resolution.

The Eritrea/Ethiopia example clearly indicates that if the boundary is not properly addressed in the settlement of a territorial dispute, there is the distinct possibility of further conflict. In the cases of both Jammu/Kashmir and the West Bank, if a permanent and adequate boundary solution is not addressed in the settlement of the territorial dispute, they could easily evolve into future boundary disputes.

Table 11.1 Evolution of the Eritrea–Ethiopia boundary dispute

Tension	Territorial Dispute	Boundary Dispute
War		
		1998–2000
High Tension	1991	
Moderate Tension		
		2004
Low Tension		
Settlement Phase		
(Boundary)		
Permanent Settlement		

4.3 De facto boundaries and acquiescence

Within territorial disputes, a *de facto* boundary can be established when hostilities between opposing forces cease. In the cases of both Korea and Cyprus, the separation of opposing forces in a territorial dispute has emerged as the *de facto* boundary.[17] Such *de facto* boundaries cannot be assumed to then become the legal (*de jure*), definitive boundary, even if title to the territory in question is unclear.[18] Nevertheless, when the boundary is addressed in negotiations during the settlement of a territorial dispute, a *de facto* boundary such as a cease fire line may prove to be the best starting point for delimitation of a *de jure* boundary, because it indicates the respective extent of control by the parties. Certainly many issues will be influential in negotiations before a *de jure* boundary is delimited, but the *de facto* line will always be the starting point unless there is significant goodwill between the parties to choose an alternative.

It is debateable whether or not the increased boundary security measures implemented by India and Israel actually constitute attempts to gain territory. India has argued that its security fence in Kashmir is located within its side of the LoC, which Pakistan would then counter is not necessarily Indian territory. Israel has argued that the path of the security barrier is to protect Israeli settlements, which, as the logic goes, must then be considered territory of Israel. The Palestinian Authority – and many outside observers – would argue that the territory was not Israeli to begin with. Both India and Israel have responded to criticism by emphasizing that in both cases the lines in question are simply cease fire or armistice lines which legally cannot be construed as international boundaries. India has emphasized that the LoC is a cease fire line and not an international boundary, therefore there is nothing to fear from the fence and security measures. Israel would give the same justification for ignoring the 1949 armistice line in the West Bank; the security barrier does not have to follow the 'green line' since it is not an international boundary.

In essence, the disparity between the two situations from a territorial perspective is that while India may be seeking to validate a *de facto* boundary (the LoC), Israel is seeking to create a new *de facto* boundary and invalidate what had been conceived by many to have been the *de facto* boundary (and some believe to have significant legal validity).[19] Perhaps, as Palestine fears, by encircling its settlements Israel is hoping that the path of the security barrier will supplant the 1949 'green line' as the starting point in future negotiations, or at least shift populations to affect further the position of a future boundary.[20] Likewise, in Jammu/ Kashmir, the fencing along the LoC by India further erodes the notion that settlement will involve the region; it instead emphasizes the LoC as the logical starting point for negotiations.

However, the true significance of cease fire or armistice lines in boundary making may not just be as starting points for negotiation, but in their *de facto* influence on the resultant positioning of populations on the ground. Because a *de facto* boundary will have affected settlement patterns on the territorial landscape, their enormous political significance in negotiations will be very influential. Endowing *de facto* lines with implied permanence, these boundary security measures complicate potential dispute resolution by reducing flexibility in negotiations and increasing the political significance of changes to such lines.[21] While fences can be removed relatively easily, changes in settlement patterns on the territorial landscape are much more difficult to undo.

There is a complicated process in international law by which a *de jure* (or legal) boundary might be created due to acquiescence and estoppel.

Briefly, this process entails the acquiescence of state A to the known presence of state B's sovereign activity within state A's territory. If state A does not protest the presence of state B, or in some way express its belief that state B does not have title to that territory, then state A may be said to have estopped its rights to that territory. Hence state B could gain legal title to that territory. Both Pakistan and Palestine do not wish to appear to acquiesce to the presence of Israel and India in territory they believe to be rightfully their own. This has also encouraged persistent official and international criticism of the boundary measures imposed by India and Israel (more significantly), including the recent 2004 International Court of Justice Advisory Opinion on the Israeli separation wall.

5 Boundary security measures in undisputed boundary areas

The recent increase in boundary security measures has not been confined to those areas of territorial or boundary disputes. Several nations around the world have dramatically increased security presence along boundaries which are not in dispute with neighbouring states. In each of the following cases, there is an agreed international boundary in place and there are no significant territorial claims or disputes along the boundary in the areas where security measures have been increased.

5.1 Botswana–Zimbabwe

In 2003 Botswana began construction of a 300 mile-long fence along its eastern boundary with Zimbabwe, roughly between the town of Francistown in Botswana and Tuli in Zimbabwe. The fence is reportedly 2.4 metres in height (although some other reports describe it up to 4 metres in height) and electrified (although it has also been reported that not all sections can be fully charged). Botswana officially claims that this fencing was erected in an effort to prevent cattle from straying into Botswana from Zimbabwe. Livestock fencing lies along the boundaries of several southern African states, since it is common when livestock diseases (such as foot-and-mouth) break out in one state for foreign markets to refuse imported livestock from neighbouring states unless boundary fencing is in place.[22]

However, Zimbabwe believes that Botswana's boundary fencing serves a very different purpose. Many communities on Botswana's side of the boundary have recently complained of a serious crime wave which has been blamed on an increase in the number of refugees fleeing Robert Mugabe's regime and the economic conditions in Zimbabwe. Whether the increase in criminal activity is a direct result of these refugees or not, it is true that such an influx of refugees is likely to have some kind of destabilizing effect, particularly in Botswana's borderland populations. Critics, particularly from Zimbabwe, have accused Botswana of erecting the fence to prevent the movement of people rather than livestock.[23] While many livestock boundary fences in southern Africa are electrified (e.g. some of the Botswana–Namibia boundary fencing), the true nature of Botswana's fencing may be thinly veiled, as livestock fences do not generally reach 3 to 4 metres in height.

5.2 Saudi Arabia–Yemen

After a protracted boundary dispute, Saudi Arabia and Yemen finally delimited their land boundary in June 2000 through a treaty signed in Jeddah. Demarcation of the boundary was undertaken in 2001 and completed in 2003. In spite of boundary demarcation, Saudi Arabia claimed that illegal arms trafficking from Yemen into Saudi Arabia continued through the vast desert sections of the boundary (the so-called 'Empty Quarter'). In an effort to deter smugglers, Saudi Arabia began erecting a barrier along a 95 km stretch of the newly demarcated boundary between two mountains, which was a known transit route for arms smuggling.

The barrier consisted of a 3 metre-high, disused above-ground oil pipeline filled with concrete stretching across the desert. Yemen quickly criticized the barrier, stating that such a barrier contravened the 2000 Jeddah boundary agreement which established a 20 km no-man's-land on either side of the boundary as a joint grazing area for the nomadic tribes in the region. The powerful Shi-ite Wayilah tribe in Yemen (which possesses its own private army) strongly objected to the Saudi separation barrier, comparing it with Israel's security wall. The nomadic tribe also rejected the boundary delimited by the 2000 Jeddah Agreement, stating in a communiqué to the Yemeni government: 'We are renewing our objection to the agreements that created a barrier between us and our lands and our property.'

Saudi Arabia responded to Yemeni criticism by stating that it was erecting the pipeline within its own territory as an effort to curb the illegal arms smuggling and that the barrier in no way resembled Israel's separation fence. Some unconfirmed reports indicated that the barrier was located within 100 metres of the boundary in some areas, but Saudi officials stated that the barrier was located north of the 20 km buffer zone. However, in February 2004 Saudi Arabia halted construction of the barrier after 42 km, presumably in response to Yemen's objections and in particular after significant pressure from Egypt and the United States. The Yemeni government released a statement in February 2004 stating that the differences had been settled and Saudi Arabia had agreed to dismantle the barrier.[24]

5.3 Bangladesh–India

In 2000 India drew up plans and began construction of boundary fencing along its 4096 km boundary with Bangladesh. At the end of 2003 Phase I of the project was nearing completion, with 857 km of fencing having been erected. Phase II, which envisions fencing an additional 2429 km, is estimated to be complete by 2007, according to India's Ministry of Home Affairs, Department of Boundary Management.[25] The position of the land boundary between Bangladesh and India is not in dispute; however, India claims that militants participating in a variety of insurgencies within northeast India have been crossing the loosely monitored boundary into Bangladesh to escape pursuit and to traffic weapons. At least two of these groups are related to tribal insurgency movements in the Indian state of Tripura. They supposedly conduct hit-and-run-style attacks in India before fleeing back into Bangladesh. However, Bangladesh refutes the notion that the militants are being harboured in its territory, stating that Bangladesh has been vigilant in combating these militants. Nevertheless, India has increased its number of boundary troops and begun fencing along lengthy sections of the boundary believed to be frequently crossed by militants, convinced that Bangladesh is not doing enough to stop the militants. In addition, illegal migration across this boundary from Bangladesh into India has increased and become problematic.

The security fence is reportedly a multi-layer barbed wire fence (apparently not electrified) built within Indian territory and set back from the boundary, providing a kind of no-man's-land of unspecified width between the fence and boundary. The landscape in many of the boundary areas is striated by numerous streams and rivers. In such areas where the boundary traverses rivers, India has erected floodlights to aid in monitoring any illegal movements through the watercourses. India has also increased the number of boundary troops in the area and the amount of surveillance and monitoring equipment along the boundary. Some Indian villages within the path of the boundary fence have contested its construction and are pursuing action in the courts. Supposedly India is restricting residents from living in dwellings within 150 yards of the boundary with Bangladesh. While Bangladesh has reacted sharply to India's boundary security measures, it has rejected calls from India for joint boundary operations and reserves much of its criticism for India's new river projects which could have a severe affect on the water supply to Bangladesh. In another sign of the times, the population of India's Manipur region just east of Bangladesh has apparently requested that the

Figure 11.2 Bangladesh–India boundary and areas where insurgents are active. Source: IBRU *Boundary and Security Bulletin*, 9.3.

boundary between India and Burma also be fenced and monitored. The regional government believes that such measures on the Burma–India boundary, which is not in dispute, would help restrict the movement of illegal weapons and drugs.

5.4 Malaysia–Thailand

In February 2004 Thailand announced plans to build a concrete fence along parts of its 600 km boundary with Malaysia, but construction has yet to begin. The plans for the boundary fence were announced after a string of attacks on police and Buddhist monks in the three southeastern provinces of Thailand (Pattani, Yala and Narathiwat) near the land boundary with Malaysia. While most of Thailand is predominantly Buddhist, these three southernmost regions have majority Muslim populations. On 29 April 2004, a string of attacks by Islamic insurgents on police outposts in Thailand's three southernmost provinces were met with a heavy-handed response by Thai police and over 100 people were killed as a result. Since those attacks, Malaysia has poured troops into the areas along the Thai boundary, hoping to stem the flight of the militants.

Thailand has long known that Islamic separatists were operating in the southeast region, but claimed that the groups often sought refuge in Malaysia across the loosely monitored boundary. Thailand admitted that insurgent groups were active within its territory, but felt that the boundary fence was necessary to prevent the separatists from seeking refuge in Malaysia. The Malaysian government was quick to state that its territory had never been used to harbour any insurgents and that it would not allow such militants sanctuary within Malaysian territory.

The boundary in the area is also a well-known smuggling route for drugs, and since the April 2004 attacks some joint surveillance measures have been undertaken by the two countries, including joint patrols along the boundary. Generally bilateral ties between Malaysia and Thailand are very good.[26] In fact, it is likely that Thailand halted its plans to construct boundary fencing when Malaysia increased its troop numbers in the boundary areas and voiced its commitment to cracking down on militants in the region. While the boundary fence is currently on hold, even against Malaysia's protests.[27]

5.5 Responses to the increase in boundary security along undisputed boundaries

5.5.1 Addressing the problems

Each of the above cases where boundary security measures have been recently increased has a unique set of circumstances. The measures being put into place do seem to reflect the nature of the perceived threat or problem. Saudi Arabia's concrete-filled pipeline barrier along its boundary with Yemen was an example of security measures being uniquely adapted to thwart the specific problem of arms smugglers crossing the vast stretches of desert. Botswana's electrified fence is liable to be a deterrent for both illegal migrants as well as stray cattle. Similar measures to deter illegal migration exist along the Mexico–US boundary in California and the Morocco–Spain boundary at the enclave of Ceuta, although the fencing and monitoring is more sophisticated. The surveillance methods and fencing being imposed by India along parts of its boundary with Bangladesh are clearly intended to monitor and deter the boundary crossings of small groups of militants. Although within the context of territorial disputes, there are obvious parallels with the measures undertaken by Israel and India directed at similar threats. Plans for Thailand's security fence and boundary security measures along the boundary with Malaysia are likely to be similar to India's practices on the boundary with Bangladesh.

5.5.2 The neighbour's retort

The one constant in each scenario is the negative response from the neighbouring state. In each case the neighbouring state has been critical of the boundary fencing or other security measures. This is despite the lack of dispute between the neighbouring states either concerning territory or the position of the boundary, in these specific areas.[28] In each case the criticism has been slightly different, but the clear consensus is that the neighbouring state has felt that boundary security measures negatively affect the relationship between the two states when no obvious dispute is felt to exist.

Zimbabwe has rejected Botswana's claim that its boundary fence is for livestock and has instead accused Gaberone of sealing off the boundary and mistreating migrants from Zimbabwe. This argument essentially ignores the basis for the fencing, namely that there is an increase in migration from Zimbabwe. Instead of addressing the cause of the problem, the reason for the increase in migration (i.e. poor economic conditions), Zimbabwe has directed criticism towards the fence itself.

Yemen may have had a sound legal argument for criticizing Saudi Arabia's boundary barrier (if it was placed less than 20 km from the boundary) based on the no-man's-land regime along their newly delimited boundary established in the 2000 agreement. However, again it might be implied the root cause of the problem (cross-border arms smuggling) was not being adequately addressed by both states. Likewise, Yemen was critical of Saudi Arabia's unilateral methods.

Bangladesh may have felt that India's boundary fencing and surveillance were a direct comment on the ability of Bangladesh to combat separatists within its own territory. Perhaps the implication was that India believed Bangladesh was being soft on or even offering safe harbour to militants.

In a similar fashion, Thailand may also have been posing the same comment to Malaysia when it announced plans for boundary fencing. Malaysia may then have felt it necessary to prove its commitment to regional security. This would then explain the connection between the influx of Malaysian troops into the boundary region and the concurrent shelving of Thailand's boundary fence plans.

5.6 Conclusions on recent increases in boundary security measures along undisputed boundaries

While the practical expressions of boundary security on the ground are unique to the terrain involved and to the threat or problem of the situation, the outward political expression as interpreted by the neighbouring state appears to be constant. The recent, unilateral boundary security escalations along undisputed boundaries tend to imply that a neighbouring state has an internal problem that is not being adequately addressed domestically. In some cases the original problem may not be the presence of militants in a neighbouring state, but the attraction of sanctuary in that neighbouring state due perhaps to lack of control in a border area. This could result in what might be termed the 'Iron Curtain effect' whereby security measures turn inward to thwart movement out of the state rather than movement into the state from outside. In the current climate of states combating militants, insurgents and terrorists, no state wants to be depicted as being weak or unable to maintain security within its own boundaries.

In addition, perhaps the increase in security measures along undisputed boundaries conveys the sense of conflict where none exists. In that sense, several neighbouring states have labelled the increase in boundary security a 'sealing' of the boundaries. But the threats (i.e. separatists or smugglers) or problems (i.e. immigration) that have prompted the boundary security measures are beyond the control of either state. In terms of territory, the threats overlap the two states. Therefore by improving its boundary security, a state essentially is attempting to take responsibility for problems exclusively within its own territory. Many times such security measures allow states to deal more effectively with domestic threats or problems. Such measures along undisputed boundaries do not legally threaten the territorial integrity of a neighbouring state as long as they recognize the agreed international boundary. The unfortunate caveat is that the neighbouring state may feel slighted that the overlapping threat or problem could not be addressed cooperatively. Such a political climate is not conducive to cooperation. Hard boundaries such as those marked by fences and walls discourage transborder cooperation which can have dramatic effects beyond the issue of security, such as impeding the economic development of borderland areas and the management of the transboundary environmental resources.

5.7 Final thoughts

Throughout this chapter, the term 'boundary security' has been used in lieu of 'boundary defence'. The nuances in definitions between the terms 'defence' and 'security' pose interesting questions for understanding the significance of this recent increase in boundary security measures. The term 'security' conjures images of jails, fencing and monitoring. Often police are associated with security, as it seems to be associated with a micro-community feeling secure. Defence has a more military connotation, with images such as fortifications and walls springing to mind. Certainly there is a large degree of overlap between the two phrases, but when looking at all the security measures described above, the question can be posed: Do they represent security or defence measures? Many have been described in the media as being 'security measures'. This may underscore the shift in public thinking from the days of fearing macro-territorial conflicts when the demand was for 'defensive' measures, to the more localized threats posed by militants/terrorists which demand 'security' measures. Therefore it might be said that the comparison of boundary defence versus boundary security might be defined by the threats being addressed.

In conclusion, let it suffice to say that the recent increases in boundary security measures along both disputed and undisputed boundaries reveal a true 'hardening' of territory around the world, a return to traditional notions of boundaries being the sites of separation. This hardening not only complicates the settlement of bilateral territorial disputes, but could also affect normal bilateral relations and inhibit worthwhile transborder cooperation. But within a global climate of fear, the sealing of territorial boundaries is a natural reaction of the nation state, and more examples of boundary security measures will likely emerge throughout the world in the near future.

Notes

1 Perhaps the best examples include the influence of environmental regulation which has encouraged the recent increase in the number of transboundary conservation areas, the decline of the rule of capture in mineral/hydrocarbon extraction (particularly offshore) and cross-border ethnic identities.

2 'Sovereignty as a particular spatiality of power and authority seems unsuitable for an increasingly globalised world' (Hudson 1998: 102).

3 Recall that Botswana and Namibia spent tens of millions of dollars adjudicating their dispute over tiny Kasikili/Sedudu Island (which is mostly submerged six months of the year) before the International Court of Justice from 1996 to 1999.

4 Natural features along boundaries have also served a defensive purpose, such as the Rhine River between France and Germany, and the Himalayas isolating Nepal from India.

5 Island disputes will usually involve problems with maritime boundaries. These will not be discussed as this work is concerned with land boundaries.

6 The auspices of the 1949 Karachi Agreement stipulated that no forces could be located within 500 yards of the cease fire line. This might be considered a form of buffer zone, but was included in the 1972 agreement.

7 United Nations, Peacekeeping and Peace and Security Section of the Department of Public Information figures as of 31 March 2004. India does

provide transport and supply to UNMOGIP but does not report violations of the cease fire and largely ignores its presence.

8 'Since the line was expected to last only until agreement had been reached over the permanent disposition of Kashmir, it was not physically demarcated at the time (1949)' (Wirsing 1998: 9).

9 In fact, in its 2002–3 Annual Report, India's Ministry of Defence refers to the 'Line of Control' as the 'International Border'.

10 UN General Assembly Resolution 181 of 29 November 1947.

11 The term 'green line' was coined as a result of the line being marked in green on subsequent official Israeli maps.

12 Although due to the fact that the line was drawn on a 1:250,000 scale map with a thick greased pencil, the line varied in width when applied on the ground, up to some 500 metres in places.

13 Israel, however, has never formally annexed the majority of territory in the West Bank.

14 The size of the wall in these areas is justified by Israeli officials as necessary to deter sniper attacks.

15 The massive section of Israel's security wall in the urban areas is slightly different from the majority of the fencing, as this section is designed to not only repel militants, but also to protect areas from sniper fire.

16 Much of the surveillance and monitoring equipment installed by India along the LoC is of Israeli manufacture, including hand-held thermal imaging devices, ground-based surveillance radar and night vision equipment. Brig. Gurmeet Kanwal 'India-Israel Defence Cooperation: Chinks in the Armour' *Observer Research Foundation Strategic Trends*, 2:23, 14 June 2004 (http://www. observerindia.com/strategic/st040614.htm#2).

17 In both Korea and Cyprus, the division is by buffer or de-militarized zone areas.

18 Clearly this would invalidate the international legal principle that title to territory cannot be acquired by force and would encourage states to gain as much territory as possible by force before reaching a cease fire.

19 US president George Bush voiced support for Ariel Sharon's plan for Israeli withdrawals on 14 April 2004, stating: 'In light of new realities on the ground, including already existing major Israeli population centers, it is unrealistic to expect that the outcome of final status negotiations will be a full and complete return to the armistice lines of 1949.' White House Press Release, 14 April 2004 (www.whitehouse.gov/news/releases/2004/04/20040414-4.html) This opinion was shared by few other world leaders.

20 In addition, any Israeli settlement east of the 'green line' outside of a bilateral agreement invalidates the basis of modern international law that territory cannot be legally gained through force.

21 See especially the Annan Plan for settlement of the Cyprus dispute.

22 The European Union, which is Botswana's biggest destination for exported beef, has in the past threatened to raise tariffs if fencing is not in place when livestock diseases occur in neighbouring states.

23 Zimbabwe has also condemned Botswana's boundary police for being heavy handed in dealing with Zimbabwean migrants.

24 There are no reports confirming that Saudi Arabia has in fact dismantled the barrier.
25 Figures can be seen at http://mha.nic.in/bmmain.htm
26 The two states are members of the Associate of Southeast Asian Nations (ASEAN) which is working towards greater regional cooperation and integration. (See ASEAN Vision 2020.)
27 During June 2004, Thailand was in talks with Burma about possibly fencing their common boundary to prevent drug smuggling.
28 There are disputes between these neighbouring countries that are irrelevant to the discussion at hand. For example, Bangladesh and India dispute sovereignty over South Talpatty Island and their maritime boundary in the Bay of Bengal. However, these are unrelated to the land boundary.

References

Dahlitz, J. (ed.) (1999) *Peaceful Resolution of Major International Disputes* (New York and Geneva: United Nations).
Laitinen, K. (2003) 'Geopolitics of the Northern Dimension: a critical view on security borders', *Geopolitics*, 8:1, pp. 20–44.
Merrills, J.G. (1999) 'International Boundary Disputes in Theory and in Practice: Precedents Established', in J. Dahlitz (ed.) *Peaceful Resolution of Major International Disputes* (New York and Geneva: United Nations), pp. 95–112.
Newman, D. (1995) 'Boundaries in Flux: The "Green Line" Boundary between Israel and the West Bank – Past, Present and Future', *Boundary and Territory Briefing*, 1:7 (International Boundaries Research Unit (IBRU), University of Durham).
Pratt, M. and Brown, J.A. (eds) (2000) *Borderlands Under Stress (International Boundary Studies Series)* (The Hague: Kluwer Law International).
Wirsing, R.G. (1998) 'War or Peace on the Line of Control? The India–Pakistan Dispute over Kashmir turns Fifty', *Boundary and Territory Briefing*, 2:5 (International Boundaries Research Unit (IBRU), University of Durham).

Chapter 12

'Getting ahead of the game': border technologies and the changing space of governance

Katja Franko Aas[1]

In June 2004, a Danish humanitarian agency put up an 8 metre-high wall at the site of a rock festival in Roskilde. The wall was a copy of the wall put up by the Israeli government on the West Bank, with a message 'make peace not walls' written on it. The Roskilde wall was put up as a protest against its original in Israel, and not surprisingly, it elicited heated objections from the Israeli embassy to the Danish government. This minor incident, and numerous other protests against the Israeli wall, can serve as a reminder of the symbolic power that walls and borders still hold today. The fall of the Berlin Wall is probably one of the most potent images depicting, and finally confirming, the fall of communism. On the other hand, we are faced with a discourse about, and increasingly perceive ourselves as, living in a global and a 'borderless' world. The imagery of glossy in-flight magazines portrays modern travel as an effortless experience where our imagination is the only limit.

This chapter seeks to address the changing imagery and material manifestations of borders and territoriality, taking the case of the European Union as a point of departure. The chapter explores a certain dichotomy between the political, economic and cultural imagery of a global, borderless world and, on the other hand, the persistent, even increasing, importance of borders for the European sense of security. I shall examine how the emerging terminology of global flows, zones and networks could offer some useful tools for conceptualizing the border today. The chapter contends that while the emerging global phenomena in a number of ways transform and transcend the traditional space of governance, characteristic of nation states, they also strengthen the salience of state borders, as well as introducing new types and logics of border governance. Rather than seeing borders and global flows as two seemingly dichotomous phenomena, the chapter proposes to see the 'zone' and the 'wall' as mutually supportive. The emerging zones and global information flows are essential in maintaining the strength of the outer walls of contemporary 'fortress continents' (Klein 2003). At the same time, the existence of border controls is vital in managing global flows and maintaining the present, intensely stratified, global order.

The 'Era of Space'

In 1972 Oscar Newman published a book, *Defensible Space,* which received much attention in architectural and criminological literature, and had a profound influence on town planning in subsequent years. In the book, Newman defined territoriality and surveillance as two categories contributing to the establishment of a 'defensible space'. Newman argued that, just as conditions of visibility and surveillance in a space reduce disorder and insecurity, so too clear definitions of borders, with the help of physical as well as symbolic barriers, encourage people's ownership of space and therefore foster security. Although quite common sense, and bordering on the obvious, Newman's findings highlight the intrinsic connection among borders, territory and security.

However, according to some analysts, the connection between territory and security is not an ahistoric entity, intrinsic to any social organization, but rather a historically specific constellation, particularly characteristic of the nation state. Following Castells (1996), Bauman (2002) describes the time when territory was primary guarantee of security as the 'era of space'. The border was then literally meant as a wall around a territory, preventing penetration by the outsiders. Exemplified by the Chinese wall, Hadrian's Wall, designs of medieval castles and cities, and, later, the Berlin Wall, the wall symbolized the borders of the state and the ability of the state to defend itself. Similarly, Mary Douglas (1994) in *Risk and Blame* persuasively shows how distinct borders are essential for a distinct sense of identity, and how communities and groups maintain their sense of identity through the control of the perceived dangers at the borders.

Bauman (1998, 2002) and a number of other observers (Hedetoft 1998) point to the vital importance of territory as a material as well as a symbolic expression of the nation state's ordering capacity and national identity: 'The physicality of territory is of course a material and economic precondition, but its real meaning is symbolic: as locus and *raison d'être* for national "homogeneity" in the orders of modernity' (Hedetoft 1998: 153). The world of nation states is thus essentially a world of territorial states exercising their power through the imposition of order on their territory. This is particularly evident, for example, if one takes a look at a map of Africa, where the clear borders drawn with almost mathematical precision reflect the affinity for order of Africa's colonial rulers. Like the town planners mentioned above, also for nation states, transparency of borders represents a precondition of a modernist order.

Today, the materiality of borders is revealed in a number of locations. The rise of so-called gated communities in a number of countries is a potent reminder of the persistent belief that walls and fences can bring at least some kind of safety. Instead of building walls around cities, like in medieval times, contemporary members of gated communities seem to be afraid of the dangers that reside within their community, thus dividing cities and suburbs into a number of smaller areas which are put under surveillance. In their illuminating study, *Fortress America*, Blakely and Snyder (1997) show that never before in US history has 'forting up' been so widespread, not just among upper class, but also among middle and lower middle class Americans. Gated communities represent 'the notion of community as an island' (Blakely and Snyder 1997: 3), an attempt of their residents to run away from the disorder and messiness of communal life, and establish some sense of control. On the other hand, the gated community also exemplifies a phenomenon taking place on a larger scale, namely the emerging global patterns of inequality and social exclusion. Fortress America is emerging also on a broader level, through the fortification of the American border. America and Europe are today being described as 'fortress continents' (Klein 2003). According to Klein (2003), fortress continents are blocs of nations, with fortified external borders, and easy internal access to cheap labour (for example, Mexican, Polish, Hungarian, etc.). While liberalizing their internal borders, fortress continents seal off their external borders, thus creating 'locked-out continents', whose residents aren't needed even for their cheap labour (Klein 2003).

Therefore, not only Israel is building a wall in an attempt to strengthen its national security, but also Europe is extensively fortifying its borders. While to Europeans, and other Western citizens, the world may increasingly appear 'borderless' and 'connected', the outer borders of Europe hold a sinister reality reflected in almost daily reports about deaths of immigrants trying to enter the fortress Europe. For coast guard officials in Italy, Greece and Spain the sight of ruined boats and drowned bodies on the shores is becoming a regular part of their work. On 2 October 2004 a boat carrying 75 migrants, on their way to the Italian island of Lampedusa, sank a few kilometres off the Tunisian coast. Only 11 people survived. However, total numbers of migrant casualties are difficult to estimate, as numerous other less-publicized deaths of migrants go unregistered. Also, Turkey and other EU neighbours are becoming affected by the growing flow of migrants and the accompanying trafficking trade. In one day, BBC reports, Turkish authorities found bodies of 24 illegal migrants, among them nine children, frozen to death. On the same day five Pakistanis were found drowned in another incident on the shores of Turkey's Aegean coast.[2] In 2001, the EU countries had 380,000 applications for asylum, and only about 1 to 5 per cent were successful, although not everyone who failed actually got deported.[3] It has been pointed out that the dangerous clandestine routes of entry into the EU, operated by various smuggling networks, are partly created and sustained by the EU's tough immigration and asylum policy. The rise in the numbers of clandestine migrants reportedly started after the EU countries in 1995 started introducing tighter visa requirements, thus forcing the third-world migrants to choose other, more dangerous, routes to come to Europe. The list of countries requiring a visa to enter the EU, the so-called 'black list', has expanded from 70 in 1985 to over 126 in 1995 (Bigo and Guild 2004).

Reducing not only numbers of granted asylums, but also of asylum applications, is increasingly becoming a mark for measuring a government's success. Thinking pre-emptively, the Norwegian government, for example, invested considerable resources not only in the fortification of its borders, but also in spreading the information about it to possible migrant populations, airing, for example, informative advertisements about tough Norwegian asylum procedures on national televisions of various potential countries of asylum. A similar 'overseas information campaign' was undertaken, among others, also by the Australian government in order to discourage illegal immigrant and asylum flows from its shores.

The point here is that, although there is an undeniable 'wall-like' quality to the Western borders, the strength of these borders also depends on a number of additional strategies, particularly on a network of information flows and fortified strategic points, which seem to diffuse the wall-like impression. In what follows, I shall examine whether the work of analysts arguing for the network-like nature of contemporary social and power relations, and the terminology of the so-called zones and space of flows, can shed some light on the current nature of borders and space of governance.

Global networks, zones and space of flows

The events of September 11 tend to be described as 'global events', 'when the whole world watched the surreal and stranger-than-Hollywood event as planes with live passengers flew into and demolished two of the largest buildings in the world' (Urry 2002: 57). New York seems to be the epitome of a global city, and the fallen twin towers the supreme symbols of its power. It is therefore no surprise that in the contemporary imagination the events of September 11 tend almost exclusively to be talked about as the attacks on the twin towers, rather than on the Pentagon and the Pennsylvania airplane.

According to Bauman (2002) the fallen Manhattan towers represent the most potent symbolic reminder of an end of an era – the era of space – the 'annihilation of the protective capacity of space'.

> The events of 11 September made it obvious that no one, however resourceful, distant and aloof, can any longer cut themselves off from the rest of the world.
>
> It has become clear that the annihilation of the protective capacity of space is a double-edged sword: no one can hide from blows, and nowhere is so far away that blows cannot be plotted and delivered from that distance. Places no longer protect, however strongly they are armed and fortified. Strength and weakness, threat and security have now become, essentially, *extraterritorial* (and diffuse) *issues that evade territorial* (and focused) *solutions*. (Bauman 2002: 88; italics original)

New York can thus be seen as the prime example of what Castells (1996) terms a global (mega)city and the so-called network society. In the context of network society, the global, technologically sustained networks of information, commodities and transportation become the primary unit of economic organization and power. The nodes of networks – global cities – thus become globally inter-connected at an unprecedented level, while the territories (and states) surrounding them correspondingly lose their importance. Castells describes the new notion of space as a space of flows, which is primarily not a place, but a process: 'A process by which centers of production and consumption of advanced services, and their ancillary local societies, are connected in a global network, while simultaneously downplaying the linkages with their hinterlands, on the basis of information flows' (Castells 1996: 386). Globally connected and locally disconnected, argues Castells, global cities and networks introduce a qualitatively new and different experience of space, as well as of social organization and stratification.

Global flows and networks thus fundamentally transform the role of the nation state and its control of the territory. The speed and distance of communication and movement make them both difficult to spacialize, and impossible to build a wall around. One of the traditional roles of the nation state – maintenance of order on a certain territory – is thus put in question, forcing some to talk of the 'withering away of nation states' (Bauman 1998: 57). It is perhaps unnecessary to repeat that the process has been deeply connected to insecurity. The events of September 11 therefore simply brought to our full attention 'the dark side of globalization' (Colin Powell in Urry 2002: 58; Lyon 2003: 109). However, insecurity had been much on our lips even before 9/11, evident in the proliferation of writing about globalization and risk. Also, the environmentalist movement has long centred on the notion of global threats, yet it seems as if the fallen twin towers and the subsequent 'war on terror' really brought the message into every single home.

Therefore, contemporary governments seem to be caught between two contradicting impulses: on the one hand, the urge towards increasing securitization of borders, and on the other hand, the awareness of the importance of global flows for sustaining the present world economic order. General Motors, for example, claims that 'for every minute its fleet of trucks is delayed at the US–Canadian border, it loses about $650,000' (Klein 2003). The British White Paper *Secure Borders, Safe Haven* clearly expresses the dichotomy. According to Walters (2004), the White Paper is one of the government's first documents clearly acknowledging not only the need to control migration, but also the beneficial potential of migratory flows. The document stresses the importance of easing movements of certain groups of people, which would benefit the economy by, for example, introducing a so-called Highly Skilled Migrant Programme and Seasonal Agricultural Workers' Scheme. The objective is therefore not to seal off the border but rather to manage it efficiently; 'not to arrest mobility but to tame it; not to build walls, but systems capable of utilizing mobilities and in certain cases deploying them against the sedentary and ossified elements within society' (Walters 2004: 248). *Secure Borders, Safe Haven* therefore clearly states the need not only for more efficient protection of the border, but also for speeding up procedures for 'genuine passengers', one of the measures being the intensified use of biometrics (Home Office 2002: 18).

The challenge here is to allow those who qualify for entry to pass through the controls as quickly as possible, maximising the time spent on identifying those who try to enter clandestinely or by presenting forged documents. […] The less time the Immigration

Service needs to spend on clearing passengers, the more they can concentrate on those who seek to undermine our laws. (Home Office 2002: 17)

How to discern between 'good' and 'bad' global mobilities thus becomes a vital task of contemporary governance. According to Walters (2004), this new task introduces a new image of the state which departs from the traditional image of a social security state. While the social security state was originally organized according to a static notion of class, now, on the other hand, the state is a globally situated entity organized according to a dynamic notion of channelling potentially risky flows of people and goods.

The pre-eminent task of government is to attract and channel flows of resources, whether investment, goods, services, and now flows of (the right kind of) people into one's territory. Gone, for the most part, is the image which underpinned social security: the figure of a coherent national economic system linked in turn to a social order comprised of strata or classes. [...] In its place we find a horizontal, or perhaps 'multilevel' space criss-crossed by movements, flows, and forces. (Walters 2004: 244)

Global travel is an intensely stratified phenomenon and the task of governance is to implement these stratifying mechanisms, rather than to control the movements of people as such; or to use Bauman's (1998: 88) words, to distinguish between those allowed to be 'globally mobile' and those 'doomed to be locally tied'. Today, we seem to have a number of images and identities for describing the global traveller. Roughly speaking, they can be merchants, following Marco Polo's tradition, seeking to expand the scope of their trade; cosmopolitans moving between various world capitals and hot spots, ceaselessly pursuing the best weather and shopping conditions; and refugees, asylum seekers and what Featherstone (2002: 2) terms 'working-class cosmopolitan migrants', with a potential of harbouring among them terrorists and religious fundamentalists.

The terminology of combating trans-national criminal networks plays a crucial role in distinguishing between the flows of global 'goods' and 'bads'. It has been argued, for example, that measures to combat trafficking have been appropriated also as immigration control measures, rather then having as their sole objective to help abused migrant women.[4] Building on Jonathan Simon's (1997) concept of 'governing through crime', Walters (2004: 247) argues that the *Secure Borders* White Paper clearly exemplifies the tendency to 'govern central aspects of global migration by strategies of criminalization and illegalization'. Building on the established image of drug smuggling global networks, the White Paper describes traffickers and smugglers as sophisticated, unscrupulous and brutal organized networks whose 'aim has been to cash in on global increases in migration flows' (Home Office 2002: 16). The government's answer seems to be threefold: increasing penalties, taking advantage of new surveillance technologies, and international cooperation (Home Office 2002).

The point here is that security is essentially connected to the globalizing processes and taming potentially risky mobilities and trans-national criminal networks. Similarly, terrorist networks, epitomized in Al Qaeida, seem to be defined by their ex-territoriality, defying the state-like nature of enemies in the previous world orders. Al Qaeida has been described as the 'McDonalds of terrorism' (Murdoch 2004) – being a 'global brand', using the media to its advantage and assuming a franchise form not unlike the ones used in the contemporary business world. The task of controlling the global flows seems to be increasingly complex, and essentially global. Borders, in a traditional sense of the word, become unable to capture the emerging trans-national and extraterritorial networks of possible threats, such as clandestine immigration, drugs and people trafficking and, of course, terrorism. Speaking about the Chechen terrorist attacks, Russian defence minister Ivanov summarized the thought: 'In essence, war has been declared on us, where the enemy is unseen and there is no front.'[5] The threat of terrorism is today presented as always potentially hidden inside the state, like a 'fifth column', as well as trying to enter from the outside.

The war on terror therefore seems to be an example of a 'stateless war' (Bauman 2002) where both sides 'militate against the imposition of constraints on the newly gained extraterritoriality of the skies or the freedom to ignore or push aside the "laws of nations" where such laws feel inconvenient for the purpose at hand' (Bauman 2002: 93). The trend is reflected in the creation of a kind of 'non-space,'[6] or territory excluded from the territory, at Guantánamo, where the usual rules of national and international law do not apply. The US government, for example, presented an argument that since Al Qaeida is an organization and not a state, the rules of the Geneva Convention do not apply to Al Qaeida combatants. The current war on terror also further reflects the 'withering of the nation state' thesis, as the boundaries between state and private attempts to combat terror and achieve security become increasingly blurred. On the battlefields of Iraq and Afghanistan, soldiers and civilian contractors have become almost indistinguishable and interchangeable.

Beyond the wall

One needs, therefore, to highlight the emergence of myriad alternative strategies of governance which transcend the state itself, and its territory, as the fundamental paradigm for providing security. These strategies are marked by the fact that they aim to take the fight against global threats beyond the borders of national territories as well as inducing the cooperation of non-state agents in the task of border control. The UK *Secure Borders* White Paper thus outlines a clear strategy of averting potentially risky migratory flows before they reach national territory. The measures employed are, among others:

- Continue to deploy our network of Airline Liaison Officers stationed overseas to help prevent improperly documented passengers travelling to the UK.

- Continue to use visa regimes for nationals of countries where there is evidence of the systematic abuse of our controls.

- Continue to deploy immigration officers abroad where this is necessary to check passengers before they travel to the UK.

- Maintain our operational arrangements for UK immigration officers conducting passport checks in France.

- Develop a new concept of screening passengers before they travel to the UK whereby they are checked against IND databases to confirm their eligibility to travel.

- Develop the use of biometric technology, for example, iris or facial recognition and fingerprints, for use in expediting the clearance of particular categories of passenger, whilst at the same time safeguarding these passengers from identity abuse by others.

- Utilise x/gamma ray scanners and CCTV to help locate those seeking to enter illegally, whilst evaluating the latest technology using thermal imaging and acoustic sensors to detect those concealed in vehicles and containers.

- Use mobile task forces as part of an intelligence-led control.

- Work together with European partners, candidate and other countries to strengthen the EU's common borders and enhance border controls on transit routes.

(Home Office 2002: 92)

Using a wide array of technologies, these measures are designed to act pre-emptively and to avert potentially risky individuals before they ever have a chance to enter the national territory. Networks of airline liaison officers, employed by a number of countries, thus work at international airports helping airlines in preventing potentially inadmissible passengers from boarding airplanes. Similarly, the pre-clearance systems allow immigration officials to carry out immigration checks at airports abroad, thus effectively moving the border outside national territory. David Lyon (2003: 123–4) points out that airports in themselves are examples of 'virtual borders, even though they are not always at the geographical edge of the territory concerned'. The objective of airport controls is to check and identify travellers prior to the arrival at their destination. The notion of borders as intervention points outside the nation state territory is also reflected in the recent expansion of the British immigration checks to certain Belgian, French and Dutch cities and ports. British immigration officials are now able to stop and check travellers before they board trains and lorries heading for Britain. The primary objective of these measures is to stop people from claiming asylum. According to British Home Secretary David Blunkett:

> All of this adds up to a further reinforcement of the border controls, the restrictions, the ability to pick up people who shouldn't be coming across the border at all. [...] This is another announcement of working with the French, the Belgians and in future the Dutch, so that we can move our border controls on the European continent and stop people claiming asylum.[7]

Or as the UK immigration services director of border control said:

> It is about *getting ahead of the game*. We don't want this to turn into a problem and by being there in Brussels it won't turn into a problem. People's behaviour will change. We have to watch where the risks [of illegal immigration] are and those risks do change. (italics added)[8]

However, the rationale of intercepting potentially undesirable individuals has been challenged by a recent ruling by the Law Lords, the highest appeal court in the UK. In a case brought up by six Roma passengers who were denied entry to the UK, the court ruled that pre-clearance measures at the Prague airport were 'inherently and systematically discriminatory and unlawful'. The measures were introduced in 2001 in order to avert large numbers of Roma asylum seekers arriving in Britain. Consequently, several hundred passengers, almost all of them Roma, were turned away as 'not bona fide tourists'. The Roma passengers were 400 times more likely to be rejected than non-Roma passengers, primarily on the basis of their appearance and skin colour.[9]

A similar rationale of 'getting ahead of the game' and preventing risks before they reach national territory is also evident in the recent proposition to establish offshore asylum camps outside the EU territory. The British government proposed in 2003 to create 'regional protection zones', which would be close to areas witnessing major flows of people, thus offering to them a 'safe haven' close to home.[10] Britain further suggested the establishment of 'transit centres' on the fringes of the EU, close to the major transit routes in countries such as Albania, Turkey, Morocco, Ukraine and Somalia. Currently, the EU has not yet found consensus about these measures; they were nevertheless favourably received by a number of member states, and pilot projects are already taking place in some African countries. Italy, for example, is moving ahead with establishing three asylum camps in Libya.[11] Furthermore, the EU already exerts considerable pressure on its neighbours, such as Turkey, the Balkans states and ex-Soviet republics, to implement better border controls and ease the EU's refugee workload.[12] A recent EU policy has been the establishment of a so-called 'circle of friends', a zone of neighbouring countries which, among other things, also cooperate in the fight against organized crime, terrorism and migration issues. By using aid and trade as financial incentives, the EU has also signed repatriation agreements with a number of third world countries, which will accept back illegal immigrants coming from or having lived in those countries. The objective of the above-mentioned strategies is clearly to shift the flows of asylum seekers to zones outside the EU. Unfortunately, these zones consist mostly of countries which have considerably poorer resources and human rights records than the EU itself.

My objective so far has been to illustrate how global governance is transcending the nation state, which is particularly evident in the EU and its various institutions. The war on terror has prompted a number of EU initiatives, although with varying success in their implementation. For example: European Common Arrest Warrant; appointment of EU 'counter-terrorism czar'; EU solidarity clause on terrorism; exchange of information about persons, groups, weapons and financial transactions, etc. The EU is also setting up an agency to help manage its external borders. Although without law-enforcement powers, the Agency for the Management of Operational Cooperation at the External Borders is to coordinate national border controls and to boost the fight against illegal immigration (Guardian Weekly 2003).

However, the British *Secure Borders* White Paper also brings to our attention another aspect of contemporary global governance. In addition to dispersing the border to third world countries, the document clearly outlines a strategy of distributing the responsibility of combating potential risks with other non-state actors. The UK and the EU, as well as a number of other countries, thus have legislation which penalizes carriers for transporting passengers without the required documents. Guild (2004) argues that these carrier sanctions effectively transfer the task of carrying of border controls from state agents to commercial agents. A third world traveller encounters the border of the EU already when trying to book an airplane ticket or contacting a travel agency. The state (and the EU) is still involved in the process, although only indirectly and at a distance, by providing carriers with necessary instructions for carrying out the controls.[13] This model of 'policing at a distance' (Bigo and Guild 2004) effectively co-opts commercial agents and consulates into the task of carrying out EU border controls and identity checks inside third country territories. This distribution of responsibility responds to what has been elsewhere described as 'responsibilization strategy' within contemporary social control (O'Malley 1996; Garland 2001). It involves a way of thinking by which governments actively enlist participation by non-state actors and agencies and thus share the burden of controlling unwanted social phenomena.

The governance of borders is thus becoming an increasingly complex and un-transparent matter, combining a number of actors on various levels and with varying objectives. It is not simply a task for state or state-like institutions, but also for private actors, ready to step in when states become unwilling or unable to control the migration challenge. For example, a director of the Tangier branch of a British logistics company recently reported: 'The situation is really getting worse and worse, it's desperate. We're finding people hidden in our lorries every single week now.' The company therefore chooses to employ its own security staff to protect its drivers and lorries from migrants, rather than putting its trust in the hands of Moroccan border police who appear to be unable and unwilling to deal with the problems.[14] Crawford (2002: 47) suggests that:

> The new governance of safety across Europe involves not only the interconnections between different levels above and below nation-state […] but also sees a fusing of public and private interests as

non-state actors (including the commercial sectors) are drawn into the networks of control. The territory of the policing of crime and insecurity is simultaneously public and private as well as local, national and transnational. Consequently, we need to move beyond the notion of a unity of law and crime control tied to the nation-state towards an understanding of a plurality of legal orders and modes of regulation ...

However, it is important to note that the era of global risk management started long before the present hype of the war on terror and preoccupation with illegal migration. The 'war on drugs' was and is a global war. The reasoning behind the war on drugs was the idea that one should prevent danger on the global level. Norway, for example, has forged a number of international alliances within the UN, EU, Interpol, World Customs Organisation, within Schengen and in cooperation with other Nordic countries as well as various NGOs.[15] Furthermore, the Norwegian police and customs have their personnel deployed in a number of ports and strategically important cities in order to improve cooperation, exchange of information and prevent possible drug trafficking.[16] The strategy to fight drugs thus defies the established notion of territoriality and borders as 'walls around territories'. The police and customs cooperation, rather, assumes the dispersed and network-like shape of the flows of goods they are trying to control.[17]

Governing a technological society

Examining the transformations of borders and the changing space of governance, one needs, however, to keep in mind the technologically mediated nature of these phenomena. The space of flows, described by Castells (1996), is essentially transmitted through and supported by information and communication technologies. Castells' network society is a society where '[b]oth space and time are being transformed under the combined effect of the information technology paradigm' (Castells 1996: 376). Thus, European border security essentially depends on a variety of trans-national information flows and technological zones, most notably the ones based on the Schengen Agreement as well as the so-called Dublin Convention, dealing with asylum issues. For example, in the period between January 2003 and March 2004, the Norwegian police had 2,242 positive hits in the Eurodac database. Eurodac is a database, established by the Dublin Convention, containing fingerprints of foreign nationals, primarily asylum seekers. The main purpose of

Eurodac is to prevent people from claiming asylum in several European countries.[18]

Schengen Information System (SIS) originates in the Schengen Agreement and its objective is essentially to dismantle the EU's internal borders while coordinating and strengthening its external borders, particularly through better police cooperation and exchange of information. The SIS is a network which allows police and other agents from Schengen member states to access and enter a variety of data on specific individuals, vehicles and objects. Hayes (2004) reports that by March 2003, the SIS created

> [r]ecords on 877,655 people, a further 386,402 aliases, and more than 15 million objects. EU officials *estimate* that there are 125,000 access terminals to the SIS. Under finalised proposals, access to the SIS is to be extended to Europol, Eurojust, national prosecutors and vehicle licensing authorities. (italics original)

Furthermore, a newly established European visa information system (VIS) will contain 'personal information supplied by people from around the world in an estimated 20 million visa applications to the EU member states every year' (Hayes 2004). These systems, with their network of nodes and tens of thousands of access points, thus fundamentally reshape the scope and nature of the European space of governance.

Barry (2002: 2) argues for the need to acknowledge the 'centrality of technology to the reconfiguration of what one can call the space of government'. If geography and territorial boundaries were before central for defining the space of government, now, on the other hand, government operates 'in relation to zones formed through the circulation of technical practices and devices' (Barry 2002: 3). Drawing on Arjun Appadurai's (1990) concept of technoscapes, Barry defines technological zones as zones of circulation where technical devices, practices and artefacts are highly connected and compatible. Loader (2004: 67) argues that when it comes to the field of European policing, this is 'an almost entirely *informationalised* activity – a practice oriented not on-the-ground delivery of visible police functions [...] but towards supporting such practices through the generation, storage and dissemination of information'. Loader argues that the argument about the inefficiency of European cross-border information sharing thus overlooks and under-estimates 'the import of the activities that *are actually taking place* on a specifically European level' (Loader 2004: 67).

New technologies thus seem both to transform the traditional space of government and to disrupt territorial boundaries, as well as appearing to state and commercial organizations to be the most efficient solution for addressing the problems of governance and security arising from these reconfigurations. Through various technologically supported strategies, such as airline liaison officers and the obligation of carriers to communicate passenger data to border authorities, contemporary governance is able constantly to expand the range of actors who participate in global risk communication networks.

However, as Ericson and Haggerty (1997: 4) point out, risk communication systems are not simply neutral channels through which knowledge is transferred: 'Rather, they have their own logics and autonomous processes. They govern institutional relations and circumscribe what individuals and their organisations are able to accomplish.' The contemporary technological paraphernalia therefore not only enables fortification of the border, it also reshapes the border according to its own logic. According to Lyon (2003), globalized surveillance results in *'delocalization of the border'*.

> [B]orders themselves become 'delocalized' as efforts are made to check travellers before they reach physical borders of ports of entry. Images and information circulate through different departments, looping back and forth in commercial, policing, and government networks. Surveillance records, once kept in fixed filing cabinets and dealing in data focused on persons in specific places, are now fluid, flowing and global. These consequences are properly 'globalized' in the sense that they signal new patterns of social activity and novel social arrangements, which are less constrained by geography. The 'delocalized border' is a prime example of globalized surveillance. (Lyon 2003: 110)

However, Lyon (2003) points out that technological surveillance, intensified in the aftermath of September 11, should not be seen simply as a 'sudden change' connected to an extraordinary event. Rather, the growing surveillance practices are symptomatic of deeper shifts in the nature of social control and governance that have been present in Western societies for some time. The information flows may have intensified after September 11, but they have been also before, in some form, part of most global control strategies.

The ability of surveillance technologies to 'delocalize' the border means not only that the border can be moved outside of national territory in order to avert potential risks, but also that the border can be dispersed and moved inside the territory. Consequently, some analysts point out that the Schengen lands are by no means a 'borderless zone' (Bigo and Guild 2004; Hyden and Lundberg 2004; Walters 2004). While abolishing internal state borders, Schengen lands have intensified internal police activities and identity checks of potentially undesirable individuals, particularly in certain zones heavily populated by third country nationals (Bigo and Guild 2004). A similar strategy is present in the establishment of the so-called 'mobile task forces' described in the British *Secure Borders* White Paper:

> Acting on improved and more effective use of intelligence, these 'Mobile Task Forces' will be sent to targeted locations anywhere in the United Kingdom. An integrated intelligence network that supports the Mobile Task Forces will enable the Immigration Service to increase resources, for limited periods of time, on identified areas of greatest risk. As the risk changes, the Mobile Task Forces will be redeployed to focus on the new areas of concern. (Home Office 2002: 97)

Biometric identity cards should therefore also be understood in this context, creating, according to Lyon (in this volume), a border which is 'everywhere'. The UK government's plans for electronic tagging and satellite surveillance of asylum seekers might also have a similar effect.[19]

Living in a technological society means, as Barry (2002: 2) points out, that various technologies dominate the sense of problems which need to be addressed as well as dominating their solutions. The task of providing security and controlling borders is today constituted essentially as a technological task, including not only information sharing but also a variety of other technologies, such as gamma ray scanners, which give clear images of bodies hidden in vehicles, heartbeat sensors, advanced heat-seeking technology, etc.

The groups most eager to resist the technological surveillance networks are the ones who daily try to penetrate the fortress-like borders of the first world. Using global communication systems is a matter of necessity for them also. Mobile phones allow human traffickers to maintain contact with their networks and potential clients across the world. According to a recent BBC report 'one smuggler sold his mobile phone containing the directory of his contacts to another smuggler for $15,000'.[20] 'Staying ahead of the game' is therefore also very much on the minds of those 'doomed to be locally tied' (Bauman 1998), although the price of failure is often paid with their lives.

Conclusion

The story of contemporary borders and governance brings up themes of delocalization, globalization, ex-territoriality and 'the end of era of space'. However, as much as these themes are coupled with the images of a borderless world, they paradoxically also mean introduction of ever more efficient border controls. Bauman (1998) points out the importance of understanding the mutual reinforcement between globalization and mobility on the one hand, and, simultaneously, the renewed emphasis on territoriality on the other hand. While globalizing and borderless for some, the contemporary condition is increasingly localizing for others (or, one could say, for the largest part of the human population).

> [R]ather than homogenizing the human condition, the technological annulment of temporal/spatial distances tends to polarize it. It emancipates certain humans from territorial constraints and renders certain community-generating meanings exterritorial – while denuding the territory, to which other people go on being confined, of its meaning and its identity-endowing capacity. (Bauman 1998: 18, italics original)

Rather than talking about globalization, Bauman and other commentators talk about glocalization, thus emphasizing globalization and territorialization/localization as two mutually reinforcing processes.

The need for borders – in a material as well as symbolic sense – may be therefore greater today than in the past. Fortress Europe, fortress America, fortress Australia and the surveillance surge in the aftermath of September 11 (Lyon 2003) are witness to the persistent materiality of the border, the threat of trans-national crime being a useful justification for the controls intended to keep the locals tied to their territory. Furthermore, the political rhetoric in most Western countries today shows a potent symbolic need for borders as a means of strengthening a sense of security and identity. The wave of nationalism and xenophobia in the EU, particularly in traditionally tolerant countries such as Denmark and The Netherlands, represents a potent reminder of the symbolic importance of territory. After all, the most recent war in Europe was a war about territory and its contested nature, particularly the great symbolic power that Kosovo held and still holds for the Serbs.

The existence of borders and the 'embrace' of locality may be therefore not only a destiny to which some are 'doomed' (Bauman 1998), but also a choice, a form of escapism of the affluent. The emerging strategies for defending the border constitute, according to Walters, a new type of governance and politics – 'a will to domesticate the forces which threaten the sanctity of home' (2004: 242). Like being tough on crime, defending the border also carries an enormous political and symbolic capital. As Bauman (1998: 117) writes:

> In an ever more insecure and uncertain world the withdrawal into the safe haven of territoriality is an intense temptation; and so the defence of the territory – the 'safe home' – becomes the pass-key to all doors which one feels must be locked to stave off the triple threat to spiritual and material comfort. [...] It is perhaps a happy coincidence for political operators and hopefuls that the genuine problems of insecurity and uncertainty have condensed into the anxiety about safety; politicians can be supposed to be doing something about the first two just because being seen to be vociferous and vigorous about the third.

Notes

1 I would like to thank the participants at the Queen's University's (Kingston, Ontario, Canada) workshop on state borders and border policing, and the participants at the Oslo Institute of Criminology's seminar about crime control and technological culture, for their helpful comments and suggestions.
2 Source: http://news.bbc.co.uk/1/hi/world/europe/2024943.stm
3 Source: http://news.bbc.co.uk/1/hi/world/europe/2042779.stm
4 I am grateful to May-Len Skilbrei and Astrid Renland for bringing the issue to my attention.
5 Source: http://www.msnbs.msn.com/id/5881958/print/1/displaymode/1098/
6 The existence of 'non-spaces' has been described as a general trait of contemporary social space (Lash 2002) – exemplified by transit lounges at airports and airports themselves, or by certain territories (such as Ceuta in northern Morocco), which are experienced as transit areas where people simply wait to get somewhere else.
7 Source: BBC News at http://newsvote.bbc.co.uk/mpapps/pagetools/print/news.bbc.co.uk/1/hi/uk_politics/
8 Source: Guardian Unlimited at http://politics.guardian.co.uk/homeaffairs/story/0,11026,1192350,00.html
9 Source: http://www.guardian.co.uk/Refugees_in_Britain/Story/0,2763,1370816,00.html
10 Source: BBC News at http://newsvote.bbc.co.uk/mpapps/pagetools/print/news.bbc.co.uk/1/hi/uk/2994034.stm
11 Source: http://www.telegraph.co.uk/news/main.jhtml?xml=/news/2004/10/02/wasy02.xml&sSheet=/news/2004/10/02/ixworld.html

12 A similar example is recent efforts by the United States in West Africa to strengthen the security forces and border controls of Mauritania, Mali, Chad and Niger. The US Pan-Sahel initiative will provide equipment and training to military units responsible for the control of the porous Saharan borders. The objective of this intervention in some of the poorest countries in the world is, to borrow the words of the US spokesman, to strengthen 'surveillance against cross-border terrorism'. Source: http://www.guardian.co.uk/international/story/0,3604,1122505,00.html

13 Guild (2004: 38) reports that at busy airports, airlines may also engage services of private agencies to carry out additional passenger checks for them, thus diffusing the responsibility even further.

14 Moroccan society largely depends on money sent back home by the migrants from Spain, which may explain the lacking interest of Moroccan authorities in border control. Source: BBC News at http://newsvote.bbc.co.uk/mpapps/pagetools/print/news.bbc.co.uk/1/hi/world/africa/

15 Source: http://odin.dep.no/hd/norsk/publ/stmeld/030005-040005/ved 008-bn.html.

16 Norway has had its police and customs officers placed in Pakistan (Islamabad and Karachi), Spain, Great Britain, The Netherlands, Russia and Austria. Norway also cooperates with other Nordic countries, and they have common personnel placed in, among others, Ankara, Bangkok, Lisbon, Rome, Tallinn, Nicosia, etc.
Source: http://odin.dep.no/hd/norsk/publ/stmeld/030005-040005/index-ved008-b-n-a.html.

17 It is important to point out that the war on drugs continues, although the public focus seems to be shifting somewhat away from the drug trade as a morally reprehensible activity in itself, to drug trade being a financial supply-line for terrorism.

18 Only four countries (UK, Germany, France and Sweden) had more positive Eurodac hits than Norway in the same period. Source: http://www.kripos.no/akt_tema/eurodac.html

19 Source: http://news.bbc.co.uk/2/hi/uk_news/politics/3243530.stm

20 Source: http://news.bbc.co.uk/1/hi/world/europe/2024943.stm

References

Appadurai, A. (1990) 'Disjuncture and difference in the global cultural economy', *Theory, Culture and Society*, 7:2–3, pp. 295–375.

Barry, A. (2002) *Political Machines: Governing a Technological Society* (London and New York: The Athlone Press).

Bauman, Z. (1998) *Globalization: The Human Consequences* (Cambridge, UK: Polity Press).

Bauman, Z. (2002) *Society under Siege* (Cambridge, UK: Polity Press).

Bigo, D. and Guild, E. (2004) 'Distancering af de fremmede – logikken i Schengen –visummet', *Tidskriftet Politikk*, 3:7, pp. 23–33.

Blakely, E.J. and Snyder, M.G. (1997) *Fortress America: Gated Communities in the United States* (Washington, DC: Brookings Institution Press).

Castells, M. (1996) *The Rise of the Network Society* (Oxford: Blackwell Publishers).

Crawford, A. (2002) 'The Governance of Crime and Insecurity in an Anxious Age: the Trans-European and the Local' in A. Crawford (ed.) *Crime and Insecurity: The Governance of Safety in Europe* (Cullompton: Willan Publishing), pp. 27–51.

Douglas, M. (1994) *Risk and Blame: Essays in Cultural Theory* (London and New York: Routlege).

Ericson, R. and Haggerty, K.H. (1997) *Policing the Risk Society* (Toronto: University of Toronto Press).

Featherstone, M. (2002) 'Cosmopolis: an introduction', *Theory, Culture and Society*, 19:1–2, pp. 1–16.

Garland, D. (2001) *The Culture of Control* (Oxford: Oxford University Press).

Guardian Weekly (2003) 'EU sets up agency to police its borders', 20–26 November.

Guild, E. (2004) 'The Borders of the European Union – Visas and carriers sanctions', *Tidskriftet Politikk*, 3:7, pp. 34–43.

Hayes, B. (2004) 'From the Schengen Information System to SIS II and the Visa Information System (VIS): the proposals explained', *Statewatch Analysis*. Available at: www.statewatch.org/news/2004/feb/summary-sis.reprt.htm

Hedetoft, U. (1998) 'Constructions of Europe: Territoriality, Sovereignty, Identity: Disaggregations of Cultural and Political Space', in S. Immerfall and J. Hagen (eds) *Territoriality in the Globalizing Society: One Place or None?* (Berlin: Springer), pp. 153–71.

Home Office (2002) *Secure Borders, Safe Haven: Integration with Diversity in Modern Britain* (London: The Stationery Office).

Hyden, S. and Lundberg, A. (2004) *Inre utlanningskontroll I polisarbete: mellan attsstatsideal och effektivitet i Schengens Sverige* (Malmø: IMER, Malmø høgskola).

Klein, N. (2003) 'Fortress continents: The US and Europe are both creating multi-tiered regional strongholds', *The Guardian*, 16 January.

Lash, S. (2002) *Critique of Information* (London, Thousand Oaks, New Delhi: Sage Publications).

Loader, I. (2004) 'Policing, Securisation and Democratisation in Europe', in T. Newburn and R. Sparks (eds) *Criminal Justice and Political Cultures: National and International Dimensions of Crime Control* (Cullompton: Willan Publishing), pp. 49–79.

Lyon, D. (2003) *Surveillance after September 11* (Cambridge, UK: Polity).

Murdoch, G. (2004) 'Democracy in Digital Times', paper given at The Materiality of Mediated Communication Conference, 17–18 May, Bergen, Norway.

Newman, O. (1972) *Defensible Space: People and Design in the Violent City* (London: Architectural Press).

O'Malley, P. (1996) 'Post-Keynesian Policing', *Economy and Society*, 25:2, pp. 137–55.

Simon, J. (1997) 'Governing through Crime', in L. Friedman and G. Fisher (eds) *The Crime Conundrum: Essays in Criminal Justice* (Boulder, CO: Westview Press), pp. 171–90.

Urry, J. (2002) 'The Global Complexities of September 11th', *Theory, Culture & Society*, 19:4, pp. 57–69.

Walters, W. (2004) 'Secure Borders, Safe Haven, Domopolitics', *Citizenship Studies*, 8:3, pp. 237–60.

Chapter 13

Immigration controls and citizenship in the political rhetoric of New Labour

Don Flynn

Government policy in the United Kingdom has moved very rapidly during the course of the past eight years in the direction of an active, interventionist state claiming the authority to monitor and direct aspects of life which had formerly been regarded as none of its concern. *Laissez faire* in the realm of civic and social affairs is being replaced with a doctrine that asserts the right of the state to know far more about citizens and residents then ever it did in the past, for reasons justified by appeals to social cohesion and integration. The promotion of a new mechanism for state scrutiny in the form of the Identity Cards Bill proceeding through Parliament, at the time of writing, is emblematic of these developments.

The New Labour government responsible for this change of direction has offered a range of reasons for its policies. These extend from the need to define a new and stronger notion of citizenship capable of asserting itself against the socially fragmenting tendencies of globalization, countering the alienation of sections of society from civic affairs, through to the protection of society from the dangers of terrorism of the 11 September 2001 variety.[1] But foremost among the reasoning of New Labour thinkers has been its evaluation of the impact of immigration on British society, which it sees as being simultaneously a force aiding the modernization and economic competitiveness of the country, and a danger because of its potential to run out of control and threaten the security of settled communities.

This chapter attempts to review the recent history of immigration policy in Britain, with a view to explaining the character of the frequent innovations that New Labour has been responsible for since its election in 1997, and also its impact on the broader issues of citizenship and the emergence of an active surveillance state.

What went before

The following argument attempts a review of the recent history of British immigration control policy prior to 1997. The inclination of this author is to concur in general terms with a number of scholars who have seen in this record the common need of post-war European governments to make extensive use of migrant labour to achieve economic growth combined with low inflation (Castles and Kosack 1985; Hollifield 1992). UK governments differed from their counterparts on the continent in their willingness to rely on *laissez faire* mechanisms of market demand to recruit this labour force (Deakin 1970; Harris 1987).[2] The conventions of the dissolving empire initially provided a means by which colonial and Commonwealth citizens could act on their own initiative to travel and seek employment in the UK. While this appeared to provide an efficient means for meeting the demand of British employers for migrant workers throughout the 1950s, it also allowed a space for nationalist political currents to agitate against alleged excessive 'coloured' immigration (Humphry and Ward 1974; Layton-Henry 1992; Brown 1999).

These tensions marked out the terrain for the immigration debate in Britain during the course of the 1960s. The unrestricted rights of Commonwealth and colonial citizens to enter the UK were ended in 1962 with the first Commonwealth Immigrants Act. In 1968 a second Act imposed control measures on British citizens who had obtained that status through connections with former British colonies: in the main, people of South Asian ethnicity. In the meantime, the Labour government, under the premiership of Harold Wilson, had attempted to tackle the problem of growing anti-immigrant racism with measures that laid the foundation for what would become 'race relations' policy. A dual approach strategy emerged, which was predicated on the idea that strict immigration controls were necessary to facilitate harmonious race relations (Deakin 1970: 106).

The final stage in the construction of the post-war system of controls was reached with the Immigration Act 1971. By the time the politicians had concluded that legislation in this form was needed, the ideological paradigm had finally settled on the notion that immigration was of marginal importance to the UK and that the role of policy was to 'severely restrict'[3] the numbers coming for settlement or work. Insofar as some degree of migration had to be permitted, the legislation allowed the Home Secretary to produce a detailed set of immigration rules directing officials in the processing of visa applications and dealing with newcomers at ports of entry. These rules were drafted in sufficiently broad terms to permit a wide degree of discretion in their implementation, which allowed a management culture to be created focusing attention on what were considered the most problematic categories of aspiring entrants. Immigration statistics suggest that these were citizens of African and Asian countries (CRE 1985).

But policies aimed at promoting harmonious 'race relations' required that black and Asian settlers be able to make the transition from immigrants to being ethnic minorities (Castles, Booth and Wallace 1987). The ambiguities of this transformation saw the sense of being 'British' clash with the facts of widespread racial injustices throughout society. This encouraged the rising generation to embrace the idea of being 'Black British' and to stretch cultural assumptions of what was entailed by 'Britishness' in the first place. The insistence of this new constituency on the salience of their experiences as Black British, and the often total incomprehension of what was involved in this discourse by politicians in the mainstream parties,[4] demonstrated that the historical linkage of ambiguous nationality to immigration status had given rise to disputes about the character of citizenship itself, and its capacity to be used in a flexible way to describe the aspirations of marginalized sections of society.

The descent into disorder

The control regime put in place by the 1971 Act proved remarkably durable across the succeeding two decades. Resort to further legislation was rare, and only in ways intended to supplement the basic form of the Act.[5] Outwardly at least the system continued to run on the tramlines laid down more than 15 years previously.

Yet this appearance was deceptive. Geared to the presumption that migration was a marginal activity capable of being managed by officials controlling entry at the UK borders, the system in fact struggled to contain pressures as the sheer numbers of international travellers entering via UK ports rose through the 1980s and '90s at an average rate of 8 per cent per annum, to reach a total of 80 million people by 1998. Though only a minority could be classed as immigrants in the accepted sense of the term, each nevertheless was subject to checks on identity and reasons for travel by officials at UK ports. In practice, the burden of stringent scrutiny fell on a relatively small group of people travelling from black Commonwealth countries, identified by immigration officers as being particularly problematic in terms of their entry to the country. The pressure on airport-based immigration staff was partially relieved from 1985 onwards with the introduction of compulsory visas, the first for any group of Commonwealth citizens, for nationals of Bangladesh, Ghana, India, Nigeria, Pakistan and Sri Lanka.

But the crucial pressures on immigration, which proved less easy to accommodate with relatively minor adjustments to operating procedures, came from two separate directions: the rise of refugee movements from the early 1990s onwards, and the re-emergence of demand for labour migration at the same time.

The bulk of the new refugee movements were associated with the key periods of the Balkans wars which accompanied the break-up of Yugoslavia. These numbers were supplemented with the arrival of asylum seekers from wars and civil turmoil further afield, with nationals of Iran, Iraq, Sri Lanka, Afghanistan, Somalia and Turkey being represented among the newcomers. Bound in principle by the 1951 Geneva Convention on the Status of Refugees, European governments nevertheless had scope to act through the use of visa controls and measures aimed at the interdiction of travellers before entering EU territory. However, doing this with any degree of effectiveness required extraordinary levels of cooperation between various national authorities, which proved much harder to establish in practice than might have been anticipated. Conflicts of interest divided southern European states from northern, and those with differing traditions of human rights jurisprudence from each other.

With regard to economic migration, the reconstruction of economies around the principle of deregulation, particularly pronounced in the UK, and a lengthy period of sustained economic growth during the 1990s, generated a demand for unskilled workers in semi-casual branches of employment in the service sector which could not be met from the domestic labour force (Jordan and Duvall 2002). In cities like London, Birmingham and Manchester, these vacancies would increasingly be filled by overseas students, working holiday-makers, asylum seekers awaiting consideration of their applications, and irregular migrants. At other levels of the skills spectrum, influential groups of employers pressed for an expansion of work permit schemes to allow the recruitment of professionals, technicians and tradespeople of all kinds. The task of accommodating this new demand within a system of immigration that still presumed that migration was essentially a marginal activity became more challenging as the 1990s moved on.

Attempts at primary legislation by the Conservative government from 1993 onwards were primarily intended to provide deterrents within the system against asylum seekers, who were identified as the chief threat to ordered immigration controls. Believing that a high proportion of asylum seekers were concerned mainly with the opportunity to obtain social and welfare benefits, it constructed a harsher reception regime which withheld all national-state social welfare support from people lodging 'in-country' asylum claims (as opposed to applications made immediately on arriving at a UK border). But as national government evaded its responsibilities to assist asylum seekers, the courts stepped in to rule that local government had to assist when they became destitute.[6] This obligation unintentionally imposed on some town hall authorities a tremendous strain and cost, and the presence of asylum seekers became an issue of intense controversy. Incidents of violence against refugee families were reported in the region of the Channel ports in the southeast, which heightened the sense of crisis over the issue.

Enter New Labour: the 1998 White Paper

New Labour came to power with a strong sense of the problems and grievances that the immigration control system was generating. Settled communities felt the injustice of family reunion policies which imposed bureaucratic obstacles on the admission of spouses and children. At the same time, the anxieties of white working-class communities in traditional Labour constituencies were there to be exploited by centre right parties and the newspapers which supported them. The new government acted promptly to make a concession to its supporters among black and Asian communities by easing some of the restrictions to family reunification, abolishing the 'primary purpose rule'[7] in October 1997. On the wider issues, the new Home Secretary, Jack Straw, promised a white paper within a year which would propose changes to other areas of immigration law and policy. The momentum for substantial reform of the system was established during these early months.

The motif of 'modernization' was adopted by the government as defining its approach to immigration reform. The need for modernization of policy arose, as was explained in the first of New Labour's two white papers on immigration, because 'piecemeal' attempts at reform during the previous 20 years had created a system which was 'too complex and too slow' (White Paper 1998). This had resulted in inefficiency and had opened the system to the possibility of 'abuse'. Modernization meant updating procedures to deal with these problems.

The significance of economic migration, which this chapter argues grew greatly during this period, was dealt with only briefly on this occasion. It was noted that, 'The UK, along with the rest of Western Europe, the USA, Canada and Australia has seen a substantial increase in the number of economic migrants seeking a better life for themselves and their families' (White Paper 1998: 1.3). It implied that, in principle, there was nothing wrong with this, but national authorities were now required to be alert to the possibility of abuse of the system.

The 1998 White Paper was centrally concerned with the vexed issue of asylum. The rise in the number of refugees coming to the countries of the EU, and Britain specifically, had risen fourfold since the late 1980s, from 4,000 in 1988 to over 32,000 in 1997 (White Paper 1998: 1.9). The conviction of the government was that the majority of these applications did not qualify for protection under the Geneva Convention, and in fact involved economic migrants looking for an opportunity to get around the strict rules restricting labour migration. But the duty to evaluate complex claims about incidents of imprisonment and torture had clogged up the administration of the system to the point that large parts of the IND were effectively paralysed by backlogs of work (White Paper 1998: 1.14).

The new leadership at the Home Office was determined to tackle what it considered an abuse of refugee rights by revising asylum reception procedures to make them much less attractive to unfounded claimants. Asylum seekers were to be dispersed to towns and regions outside the main areas of immigrant settlement, subjecting them to a strict regime of surveillance to ensure they remained there. Further, their support was to be provided through a system of special vouchers instead of cash payments, making their movements particularly visible in local communities. Trapped within a system that insisted on their high visibility at all times, asylum seekers could be processed and, for the majority, removed from the country much more efficiently.

The White Paper was also required to take into account the implications of the Human Rights Act 1998 – the so-called 'Bill of Rights' for the United Kingdom – which was presented by the government as a cornerstone of its legislative programme (Klug 2000). Under these new provisions, judges would for the first time be empowered to adjudicate on whether a particular action by public authorities infringed rights guaranteed by the European Convention on Human Rights (ECHR). This would impact on legislators and policy makers, in that they would be required to consider whether their activities involved measures which could be ruled against as an infringement in the courts.

As far as immigration policy was concerned, the protection of human rights was considered to require the introduction of a right to formal legal appeal on human rights grounds to persons who believed that rights under the ECHR had been infringed by a negative decision of the authorities (White Paper 1998, Chapter 7). The 'asylum procedures' chapter offered more, setting out the fact that under a human rights regime, asylum decisions would have to take explicit account of the responsibilities of the UK authorities to comply with the 1951 UN Convention Relating to the Status of Refugees, the 1966 International Covenant on Civil and Political Rights, the 1984 UN Convention Against Torture and other Cruel, Inhuman or Degrading Treatment or Punishment, and the ECHR (White Paper 1998, Chapter 8). This new right of appeal on human rights grounds has had a major impact on the operation of immigration and refugee policy (Henderson 2003).

It is possible to see in the 1998 White Paper all the elements of the New Labour approach assembled and put on the agenda – modernization, a positive valuation of past migration and current diversity, and the new dimension of human rights – but placed in the limited context of a discussion about overcoming the failings of a collapsing immigration control system. As such, the reforms appeared largely as safeguards rather than radically formulated new principles to steer migration policy. Another three years and a further white paper would pass before these considerations were lent any greater clarity.

The sharpening of ideas: the 2002 White Paper

The 1998 White Paper, and the legislation which followed,[8] was not a significant success in terms of the developing immigration situation. The theory that asylum seekers could be deterred by dispersal and vouchers was disproved by the significant growth in refugee numbers over this period. Over 71,000 fresh applicants arrived in 1999, and a further 80,000 in 2000, most coming as a consequence of the wars in the Balkans and civil conflicts in other regions. Attempts at the interdiction of refugee movements at the EU borders had produced the perverse effect of strengthening the role of agents and facilitators in obtaining entry to the territory of member states. The UK had emerged as a favoured destination for these networks, resulting in the establishment of a Channel crossing staging post at the Red Cross-managed Sangatte refugee camp, near Calais (Cohen 2004). The highly publicized disruption caused to Channel Tunnel rail services during the period after the 1999 Act, and the continuing high volume of new applicants, advertised the fact that New Labour had still not found the key to the orderly management of migration.

Public opinion on the effects of the government's policies was in the main hostile to the newcomers, but an important though smaller group reacted in an opposing way. The voucher scheme combined with compulsory dispersal was viewed by many within New Labour's coalition of supporters as an outrage. The deliberate isolation of vulnerable people beyond the fringes of the cash economy offended against values of decency and hospitality. After the murder of a Kurdish asylum seeker, Firsat Dag, on the Sighthill estate in Glasgow in 2001 public attention was focused on the conditions dispersed asylum seekers were being expected to endure.[9] The Jamaican-born leader of the Transport and General Workers Union, Bill Morris, normally considered close to the New Labour government, responded to the accounts of violence and discrimination against asylum seekers by proposing to bring the entire issue onto the floor of that year's Labour party conference, thereby threatening the government with the prospect of a major breach with its supporters on asylum policy.

The critics of government policy effectively won this round of the campaign. A ministerial re-shuffle in the summer had seen Jack Straw replaced with David Blunkett as Home Secretary, a politician steeped in the traditions of northern English municipal socialism (Blunkett 2001). Blunkett immediately saw his task as imposing a more focused agenda on his department, structured around notions of civil renewal and the strengthening of community. From this perspective the abstractions of human rights looked like the obsessions of the southern 'chattering classes', and as such stood in the way of policies which first and foremost would offer 'security' to ordinary citizens, and a space in a society which they were confident resembled the core values of their traditional local communities.[10]

He moved quickly to defuse the row over refugee dispersal. It was obvious that the voucher system for supporting asylum seekers would be abandoned to head off the threatened revolt at the party conference. However, when he rose to speak at that assembly on 1 October 2001, the smoke from the terrorist attacks on New York and the Pentagon on 9/11 was still very much in the air. The security element of Blunkett's concerns was powerfully reinforced, and it was clear that these would be prominent in the immigration debate thereafter.

The immediate promise was for a second fundamental review of policy, and a second white paper was eventually published in February 2002. *Safe Borders, Secure Haven* differed from its predecessor in being uncluttered by the need to address the chaos caused by the failed policies of the Tory epoch. It aimed at the onset for the integration of a sweeping worldview dealing with globalization and its consequences for local communities. The contexts of citizenship and social cohesion extended the range of discussion from matters relating to the admission of immigrants, through to the supervision of migrant communities, and the circumstances in which their integration into wider British society would be provided for. There was a retraction from New Labour's initial idealism about the potential of human rights in the White Paper's discussion of refugee and asylum issues.

From the outset the White Paper posed the problems of migration within the framework of citizenship and nationality. Migration is potentially unsettling because it leads to changes in national culture and identity. Tensions can be raised and long-established senses of belonging can be undermined (White Paper 2002: 9). But a later reference to the civil disturbances which took place in the northern towns of Oldham, Burnley and Bradford in the summer of 2001 suggested a more fundamental problem: even without the tensions allegedly induced by migration, the sense of culture and national identity was already fragile in the UK:

> [...] globalisation of communication media and information technology has opened up national cultures to diverse influences, and provided channels of mutual interaction between different parts of the world that literally know no boundaries. Social changes such as the decline of old certainties of class or place, and the emergence of new political institutions alongside the nation state, have also contributed to these changes in identity and belonging. (White Paper 2002: 9–10)

The formulation of new policies on citizenship, intended to promote this lost sense of belonging, are therefore required not only because of the experience of migration, but because of developments arising from globalization. In fact, these efforts to focus interest on the forms modern citizenship might take precede both white papers and go back to days before government when Etzionian ideas of communitarianism were being investigated by New Labour theorists. The task of 're-moralising' the nation, and the role which education might play in promoting the core values of community were strongly present in the adoption of citizenship studies in the school curriculum as a part of New Labour's education policy. In this form, however, they were criticized by Tory opponents as faddish and a manifestation of the 'nanny state's' desire to interfere in matters which were not its proper concern.

The disturbances in the northern cities in 2001 changed the context and shifted citizenship from theoretical abstractions to something with much more grit. The fact that the protagonists during the riots had been groups of whites and Asian youths – the latter overwhelmingly of British birth and education – exoticized the discussion and associated it with the entry of foreign elements into settled British communities. Rooted in these points, a conversation about equipping newcomers with the basic principles of how to live and behave in British society injected new hope that the issues New Labour was trying to talk about might become more widely understood.

As the White Paper said, 'Historically, the UK has had a relatively weak sense of what active citizenship should entail. Our values of individual freedom, the protection of liberty and respect for difference, have not been accompanied by a strong, shared understanding of the civic realm' (White Paper 2002: 10–11). The business of integrating immigrants was seen as a welcome opportunity to explore this long-neglected social space. Doing it this way allowed its authors to say categorically that a modern civic culture would not be able to prosper on the basis of a 'narrow and out-dated view of what it means to be "British". The government welcomes the richness of the cultural diversity which immigrants have brought to the UK – our society is multi-cultural, and is shaped by its diverse peoples. We want British citizenship positively to embrace the diversity of background, culture and faiths that is one of the hallmarks of Britain in the 21st Century' (White Paper 2002: 29).

But if British citizenship was not to be narrow, what would be the extent of its breadth? The Human Rights Act 1998 was referred to as providing 'a source of values that British citizens should share'. At this point we are given an indication of what is likely to lie outside the scope of these values, in particular 'some cultural values which conflict [...] such as those which deny women the right to participate as equal citizens' (White Paper 2002: 30). And the ability to speak a 'common language' was raised as a reference point, so that people could participate as active citizens in economic, social and political life.

By such hints the role of immigration policy in shaping citizenship gradually emerged. People would need to be 'prepared for citizenship'. It should be a 'significant life event'. It was a point at which people committed themselves to being a part of British society. To get there, applicants should be able to demonstrate a level of knowledge about British society which implied acceptance of its broad traditions. The government had made it clear that this knowledge would be of a general kind, rather than detailed insights into history or society. A working group set up under the chairmanship of Professor Sir Bernard Crick would later set out its advice that it should contain a broad sense of the direction of British history, together with ideas about how healthcare or education and schools worked, as well as a basic knowledge of key institutions, like Parliament and the monarchy. Language tests would similarly be expected to demonstrate a practical facility in English (or Welsh or Scottish Gaelic).

Other chapters explain why an active approach to citizenship and population formation was now being expressed. New Labour had accepted the case for economic migration and believed that British employers needed to have access to global labour markets across all levels of the skills spectrum. The integration of new high technology sectors across the globe meant that many highly qualified people living in developing countries were motivated to work for at least a part of their careers in the UK (Castles and Miller 2003). Beyond the demand for the highly skilled, the growth of living standards in the cities of the UK had produced a new service sector catering to the lifestyles of the affluent middle classes. Deregulation of labour markets meant that many of these would be provided in conditions which had traditionally generated demand for low-skilled migrants (Harris 1995). The modern immigration policies which New Labour envisaged would manage the admission of large numbers of migrants also imposed on these workers conditions of residence which ensured their subservience to the often demanding conditions of life in the '3D' jobs (dirty, demanding, dangerous) which were increasingly the norm.

The White Paper chapter on 'working in the UK' set out the arguments for a pro-active policy of managed economic migration to meet the needs of British employers. It envisaged a rigidly structured system, capable of differentiating between skilled workers in sectors with acknowledged shortages (to be fast-tracked); employers unable to fill a specific vacancy from the domestic labour market (standard work permit procedures); and employers with seasonal needs for sizable workforces on a casual basis who were not able to mobilize sufficient numbers to fill vacancies on the short timescales they operated on (seasonal and temporary work schemes). The problem in tying managed migration to this highly differentiated labour market is that the system of management must mirror this complexity and be sufficiently sophisticated to respond to all these needs in a flexible fashion. What emerged in practice was a highly stratified system, with over 22 schemes being officially acknowledged as a part of managed migration, with the potential for further layers being added as new situations were generated (Morris 2004).

This system sought to allocate differential rights to migrant workers, covering such issues as permitted length of residence, the possibility of changing employer, access to welfare benefits and services, family reunification, and eligibility to eventual rights of settlement. The pattern of allocation was itself a function of such factors as skill level, nationality and gender, with evidence that ethnicity was also a component at an informal level.[11]

A system of this sort could be expected to generate friction, with many categories of migrants being frustrated in ambitions and plans for their migration. Policing the different categories of migrant workers imposes heavy costs on administration. Under New Labour's scheme, the state authorities divest themselves of some of these by enrolling other parties to undertake tasks of monitoring and surveillance. These include employers, social security agencies, education services (many casual workers are also students), healthcare services, local authorities, and potentially such private sector actors as banks and other financial service providers.

This level of policing might be sufficient for the majority of migrant workers, and most will remain in compliance with whatever conditions are imposed on them. But it is realistic to suppose that a significant fraction will experience difficulties from a range of sources, such as encountering exploitative employers, discovering that they have been unable to recover the costs of their migration (particularly for those from distant countries, or whose admittance into the system has been facilitated by expensive agents), or whose life circumstances change and who need, or simply want, to remain longer than was originally permitted. In the face of this the state has the need to be continually overhauling its capacity for surveillance and supervision, and ultimately the power to intervene to deal with delinquent migrants.

Against such contingencies the need for close supervision of migrant communities can be understood. Home Office statistics for the year 2002 suggest that 320,000 people were admitted in eight managed migration schemes during the previous 12 months. Blunkett made it clear that he did not favour the setting of government-inspired caps on the numbers admitted.[12] A 'modern' immigration policy therefore has to contemplate the management and supervision of potentially large numbers of people whose official designation as being outside the mainstream of life will lead to widespread alienation from the values of the society on whose periphery they temporarily reside.

The issue of the surveillance and control of migrants figures prominently in the White Paper. The starting point for the discussion is proposals for improved techniques aimed at keeping asylum seekers in the UK under close observation, through the use of induction centres, accommodation centres, reporting centres, and a new asylum identity card, the biometrical Asylum Registration Card (ARC). This latter item has been used to test out the technology needed for a general identity card scheme, which at the time of writing is being piloted through Parliament in an Identity Card Bill.

The main rationale advanced by the government for a national identity card scheme has been precisely that of managing migration, and to a lesser extent, fighting fraud.[13] True to New Labour's approach to the tasks of modernization, the scope for using technology and management techniques imported from the private sector is seen as vast. The White Paper sets this out in a chapter dealing with the issue of 'fraud' (White Paper 2002, Chapter 5). It states that there would be more coordination between government departments and other concerned parties; IT would be upgraded, and databases developed to track and record movements. Presented as a convenient way of demonstrating entitlement to a range of state services for those who held them, the argument was spiced up in further discussions to include the assertion that people would be proud to possess such a card, because it would be a palpable badge confirming their membership of the community. Blunkett made a statement to the Commons on 11 November 2003, saying that identity cards were 'about asserting our sense of identity and belonging, about our citizenship, and reinforcing the balance between rights and responsibilities'.[14] They also appear to be about the establishment of a database containing specific personal identifiers for the entire population, with the potential for monitoring the movement and transactions of millions of people.

To summarize, the significance of the second White Paper lies in its assertion of a vision of a modern immigration policy, aiming for the management of new forms of migration established under the impetus of globalization, and the benefits which the UK expected to derive from this in terms of economic growth and cultural diversity. The problems anticipated with these developments were seen as an increase in anxiety due to a loss of the sense of belonging on the part of established communities and the historical weakness in the core values which were accepted as defining British society. Further, the ordered management of the new migrations would place huge demands on administration which could only be met by increased international cooperation, particularly at the level of the EU, and a massive investment in organization and technology to ensure that flows were properly structured and adequately policed.

The solutions to all the issues raised implied a reconstruction not just of migration management techniques, but also of wider conceptions of citizenship in order that the sense of belonging could acquire updated meaning and be properly expressed within the new system of rights and responsibilities that would arise. In considering all these points it could be said that a paradigm was being constructed which presumed the type of society receiving migration on the scale envisaged would be very different from that constructed by the *laissez faire* traditions of old Britain.

New Labour rhetoric in effecting change

In this final section we will try to set out thoughts on the ways in which the New Labour mode of political discourse is facilitating the types of changes needed for the introduction of the managed migration it envisions as a major component of its policies. We will also suggest reasons why there are likely to be limits to the progress which New Labour can make in this direction, and the implications this will have for public debate in the future.

Alan Finlayson has argued for attention to be paid to the rhetorical form of a political party's 'pitch' to the electorate on the grounds that, 'Politics is concerned not only with deploying the force of words in order to achieve some desired effect but in giving force to words so that their usage can come to have such effects' (Finlayson 2003: 67). A political argument is rhetorical in that 'it functions to persuade and motivate'. Finlayson uses the example of 'modernization' to make his point, but a term like 'citizenship' could equally be designated as an '"up" word, that makes things sound exciting, progressive and positive'. But crucially it:

> [...] is also ideological in that this rhetorical usage helps generate an appearance of structured and unified thinking beyond which is either nonsense or (by implication) outdated thinking. It helps to render 'natural' and un-contestable that which is not necessarily so. Because the same word is used to describe constitutional reform, changes to the police force, health service and educational system, it seems that some sort of coherent approach is underpinning policy. Along with this unifying effect there is (as a necessary corollary) a simultaneous exclusion. That which is not modern is not of New Labour's New Britain, and that which is not part of it cannot lay claim to be modernised. (Finlayson 2003: 67)

This paper has argued that New Labour's approach to the reform of immigration policy in Britain has been structured around the concept of 'modernization', with the pivotal ideas being adaptation to the new realities of globalization and the importance of diversity in multiplying the complexity of markets and the potential for trade and higher levels of economic growth. The insistence on linking modernization to market-led growth also assumes a particular style of discipline being exercised over flows, with economic migration being privileged over humanitarian and secondary movements, and channelled precisely into the sectors and niches in which the demand from employers is greatest. This implies a tremendous complexity in the ways in which migration is organized, because the needs of employers, for workers of various skill levels, for employment on different types of contracts, for workers of particular national or cultural backgrounds, age groups, tolerance for particular types of work, etc., is itself very complex. But while the need for this complexity is challenging, the emergence of new management techniques and new technologies of supervision and control hold out the hope of a system of managed migration which extends seamlessly, from the issuing of visas in countries of origin, to maintaining the integrity of the channels and corrals in which migrant labour is to be confined, through to the eventual integration of the chosen fractions deemed worthy of the grant of citizenship.

It must be clear that a political formation which is propounding these extensive programmes of reform is not simply maintaining the racist and restrictive traditions of Britain's post-war immigration control legislation. And yet racism and restriction remain present within the new techniques of management, in the form of 'institutional racism'[15] and the cultural focus on the values of citizenship, which generate inevitable tensions between administrators and those whose cultural stance is considered problematic. Managed migration will be restrictive because it will assert the right of the state to say no, but this time on a great deal more issues than the simple question of admission into the country. It will routinely refuse permission to migrant workers to change employment when better pay or career prospects are in view. It will decide that six months, one year or two years is long enough for different groups of migrant workers, whether applications to assist with housing costs or deal with short-term unemployment will be refused, and primarily healthcare withheld from workers suffering from infections and injuries deemed non-urgent. Family re-unification will be contested by a state which has decided that it is not appropriate for workers whose presence is required only for short-term, casual employment; and refugees will be informed that 'sustainable protections options' are available for them overseas, obviating their old rights to live and settle in a safe European country.

New Labour has been assessed by a number of critical commentators as a formation which has its strengths in essentially sociological pre-sumptions about the nature of modern society, and its weaknesses in its poverty of appreciation of politics (Finlayson 2003; Leggett 2004; Marquand 2004). The review of the white papers attempted here gives substance to this viewpoint, in their presumption that the case for reform can be made primarily on grounds of economic efficiency and the contingencies of social cohesion. They assume the resumption of the type of stability which proved possible after the Immigration Act of 1971, when immigration pressure was regulated by low domestic demand and the relative isolation of immigrant communities seeking to contest the basis of control. Yet neither of these conditions applies at the present time, and what is more, New Labour policy itself justifies its reformist stance on the grounds that demand, being rooted in the workings of the global economy, will remain high, and that the centrality of human rights, anti-racism and social cohesion will mean an intense engagement with the lives of immigrant and black and minority ethnic communities. That this will require permanent change and adaptation is intrinsic to the New Labour vision of modernization, which sees it imposing on society the unending demand continually to change and transform. This has certainly been the history of immigration policy under New Labour, with two major White Papers and three major Acts of Parliament during the seven short years it has been in office. Yet the end is still not in sight and its core principles seem as contentious and difficult as ever. Maybe this turmoil will eventually take immigration policy beyond the parameters of New Labour altogether, and in the direction of a global society its ideologues had never thought possible.

Notes

1 For a presentation of the ways in which these themes have been elaborated in New Labour's thinking, see Blunkett (2001).

2 The existence of a government European Voluntary Workers scheme immediately after the war, which recruited and directed the work of 180,000 mainly Polish and Ukrainian workers was a significant exception to the general *laissez faire* approach of government, albeit for a relatively short period of time.

3 This formulation was used to explain the *raison d'être* of immigration control policy in the mission statement of the Immigration and Nationality Directorate (IND) throughout the 1980s and up to its amendment by New Labour in 1998.

4 A good example of this was provided by the 'Labour says he's black, we say he's British' advertising campaign which was run by the Conservative party in the early 1990s. Embarked upon as an attempt to demonstrate the non-racial credentials of the Conservatives, campaign strategists were horrified by the negative reaction of almost all minority ethnic communities, who typically responded by asserting the fact that they were both black and British.

5 Carriers liability legislation was brought onto the statute book in 1987, allowing the immigration authorities to impose fines on air and sea lines carrying passengers who had not obtained the visas required under the provisions of the immigration rules. The Immigration Act 1988 tidied up a

number of items which were perceived as loopholes in the main legislation, such as removing the obligation to facilitate the admission of family members of a Commonwealth citizen who had resided in the UK at 1 January 1973 (the date when the 1971 Act came into force), and a new prohibition on the admission of subsequent wives in polygamous marriage cases.

6 *R -v- LB Hammersmith, ex parte M*, reported in *The Times*, 19 February 1997.
7 The primary purpose rule required the spouses and fiancé(e)s of people settled in the UK to demonstrate they were not primarily motivated to marry because of the immigration advantages which would be conferred. The obstructive impact of the rule fell largely on people from the countries of the Indian subcontinent – see Sondhi (1982) and Sachdeva (1992).
8 The Nationality, Immigration and Asylum Act 1999.
9 See, for example, the report on the health of asylum seekers published by the British Medical Association and the Medical Foundation for the Care of Victims of Torture in October 2001.
10 See John Kampfor's interview with David Blunkett, *New Statesman*, 5 July 2004.
11 For example, Asian and African nurses are employed disproportionately in the private care sector, with fewer opportunities for career development and hence less access to the greater privileges associated with higher status migrants.
12 Blunkett: 'No UK immigration limit', *The Guardian*, 13 November 2003.
13 See *Legislation on Identity Cards: A Consultation*, Secretary of State for the Home Department, April 2004.
14 Hansard, 11 November 2003, Column 173.
15 For the meaning and significance of the concept of institutional racism, see the Macpherson Report of the Inquiry into the Death of Stephen Lawrence, Home Office, February 1999.

References

Blunkett, D. (2001) *Politics and Progress: Renewing Democracy and Civil Society* (London: Demos).
Brown, A.R. (1999) *Political Languages of Race and the Politics of Exclusion* (Aldershot: Ashgate).
Castles, S. and Kosack, G. (1985) *Immigrant Workers and Class Structure in Western Europe* (Oxford: Oxford University Press).
Castles, S., Booth, H. and Wallace, T. (1987) *Here for Good: Western Europe's New Ethnic Minorities* (London: Pluto Press).
Castles, S. and Miller, M.J. (2003) *The Age of Migration: International Populations Movements in the Modern World* (Basingstoke: Palgrave Macmillan).
Cohen, N. (2004) 'The Sangatte legacy', *The Observer*, Sunday 13 June.
CRE (1985) *Immigration Control Procedures: A General Investigation* (London: CRE).
Deakin, N. (1970) *Colour, Citizenship and British Society* (London: Panther).

Finlayson, A. (2003) *Making Sense of New Labour* (London: Lawrence & Wishart).

Harris, C. (1987) 'British Capitalism, Migration and Relative Surplus-Production', in *Migration*, January 1987, Berlin.

Harris, N. (1995) *The New Untouchables: Immigration and the New World Worker* (Harmondsworth: Penguin Books).

Henderson, M. (2003) *Asylum and Human Rights Appeals* (London: ILPA/Refugee Legal Group).

Hollifield, J.F. (1992) *Immigrants, Markets, and States: Political Economy of Postwar Europe* (Harvard University Press).

Humphry, D. and Ward, M. (1974) *Passports and Politics* (Harmondsworth: Penguin Books).

Jordan, B. and Duvall, F. (2002) *Irregular Migration: The Dilemmas of Transnational Mobility* (Cheltenham: Edward Elgar Publishers).

Klug, F. (2000) *Values for a Godless Age: The History of the Human Rights Act and Its Political and Legal Consequences* (Harmondsworth: Penguin Books).

Layton-Henry, Z. (1992) *The Politics of Immigration* (Oxford: Blackwell Publishers).

Leggett, W. (2004) 'New Labour's Third Way: From "New Times" to "No Choice"', in Hale, Leggett and Martell (eds) *The Third Way and Beyond: Criticisms, Futures, Alternatives* (Manchester: Manchester University Press).

Marquand, D. (2004) *The Decline of the Public* (Cambridge: Polity Press).

Morris, L. (2004) *The Control of Rights: The Rights of Workers and Asylum Seekers Under Managed Migration* (London: JCWI).

White Paper (1998) *Fairer, Faster and Firmer – A Modern Approach to Immigration and Asylum* (London: The Stationery Office).

White Paper (2002) *Secure Borders, Safe Haven: Integration with Diversity in Modern Britain* (London: The Stationery Office).

Chapter 14

Freedom of movement inside 'fortress Europe'

Willem Maas

Introduction

Much attention has been focused on those seeking to enter 'fortress Europe' – whether the concept is understood to refer only to the EU Schengen countries or to include non-EU Schengen countries, the United Kingdom and Ireland, or the countries which joined the Union in May 2004. Yet internal mobility within 'fortress Europe' is at least as worthy of consideration.

The rise of freedom of movement rights in Europe – now codified with the legal category of European Union citizenship – represents a startling reversal of the historical tradition of state sovereignty. States have historically been defined in terms of insiders (citizens) and outsiders (foreigners). The new supranational rights supersede this traditional distinction by reducing or even removing the ability of European states to discriminate between their own citizens and those of other EU member states. Borders within the European Union still matter, but the remaining barriers to freedom of movement within 'fortress Europe' are practical rather than legal, and even they are rapidly disappearing.

Exceptions to the European free movement regime still exist – such as the case of individuals deemed to pose a significant threat to public health or public security. But the rights of free movement have now been extended to virtually all European citizens, even though there will be a phase-in period for workers from most of the new accession states. By contrast, third-country nationals – citizens neither of the host state (first country) nor of another EU Member State (second country) but of a non-EU state – continue to be denied freedom of movement rights within the Union, despite the efforts of the Commission and some national governments to extend them the same rights as those enjoyed by EU citizens.

Exceptions to Schengen also continue to exist, as with special events such as the European soccer cup, for which Portugal in 2004 (just as Belgium and the Netherlands in 2000) was granted a temporary exemption on the requirement to abstain from checking the identification of individuals crossing Portuguese borders. On the whole, however, the picture that emerges for freedom of movement within Europe is one of a continent in which Europeans can move about freely, and in which state borders (though clearly not the borders between 'fortress Europe' and the rest of the world!) have lost most of the significance they once possessed. This paper lays out the development of the Schengen system and places it within the context of European Union citizenship.

Signing Schengen

On 14 June 1985, in the Luxembourg town of Schengen, representatives of Belgium, Germany, France, Luxembourg and the Netherlands agreed to eliminate border controls between their countries. The agreement was signed on the same day that the new European Commission, headed by Jacques Delors, released its White Paper entitled *Completing the Internal Market*, which laid out the single market program and inspired the Single European Act and the Maastricht Treaty. The signing ceremony occurred on a ship anchored on the Moselle River at the point where the borders of West Germany, France and Luxembourg meet. To add to the symbolism, the boat sailed through the waters of the three countries following the signing. The Belgian secretary of state for European affairs affirmed that the ultimate goal of the agreement was 'to abolish completely the physical borders between our countries' (United Press 1985). For Luxembourg's minister of foreign affairs, the agreement marked 'a major step forward on the road toward European unity', directly benefiting the nationals of the signatory states, and 'moving them a step closer to what is sometimes referred to as "European citizenship"' (United Press 1985). Schengen was an example of the 'two-speed Europe' that some regarded as the best way out of the institutional paralysis resulting from the Community's expansion to ten members. Faced with resistance on the part of three of the newer Member States – Denmark, the UK and Greece – five of the original six pushed ahead with plans to eliminate border controls. Italy was not invited to join because of fears of inadequate policing of the long Italian coastline, while Ireland opted not to join in order to stay in the Common Travel Area that it shared with the UK.[1]

Following lengthy preparations, the five Schengen states signed an implementing Convention on 19 June 1990, agreeing to remove internal border controls while coordinating control at external borders. Under the supervision of the Joint Supervisory Authority, an independent body established in Brussels and composed of representatives of the national data protection authorities, this coordination was to be achieved largely through the use of the Schengen Information System (SIS), a database shared by all Schengen states. SIS would contain information on persons and on stolen or missing vehicles and objects such as identity papers.[2]

As discussions on implementation continued, Italy signed the Agreement on 27 November 1990, while Spain and Portugal joined on 25 June 1991. Whereas Spain and Portugal were soon judged to have met the conditions for effective border control, Italy was not. Meanwhile, proposals to incorporate the Schengen policies into the Maastricht Treaty failed. Incorporation into the Treaty would have given the Community institutions (Commission, Parliament, Court) roles in the Schengen *acquis*; without incorporation, Schengen continued as an inter-governmental bargain. Originally intended to be an interim arrangement leading to the complete abolition of border controls within the EU, the Schengen laws and regulations had continually expanded. Yet extending Schengen to all Member States was blocked by the diplomatic impasse between Spain and the United Kingdom over the status of Gibraltar (Handoll 1997). Nevertheless, more states joined: Greece agreed to join on 6 November 1992, following its ratification of the Maastricht Treaty, while Austria signed the Schengen Agreement on 28 April 1995.

Full implementation of the Schengen Treaty began in July 1995 with the removal of internal border controls between six of seven Schengen states: Germany, the Netherlands, Belgium, Luxembourg, Spain and Portugal. France invoked internal security and decided to use the safeguard clause of the Treaty, allowing the temporary continuation of passport controls on its borders with Belgium and Luxembourg (but not with Germany and Spain, which were opened). An important aim of these controls was to check the importation of drugs, notably from the Netherlands.[3]

Meanwhile, Greece had not yet adapted its legislation, while Italy and Austria were judged to have not yet completed the physical preparations needed for secure controls at external borders. This judgement reflected the worry, especially on the part of Germany, that large numbers of migrants were entering Europe illegally across the Italian and Austrian borders, and that the Austrian and Italian authorities had not done enough to stop them. Before a settlement was reached in July 1997, Austria threatened to block the Amsterdam Treaty if it continued to be excluded from Schengen (BBC News 1997). In order to comply with Schengen external border control conditions, Austria deployed over 6,500 new personnel along the external border, bought new technical equipment, and laid down the SIS IT infrastructure (Karanja 2002).[4] This satisfied Germany and the other Schengen states, and Austria, together with Italy, fully joined Schengen on 1 April 1998 (*European Report* 1997). Meanwhile, Greece finalized the necessary legislation in 1997, but it took another two years to prepare all necessary procedures, and the full implementation of the Schengen *acquis* took place from 1 January 2000 for land and sea borders and 25 March 2000 for air borders (Hellenic Republic 2004).

The Treaty of Amsterdam incorporated the Schengen arrangements into the *acquis communautaire*, the body of community law, upon its entry into force on 1 May 1999. The Council replaced the Schengen Executive Committee, the Schengen secretariat staff moved to the Council's general secretariat, and new Council working groups were established to deal with Schengen. Furthermore, the Council decided which of the Schengen rules would be incorporated into the *acquis communautaire*, and hence be susceptible to control by Community institutions (Commission, Parliament, Court) and form part of the legal rules which countries seeking EU membership must adopt into their own national legislation.

Denmark, Finland and Sweden signed the Schengen Agreement on 19 December 1996. At the same time, the Schengen states signed a cooperation agreement with the non-EU members of the Nordic Passport Union (Norway and Iceland) giving them observer status (though not voting rights) on the Schengen Executive Committee. Though acts continue to be adopted by the EU Member States alone, they apply to Iceland and Norway as well, and their application is vetted by a committee composed of representatives from the Icelandic and Norwegian governments and members of the European Council and the Commission (Commission 2004a).

On 1 December 2000, the Council decided on the application of the Schengen *acquis* in Denmark, Finland and Sweden, and in Iceland and Norway. The Council decided that, as of 25 March 2001, the Schengen arrangements would apply to these five countries of the Nordic Passport Union.

The United Kingdom and Ireland remain outside Schengen. The UK requested in March 1999 to participate in police and legal cooperation in criminal matters, the fight against drugs, and the Schengen Information System. The Council's approval was achieved only on 29 May 2000 because the dispute between Spain and the United Kingdom regarding Gibraltar delayed the process. Ireland also asked to participate in the Schengen Information System on 16 June 2000 and on 1 November 2001. On 28 February 2002 the Council adopted a decision on Ireland's request which took effect as of 1 April 2002 (Commission 2004a).

The Schengen states now include Austria, Belgium, Denmark, Finland, France, Germany, Iceland, Italy, Greece, Luxembourg, the Netherlands, Norway, Portugal, Spain and Sweden. On 19 May 2004, the Commission agreed to allow Switzerland to join the Schengen treaty within three years (Government of Switzerland 2004).

The Schengen system will ultimately apply to all new Member States, but full participation in it will be based on a two-step process: 'The new Member States will first need to achieve a high level of external border control upon accession whereas the lifting of internal border controls with current Member States will take place only at a later stage, subject to a separate decision by the Council' (Commission 2001).

Schengen measures

Schengen's key measure is the removal of checks at common borders, replacing them with external border checks. This main measure has led to a number of related ones:

- a common definition of the rules for crossing external borders;
- separation in air terminals and ports of people travelling within the Schengen area from those arriving from countries outwith the area;
- harmonisation of the rules regarding conditions of entry and visas for short stays;
- coordination between administrations on surveillance of borders (liaison officers, harmonisation of instructions and staff training);
- the definition of the role of carriers in the fight against illegal immigration;
- requirement for all non-EU nationals moving from one country to another to lodge a declaration;
- the drawing up of rules for asylum seekers (Dublin Convention);
- the introduction of rights of surveillance and hot pursuit;
- the strengthening of legal cooperation through a faster extradition system and faster distribution of information about the implementation of criminal judgments; [and]
- the creation of the Schengen Information System (SIS). (Commission 2004a)

237

Each of these deserves separate attention, though let me simply note here the Council's formulation: 'Free movement within the territory of the Schengen States is a freedom which as a counterpart requires not only the strengthening of the common external borders and the administration of third country nationals, but also enhanced co-operation between law enforcement authorities of Schengen states' (Council 2003b).

The Commission's resources for coordinating these measures remain paltry: the Justice and Home Affairs DG has a unit devoted to citizenship, racism and xenophobia, the Charter of Fundamental Rights, and the Daphne program (designed to combat violence against children, young people and women), and another unit devoted to free movement of persons, visa policy, external borders and Schengen, along with other units. In 2002, the unit devoted to free movement of persons, visa policy, external borders and Schengen had just seven officials, in addition to three bureaucrats seconded from Member States. Created as a separate DG in 1999, the entire Justice and Home Affairs DG has just 180 officials.[5] It has been growing fast, but its small size reflects the fact that cooperation on the Schengen *acquis* developed through inter-governmental coordination, first outside the Community altogether and then, with the Amsterdam Treaty, within the Council.

Customs cooperation

The goal of removing all barriers to the free movement of persons is accompanied by the same goal with regard to the free movement of goods. Thus it is instructive to examine European customs cooperation to draw parallels with the free movement of persons. On 11 February 2003, the European Parliament and the Council adopted an action program for customs in the Community, entitled Customs 2007 (Council 2003a). The program is scheduled to run from January 2003 to December 2007 and is intended to ensure that the customs administrations of Schengen states:

> (a) carry out coordinated action to ensure that customs activity matches the needs of the Community's internal market...; (b) interact and perform their duties as efficiently as though they were one administration and achieve equivalent results at every point of the Community customs territory; (c) meet the demands placed on them by globalisation and increasing volumes of trade and contribute towards strengthening the competitive environment of the European Union; (d) provide the necessary protection of the financial interests of the European Union and provide a secure and

safe environment for its citizens; [and] (e) take the necessary steps to prepare for enlargement and to support the integration of new Member States. (Council 2003a)

Furthermore, the common customs policy 'shall continuously be adapted to new developments in partnership between the Commission and the Member States in the Customs Policy Group, composed of the heads of customs administrations from the Commission and the Member States or their representatives' (Council 2003a). This goes beyond the level of mutual aid specified in the Conventions on Mutual Assistance between Customs Administrations: Naples I of 1967 and Naples II of 1998.[6] Thus the Commission and the Member State customs administrations have established regular interactions so that they may indeed work together as efficiently and effectively as a single administration which achieves equivalent results throughout the Community customs territory, and meet the other aims specified by the Parliament and Council.

In order to achieve these goals, the Commission and the Schengen states agree to ensure the smooth functioning of a number of communication and information exchange systems:

(a) the common communications network/common systems interface (CCN/CSI)...;
(b) the data dissemination system (DDS);
(c) the new computerised transit system (NCTS/NSTI);
(d) the information system on the integrated tariff of the Community (TARIC);
(e) the information system for transfer of origin stamps and the transmission of transit stamps (TCO/TCT);
(f) the European customs inventory of chemical substances (ECICS);
(g) the European binding tariff information system (EBTI/RTCE);
(h) the tariff quota surveillance management system (TQS);
(i) the inward-processing relief system (IPR);
(j) the Unit values system;
(k) the Suspensions information system; [and]
(l) other existing IT Community systems in the customs area to ensure their continuity.[7]

Each of these systems is necessary to maintaining an efficient common customs policy. For example, the European Binding Tariff Information (EBTI) system is a key instrument for implementing the Common Customs Tariff and is intended to simplify procedures for importers and exporters to get the proper classification of the goods. Customs authorities of the Member States issue importers and exporters with Binding Tariff Information in advance, so that they know the tariff classification of the goods they intend to import or export. Such BTI is introduced into a database run by the Commission and is legally valid in all Member States, regardless of the Member State which issued it (Commission 2004b).

Overall, the Parliament and Council allocated €133 million to the Commission for the implementation of the Customs 2007 programme for the period 1 January 2003 to 31 December 2007 (Council 2003a). This is in addition to the funds that the Member States will devote to carrying out their duties under the Schengen *acquis*.

Recognizing that within 'the framework of the creation of an area of freedom, security and justice, the free movement of goods, persons and capital leads to a reassessment of control measures within the European Union', the Council in October 2003 resolved, among other things, to define a strategy for customs cooperation within the framework of the creation of an area of freedom, security and justice, based on the following aims:

(a) to consider new forms of cooperation, including the examination of the need for common analysis in the fight against cross-border organised crime and to protect citizens and the economy and to consider a common approach to training among their customs administrations...;

(b) to take practical steps towards implementing these new forms of cooperation, such as to: improve operational cooperation; ensure an effective role at the external borders of the European Union; consider the creation of a permanent Operational Coordination Unit which will support the JCO; ensure an institutional approach based on cooperation between customs, police and other relevant border agencies; further develop Third Pillar IT systems...;

(c) to improve and make more flexible the existing cooperation process, mainly by means of new or improved legal mechanisms and a structured and measurable approach to sharing good practice, so as to meet the expectation of an effective approach to seizing illicit goods and combating cross-border organised crime throughout the European Union; and

(d) to enhance public confidence in customs, by demonstrating tangible results through customs cooperation and ensuring an increased awareness of customs role in relation to law enforcement.[8]

Key here is the determination to extend to all EU Member States the lessons learned from the Schengen *acquis*. Of course, Articles 29 and 30 of the Treaty on European Union (as amended at Amsterdam) already provide for closer cooperation among the customs administrations of the Member States in order to contribute to the creation of an area of freedom, security and justice for Union citizens. But this has yet to result in practical developments, as the language of the Council resolution cited above indicates.

Coordination on visas to third countries: the United States

All the pre-accession EU Member States except Greece (i.e. Austria, Belgium, Denmark, Finland, France, Germany, Ireland, Italy, Luxembourg, the Netherlands, Portugal, Sweden, Spain and the UK) have a waiver agreement with the United States. Conversely, only one of the new member states, Slovenia, has a waiver agreement. The other nine new members (i.e. Cyprus, the Czech Republic, Estonia, Hungary, Latvia, Lithuania, Malta, Poland and Slovakia) do not. The new Member States, particularly Poland and the Czech Republic, have suggested that they would invoke the solidarity clause of the Schengen Convention. This could mean that all Schengen states would be required to act uniformly, requiring visas from US citizens. Rather than seeing the solidarity clause invoked, the European Commission prefers to negotiate with the US that all the new Member States can join the visa waiver as a bloc when they join Schengen, expected in 2006 (*EU Observer* 2004b). Greece has not invoked the clause 'in order not to create major trouble for other member states', according to Jonathan Faull, Director General of the Commission's Justice and Home Affairs DG. He also suggested that the reciprocity clause would be amended to 'introduce some flexibility' (*EU Observer* 2004a). This highlights the continuing tension between Member States which face different requirements for persons and goods leaving for third states, yet must agree on common requirements for persons and goods arriving from those third states.

Citizenship

The free movement of both people and goods can be conceptualized through the lens of European Union citizenship. The key right of EU citizenship, which was formally introduced in the Maastricht Treaty of 1992 (although its core precepts had characterized the development of

European integration since the 1950s) is free movement of persons (Maas 2004). The development of Schengen came about not merely because of economic calculations – though the desire to reap the economic benefits of increased mobility no doubt played a role – but because of the political value to creating a borderless Europe in which European citizens can travel freely.

Since the Schengen program can be situated within the development of EU citizenship, it can also draw criticism from those who disagree with the project of creating European citizens. The key source of opposition to the rights of EU citizens is found within populist parties. Thus, in the 2002 election campaign in the Netherlands, populist Pim Fortuyn campaigned to re-introduce border controls within the EU, a perspective shared by the French far-right party Front Nationale (Gollnisch 2002). Similarly, the Austrian Freedom Party is opposed to freedom of movement for new EU citizens from the accession states, a perspective shared by the Danish People's Party.[9] In addition to the positions of populist political parties, there also exist religious pressures to back out of the Schengen agreement, although they too remain marginal. Thus, for example, the Greek Orthodox Church warned in its 1997 Easter encyclical, read out in all Greek Orthodox churches during Easter services, against the threat that the Schengen agreement poses to 'our Orthodoxy' (cited in Fokas 2000).

Conclusion

The project to abolish completely the physical borders between European states formally commenced with the signature of the Schengen Agreement by representatives of Belgium, Germany, France, Luxembourg and the Netherlands on 14 June 1985, the same day that the Commission released its White Paper entitled *Completing the Internal Market*, which laid out the '1992 program'. Over the past 19 years, the Schengen *acquis* has grown to include almost every Western European state, and plans are well underway to ensuring that the entire European continent will become borderless. This striking development has not proceeded without problems, as the challenges to coordinating the customs and immigration regimes of 13 and more member states are significant. Furthermore, there remain significant issues surrounding the free movement of third-country nationals, individuals who are not citizens of EU Member States. For Europeans, however, the development of rights of free movement has been remarkable. This chapter charted the development of the Schengen *acquis* and discussed some of the remaining issues and tensions, before arguing that the project of eliminating border controls between the European states flows from the development of European Union citizenship.

Notes

1 There are generally no passport controls within the Common Travel Area (which includes the Isle of Man and the Channel Islands in addition to Ireland and the UK), although Ireland has at times instituted controls on crossings from Northern Ireland. Over two-thirds of journeys leaving Ireland have Britain as their destination, so the Irish government calculated as too high the cost of leaving the Common Travel Area in order to join Schengen.

2 Article 94 of the Convention contains a detailed list of categories of data that can be stored in the system. Data on persons may include: (a) surname and forenames, any aliases possibly entered separately; (b) any specific objective physical characteristics not subject to change; (c) first letter of second forename; (d) date and place of birth; (e) sex; (f) nationality; (g) whether the persons concerned are armed; (h) whether the persons concerned are violent; (i) reason for the alert; (j) action to be taken. Sensitive information (e.g. concerning racial origin, political, religious or other beliefs, or information concerning a person's health and sexual activities) may not be entered. The purposes for which alerts may be entered are given in Articles 95 to 100. An alert for a person may be entered in the SIS for the following reasons: arrest for the purpose of extradition (Article 95); to determine the whereabouts of a missing person, of minors or of persons whose detention has been ordered by the competent authorities (Article 97); arrest for the purpose of appearing in court, either as a suspect or a witness, or at the request of the judicial authorities in connection with a criminal investigation or for the purpose of serving a custodial sentence (Article 98); discreet surveillance and specific checks, conducted for the purpose of prosecution in connection with a criminal offence, averting a threat to public safety or national security (Article 99); in the case of aliens, refusal of entry to the Schengen area pursuant to a decision taken by the competent administrative or judicial authority subject to national laws, a decision based on the danger posed to national security and public order or a decision based on the fact that the alien concerned has contravened national provisions governing entry and residence (Article 96). Data on objects may include: (a) motor vehicles with a cylinder capacity exceeding 50 cc which have been stolen, misappropriated or lost; (b) trailers and caravans with an unladen weight exceeding 750 kg which have been stolen, misappropriated or lost; (c) firearms which have been stolen, misappropriated or lost; (d) blank official documents which have been stolen, misappropriated or lost; (e) issued identity papers (passports, identity cards, driving licences) which have been stolen, misappropriated or lost; (f) banknotes (suspect notes). (Joint Supervisory Authority 2004)

3 There continue to be regular news reports of (mostly North American) students and tourists caught with marijuana on checks on the Amsterdam to Paris Thalys trains.

4 The article mentions that the Austrian authorities claimed to have spent 3 billion Austrian Schillings preparing Austria for Schengen implementation. But this seems highly unlikely, since that corresponds to €218 million.

5 Source: http://europa.eu.int/comm/dgs/justice_home/freemovement/wai/dg_freemovement_en.htm (last accessed 3 March 2005).

6 OJ C 24, 23 January 1998, 1. The text of Naples II is also available at http://europa.eu.int/scadplus/leg/en/lvb/l33051.htm (last accessed 3 March 2005)

7 Ibid. Chapter II, Article 5 § 1.

8 Council resolution of 2 October 2003 on a strategy for customs cooperation, OJ C 247, 15 October 2003, 0001-0003.

9 In the 2001 elections, the Dansk Folkeparti, a populist party with an anti-immigration platform, took out full-page newspaper advertisements with a caption reading 'Do you really want to open our borders to 40 million Poles?'

References

BBC News (1997) 'Background to Schengen Agreement', 28 November. Available at: http://news.bbc.co.uk/1/hi/special_report/1997/schengen/13508.stm (last accessed 3 March 2005).

Commission of the European Communities (2001) *The Free Movement of Workers in the Context of Enlargement*, 5.

Commission of the European Communities (2004a) 'The Schengen acquis and its integration into the Union'. Available at: http://www.europa.eu.int/scadplus/leg/en/lvb/l33020.htm (last accessed 3 March 2005).

Commission of the European Communities (2004b) 'Binding Tarriff Information'. Available at: http://europa.eu.int/comm/taxation_customs common/databases/ebti/index_en.htm (last accessed 3 March 2005).

Council of the European Union (2003a), Decision No 253/2003/EC of the European Parliament and of the Council of 11 February 2003 adopting an action programme for customs in the Community (Customs 2007), OJ L 036, 12 February 2003, 0001-0006 and OJ L 095, 11 April 2003, 0036-0037.

Council of the European Union (2003b), *EU Schengen Catalogue, Vol. 4* (June), p. 32.

EU Observer (2004a) 'EU and US in tussle over visa arrangements', 27 April.

EU Observer (2004b) 'US grants more time for new passports', 11 August.

European Report (1997) 'Schengen: Germany, Austria and Italy agree to scrap border checks in April', 23 July.

Fokas, E. (2000) 'Greek Orthodoxy and European Identity', in A. Mitsos and E. Mossialos (eds) *Contemporary Greece and Europe* (Aldershot: Ashgate).

Gollnisch, B. (2002) 'Il faut instaurer un contrôle des frontières en revenant sur les accords de Schengen', *Le Monde*, 30 December.

Government of Switzerland, Integration Office DFA/DEA (2004) 'Bilateral Agreements II Switzerland – EU'. Available at: http://www.europa.admin. ch/nbv/off/e/index.htm (last accessed 3 March 2005).

Handoll, J. (1997) 'The Free Movement of Persons', in B. Tonra (ed.) *Amsterdam: What the Treaty Means* (Dublin: Institute of European Affairs), p. 134.

Hellenic Republic, Ministry of Foreign Affairs (2004) 'The Schengen Acquis'. Available at: http://www.mfa.gr/english/foreign_policy/eu/acquis.html (last accessed 3 March 2005).

Joint Supervisory Authority (2004) 'The Schengen Information System'. Available at: http://www.schengen-jsa.dataprotection.org/ (last accessed 3 March 2005).

Karanja, S. (2002) 'The Schengen Information System in Austria: an essential tool in day to day police and border control work?' *The Journal of Information, Law and Technology*, 1

Maas, W. (2004) 'Creating European Citizens', PhD Dissertation, Department of Political Science, Yale University.

United Press International (1985) 'Five EC Members Agree to Eliminate Border Checks', 14 June.

Index

scanning 24
Schengen Agreement 106, 234–7
  measures 237–8
Schengen Information Systems I and
  II 56, 106–7, 207
Schengen space 52
searchable databases 68
Seasonal Agricultural Workers'
  Scheme 199
Secure Borders, Safe Haven 199–200,
  200–1, 202, 205, 209, 221–7
Secure Flight 126
securing identity 92, 93
security
  blurring of public and private space
    86–8
  of the database 89, 90
  of identity 87
  identity and the space of the
    database 93–4
  and territoriality 195–7
  through ID cards 72–3
  see also border security; boundary
    security measures; national
    security
security barrier, Israel-Palestine 180
Security Perimeter, Canadian-
  American border 57
self
  less protection from covert
    intrusions 24
  new ways of defining 23
self-disciplining docile body 100–1
self-disclosure, at airports 44–5
self-policing, at airports 44–7
self-sorting, by travellers 44
sense borders 14, 19–22
September 11
  Canadian-US border management
    57
  concerns about mobile population 1
  dark side of globalization 199
  enhancement of US tracking
    capacity 158–9
  formation of US Customs and
    Border Protection Agency 109

less concern for invasion of privacy
  14
Mexican-US border 52
NSEERS as reaction to 153
processing passenger data
  after 113–33
re-awakening of international
  boundaries 175
urgency for and talk about ID cards
  71, 77
shadow self 23
Simla Agreement (1972) 177
smart ID cards 67, 68, 69–70, 71–3,
  76–7, 159, 209, 226
Smarter Border Accord 57, 125, 159
smugglers 62, 209
social classes, experience of borders
  37
social construction perspective,
  borders 54
social control
  by police 105
  formalized 98
  in a surveillance society 98–9
  surveillance technologies and
    equality in 101–2
social control organizations, blurred
  borders 25–6
social institutions, transitory control
  43
social sorting 3, 43, 67, 101–2
society, as systems 13
sociocultural concerns, biometrics
  88–91
sovereign power, at borders 38, 39
space of the database
  biometrics politics 92–3
  identity and security 93–4
space of flows 9, 198, 206
space of power, border as 61–2
special registration (NSEERS) 141,
  142–4, 147
Special Service Request field, PNR 117
standardization, PNR 119
state borders 9
  formalized social control within 98